In the Context of Eternity

A Short History of the
Christian Church

GW00401688

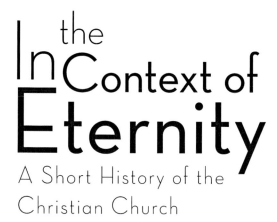

the In Context of Eternity

A Short History of the Christian Church

by

David Arnold

Grosvenor House
Publishing Limited

The right of David Arnold to be identified as the author of this
work has been asserted by him in accordance with Section 78
of the Copyright, Designs and Patents Act 1988

The book cover picture is copyright to titoOnz

This book is published by
Grosvenor House Publishing Ltd
28-30 High Street, Guildford, Surrey, GU1 3EL.
www.grosvenorhousepublishing.co.uk

A CIP record for this book
is available from the British Library

ISBN 978-1-78148-448-7

For my twin brother

John

and in gratitude to
The Religious, Royal and Ancient Foundation of Christ's Hospital,
where we first encountered the mystery and splendour
of the Christian Faith.

Acknowledgements

First I must thank Canon Derek Tansill, formerly Vicar of the Parish Church of St Mary the Virgin in Horsham, who, knowing of my interest in ecclesiastical history, asked me to give a series of talks over a period of a year on the history of the Christian Church to about forty or fifty members of the congregation. Later I turned them into more formal lectures for an evening class at the College of Richard Collyer in Horsham, and now they have been turned into this book.

Next I must thank a number of friends who have kindly read and offered their criticisms of all or part of the text. Professor the Reverend Colin Morris, who taught me at Pembroke College, Oxford, read the medieval chapters, the Reverend Dr Peter Newman Brooks, who taught at Cambridge University, read the chapters on the Reformation period, and both Professor Christopher Holdsworth, formerly of Exeter University, and my brother, the Very Reverend Dr John Arnold, Dean Emeritus of Durham and formerly President of the Conference of European Churches, read the whole text. In each case their comments were a great help. It is scarcely necessary to add what is obvious: that the faults are my own.

My further thanks to Bryan Magee, philosopher and teacher of philosophy, television broadcaster, Member of Parliament and prolific author, whom I first met when we were both at school, for kindly giving me permission to include on pages 26 and 27 an extended quotation from his *Confessions of a Philosopher*.

Finally I offer my thanks and gratitude to my wife, Catherine, who has lived patiently and tolerantly with the theological controversies and political upheavals of the Christian Church, has read the whole text to try to ensure its accessibility, and even found time, while working for the RSPCA and doing most of the housework, to help me make the index.

David Arnold. May 2015.

Foreword

In the context of eternity the history of the Christian church is a brief moment in time. The planet we live on has sustained life of some sort for anything up to four thousand million years and could continue to do so for untold millions of years to come. In that context the last two thousand years is the equivalent of no more than a few seconds in a year. Yet they are important to us because they help us to make sense of the world in which we live, and it is easier to establish some connection with the relatively recent past than with events long ago. But the great German historian Leopold von Ranke once suggested that 'every age stands in its own relationship with God', and an important part of the intention of this book is to give as much attention to events one or two thousand years ago as to those of more recent times. Thus the period from the baptism of the Emperor Constantine in 337 AD to the rise of Islam in the seventh century rates as much attention as the period a thousand years later from the late medieval and Renaissance papacy, through the era of the Reformation and Counter-Reformation, to the end of the seventeenth century wars of religion.

It has been characteristic of historical writing about the history of the Christian church that little attention is given to the Jewish, Greek and Roman background, more attention is given to developments in the West than to those in the East, and far more to the events of the last five hundred years than to the more distant past. Typically a history of the first two thousand years of Christianity devotes about twice as much space to the last five hundred years as to the previous one and a half thousand, and is likely to be arranged in sections something like this:

1. The lives of Jesus and St Paul, and the story of the early church as it spread through the Roman Empire until, say, the death of St Augustine in 430 AD.

2. The thousand years or so from the barbarian invasions of the fifth century through the so-called Middle Ages to the time of the Renaissance popes.
3. From 1500 to 1648 – the Protestant Reformation, the Catholic Counter-Reformation and the religious wars of the sixteenth and seventeenth centuries.
4. From 1648 to 1870 – the divisions of Protestantism, the vicissitudes of the Roman Catholic Church and the subjugation of the Orthodox Church in the East.
5. Evangelism in America, Asia and Africa during the second half of the second millennium and the export overseas of the divisions in the European churches.
6. From 1870 to 2000 – the development of the church amid the revolutions and wars of the modern world, and its adjustment to new political systems and to post-Christian society.

It is worth noticing that more than half of the time involved, from the fifth century to the sixteenth, usually takes up only a sixth of the total space. How that works in practice can be seen by looking at some of the general histories of Christianity published in the second half of the twentieth century (See the suggestions for further reading on page 281). There is usually some emphasis on the early centuries, though not as much as on the last five, and far less attention is given to the period of over a thousand years in between.

That tendency to neglect the period between the fall of the Roman Empire in the West and the era referred to as the Renaissance and Reformation is not only characteristic of the history of the Christian church. It is also true of the popular view of history generally. At one time there were the ancient civilisations of Greece and Rome. Some time later there came into existence the modern world in which we live. In between there was a period of history which, for want of a better name, is called the Middle Ages – from the fall of the Roman Empire in the West in the fifth century until, perhaps, the discovery of the New World by Christopher Columbus in 1492.

That view of history carries with it the implication that ancient history came to an end in the fifth century, nothing very much of any significance happened for the next thousand years, and then in about the fifteenth century there was a renaissance, a rebirth, of the ancient world, and history took up again where it had left off a thousand years earlier. That is mistaken on every count. The Roman Empire continued in the East for a thousand years after its collapse in the West, and in the West it was what happened in those thousand years which led on to the developments known as the Renaissance and the Reformation. In the centuries after the birth of Christ two entirely different forces had a powerful impact on the Roman Empire and on each other. One was Christianity. The other was Barbarism. Over the next thousand years that extraordinary intermingling of the Roman Empire, Christianity and Barbarism produced in Western Europe the most dynamic society the world has ever known. It may not be as attractive as ancient China or the Egypt of the Pharaohs, or even the Roman Empire, but it achieved more than any of them, and its achievements arose from that explosive mixture.

The Roman Empire was essentially all the land around the Mediterranean Sea. It developed during the period when Rome was a republic, but the empire only came into existence shortly before the birth of Jesus of Nazareth, after the upheaval and civil wars which followed the assassination of Julius Caesar in 44 BC, and out of which Julius Caesar's nephew, Caesar Augustus, emerged as the first Roman Emperor. It was in the reign of Caesar Augustus that Jesus was born and it was in the reign of his successor, the Emperor Tiberius, that he was executed.

The empire had a natural border in the South where it met the desert and in the West where it met the sea. To the East was the Persian Empire, and the border fluctuated according to the relative strengths of the Romans and the Persians. In the North there were barbarian tribes: Goths and Huns, for example, and Saxons and Franks. The only significant features which formed some sort of border in the North were the rivers Rhine and Danube and a wall which the Romans built in the area in between. Internally Rome provided peace, stability and civilisation, but throughout the history of the Roman Empire there was always fighting along the northern border, and eventually, in the fifth century, the western part of the empire fell to the barbarians. Edward Gibbon, the eighteenth century author of *The History of the Decline and Fall of the Roman Empire*, in the last pages of chapter 38, ascribed that decline and fall partly to the enfeebling effects of the spread of the Christian church and its influence. But the real problem was that the Roman Empire was attractive, the barbarians invaded because they wanted a share of what they found appealing, and there were too many of them for the Romans to be able to keep them out.

In the East the Roman Empire survived for another thousand years, and the Christian church survived as the official church of that empire. Despite the collapse of the empire in the West, the church survived there as well and its bishops converted the barbarian tribes to Christianity. The bishop of Rome, by then usually known as the pope, could even be seen as in some sense the successor to the Roman emperors, because he remained in Rome, while the barbarian kings were perpetually on the move; and in the seventeenth century the papacy was described by the English political theorist, Thomas Hobbes, as 'none other than the ghost of the old Roman Empire sitting robed and crowned upon the grave thereof.' Eventually nation states grew out of the barbarian kingships, and somehow the modern world, the world of the scientific revolution, of capitalism, and of the liberal democracy of the United States of America across the Atlantic all emerged out of the interaction of Christianity and Barbarism on the ruins of the Roman Empire in the West.

The intention of this book is to tell the story of how the Christian church came to develop the way it did, how Christians developed their beliefs and organisational structures, and how they came to disagree with each other over a variety of issues. It pays attention to the Jewish, Greek and Roman worlds out of which the church emerged, and it deals with developments in the East, including the rise of Islam. It pays due attention to the so-called Middle Ages, looks at developments in the wider world, and aims to do these things briefly and succinctly, showing as it does so something of how the church influenced and was influenced by the societies within which it developed.

Contents

Section 3 Christendom Divided
(the 660s to 1000 AD)

Section 4 The High Middle Ages
(1000 AD to the 1330s)

Section 5 The Era of Reform
(the 1330s to the 1660s)

Prologue

Chapter 1

Israelites, Jews and Greeks

The Creation Myth

One way of looking at the origins of Man is to start at the beginning of the *Book of Genesis*, the first of the books of the Bible. It was written less than two and a half thousand years ago, only four hundred years or so before the birth of Christ, and it starts with a creation myth. Myths are stories which do not have to be literally true but are told to illustrate important truths. Many human societies have had creation myths and in the first chapter of *Genesis* there is a brilliant, beautifully clear description of how 'in the beginning God created the heaven and the earth.'

He did it in six days and then rested on the seventh. On the first day he created light and darkness, on the second air and water, on the third land. Then in the next three days God put things into that which he had already created: sun, moon and stars on the fourth day, birds and fishes on the fifth, plants and animals, including mankind, on the sixth. The description of the creation of mankind is worded like this in the English translation commissioned by King James I early in the seventeenth century: 'So God created Man in his own image; in the image of God created he him; male and female created he them.'

It is worth noticing the idea that mankind is somehow made in the image of God, and it is also worth noticing that God created both male and female right from the beginning. That needs to be stressed because chapters two and three of *Genesis* are written on the assumption that the first man was originally on his own. But that is a separate story, written much later, which provides an entirely different description of how women came into existence. It is a good example, right at the beginning of the Bible, of how historians need to be careful about their sources. A literal interpretation of ancient documents will lead to problems, especially when the authors were telling stories to illuminate what they saw as the truth rather than trying to give an accurate factual account. One should not be too surprised to find contradictions in the Bible. Chapter one is a brilliant and beautiful creation myth. Chapters two and three give a different account of the creation of mankind and go on to tell the story of the Garden of Eden and the Fall and describe how everything went wrong.

Adam and Eve

To begin with God gave the first man, Adam, a garden in Eden and everything was perfect, except that he was lonely. A man usually needs a woman. A survey was conducted some years ago into levels of contentment in married and unmarried men and women. The outcome was that the most contented group was married men, next were unmarried women, third were married women and least contented of all were unmarried men. However that may be, apparently Adam did not have a woman, despite the comment in chapter one about God creating both male and female. In this second story Adam was lonely, so God put him to sleep, took out one of his ribs and from it created a woman, and the two of them were naked and unashamed (*Genesis 2. 21-25*). Everything was fine, except that there was a rule that they must not eat the fruit of the tree of the knowledge of good and evil. But a serpent tempted Eve. She in turn tempted the man, who ate the fruit, and when God caught them, the man blamed the woman, she blamed the serpent, God drove them out of the Garden of Eden, and everything had gone wrong. That is what is known as the Fall.

The Fall

The Fall is not a single event which happened untold years ago. The story of what happened in the Garden of Eden illustrates something which is happening all the while. It happens whenever human beings fall short, as we all do, of an ideal of perfection. In relations between nation and nation, between one racial group and another, between husbands and wives, parents and children, employer and employee, teacher and taught, and in the way human beings treat animals there is too often cruelty where there should be concern and love.

No wonder that people ask such questions as 'Where did it all go wrong?', or 'Why does so much go wrong?' The story of Adam and Eve and the Fall draws attention to a whole range of questions – without necessarily providing the answers. Why are the sexes so strongly attracted to each other? Why do human beings feel shame and wear clothes? Why do women put up with brutal and insensitive men? Why is childbearing so painful? Come to that, why do we find snakes and many other creatures both frightening and repulsive? Above all, why are we so ready to blame each other when things go wrong, and what on earth is meant by the presumptuous suggestion that Man (and I take that to mean humankind – not man as distinct from woman) is made in the image of God? The story of the Garden of Eden, like most good stories, whether they are myths or historical accounts, raises more questions than it answers.

The Evolution of Man

Anyone wanting an answer to these questions needs to look not only at the Bible but also at the way in which the human animal has evolved. In particular it is worth considering the extraordinary evolutionary development which led a creature which at one time had gone on all fours to adopt an upright posture. The first creatures which could reasonably be called men developed through the evolutionary process by natural selection until about two and a half million years ago they stood up and are recognisable to us as human beings – even if very primitive ones.

The adoption of an upright posture proved to be immensely important and brought with it enormous advantages. One was that it freed the hands to make things. Another advantage was that men and women became attractive to each other and capable of bonding with each other, both physically and emotionally, in different ways from other animals. But by far the most important consequence was that it made possible the development of a large brain capable of thinking in quite different ways from other animals. Man is capable of conscious thought. Not only does he have the capacity to think; he can even be conscious that he is thinking. He is capable of creative thought and can use his mind and his hands to turn what he imagines into physical reality. He is capable of thinking logically and constructing rational arguments. He can construct images in his mind and speculate on what may have happened in the past and might happen in the future. He can make judgements about moral issues, think about his own emotions and make decisions which do not necessarily accord with those emotions. However much he is conditioned by circumstances and by his inheritance, he appears to have (and certainly acts as if he has) what is called 'free will.' That is what it is to be human, and it is possibly about as close as one can get to what is meant by the idea that Man is in some sense 'made in the image of God.'

But the good always carries with it the possibility of its opposite. Human beings can use their hands and the tools they manufacture for destruction as well as for creation. Human sexual relationships can be a source of joy, but they can also lead to bitter disappointment and distress. Men can think beautiful thoughts, but they can also think evil thoughts. They can think creatively, but they can also think destructively. The bad is the price paid for the good. We know the difference between good and bad, and all too often choose the bad rather than the good. So perhaps it is not surprising that we are told that 'God saw that the wickedness of man was great in the earth and that every imagination of the thoughts of his heart was only evil continually' (*Genesis 6. 5*).

The upright posture brought with it disadvantages as well. Bending to till the soil is back-breaking work, and a female pelvis adapted to upright walking results in painful childbearing. That may explain why God tells Eve that she shall bring forth her children in sorrow (*Genesis 3.16*). The story of the Fall may not tell us anything about evolution, but evolution does tell us quite a lot about some of the issues raised by the story of the Fall.

The Israelites

Some two and a half million years after Man had come into existence, and some one thousand, five hundred years before Christ, we hear of Hebrew nomads from what is now Iraq travelling through the desert led by the patriarch Abraham, then by his son Isaac, and next by his grandson, Jacob, whose name God changed (*Genesis 35. 10*)) to Israel, which meant 'Ruling with God.' Israel had twelve sons from whom were descended twelve tribes. As a consequence of famine their descendants spent some time, probably rather more than a hundred years or so, in slavery in Egypt. Eventually they were led out of captivity by the most important leader in their history, Moses, and the foundation of their religion is tied in with that deliverance. The so-called Children of Israel formed a confederation of tribes bound together by common descent, by history and by religion. The three things were inextricably interwoven.

The Israelites interpreted historical events as the working out of the purposes of their god, who had delivered them from slavery, chosen them as his people and entered into a covenant with them. They should worship him, trust him and obey his laws. He would protect them and guide them through history. Much of the Old Testament is concerned with explaining their history in terms of this covenant. It is written to show how the people flourished when they followed the God of Israel and suffered when they turned from him to worship other gods.

The Ten Commandments

When Moses led them out of captivity, they returned to a nomadic life and travelled from one pasture to another in the deserts of the Middle East. Moses gave them ten rules (*Exodus 20. 1-17*) by which to live their lives, and these rules can for convenience be divided into two groups of five.

He began with fundamental issues. They should worship just one god, they should not worship other gods or make idols, they should respect their own god enough not to use his name casually, and they should work six days of the week but rest on the seventh and treat it as a time to worship their god. He then added a fifth law, that they should respect their parents. After that he moved on to a group of five more rules aimed at making their society work smoothly. Do not kill people; do not take or have sex with anyone else's wife or husband; do not steal other people's property; do not lie about them; do not even envy them.

Those commandments look to many people like clear rules of universal application, as beautiful and memorable in their simplicity as the description at the beginning of Genesis of how God created the World in six days. But they are open to interpretation. No doubt it is wrong to kill members of one's own tribe or to commit adultery or steal within one's own tribe. It was by no means clear that the same rules applied when dealing with other people.

Israel and Judah

A generation later, when Moses had died, Joshua, the son of Nun, led the Israelites westwards out of the desert, and they looked down on the fertile land between the River Jordan and the Mediterranean, a land flowing with milk and honey, inhabited by a range of tribes known to us as Philistines, Canaanites, Midianites, Amalakites, Perizzites, Jebusites, Hittites and so on. The whole area is sometimes referred to as Canaan, after a dominant tribe which lived in the North of what is now Israel, and sometimes Palestine, a version of Philistia, after the Philistines who lived in the south-west. The Israelites emerged from the desert and bit by bit, battle by battle, seized the land, property and women of the tribes settled in the area, which, they were persuaded, was a land promised to them by their god, so long as they kept their covenant with him.

Eventually they established the Kingdom of Israel, which was ruled in about 1000 BC by a powerful warlord whom we know as King David. His kingdom embraced all twelve of the tribes known collectively as the Children of Israel. But after the reign of David's son, King Solomon, who built a great temple to the Israelites' god in his father's City of Peace, Jerusalem, the kingdom broke up into two. Most of the tribes continued under the leadership of a warlord who became King Jeroboam of the Kingdom of Israel, but two tribes in the South, Judah and the small tribe of Benjamin, formed the Kingdom of Judah, which continued to be ruled by the descendants of David and Solomon.

Much of the Old Testament is about the rivalry between these two kingdoms. It is also about the conflict between those who were inclined to mix and inter-marry with Canaanites, Perizzites, Jebuzites and all the other peoples of the area and worship other gods, and those who were anxious to keep the exclusive covenant with their own god.

Prophesy

It is in this period of the separate northern and southern kingdoms that there begins the tradition of prophecy. Prophets such as Amos and Hosea in the North or Isaiah and Micah in the South condemned the corruption of their own societies, appealing to long-established moral standards associated with the will of God, and threatened dire consequences if the people continued to go a-whoring after strange gods. Amos called for justice, Hosea wanted greater loving-kindness and mercy, Isaiah demanded that the Jews should turn away from sin and obey God, and Micah summed up their messages, asking the question, 'What doth the Lord require of thee, but to do justly, and to love mercy, and to walk humbly with thy God?' (*Micah 6. 8*).

Isaiah had also foretold the coming of the Prince of Peace, who would sit upon the throne of David, ruling 'with judgement and justice from henceforth even for ever' (*Isaiah 9. 6 and 7*). Micah looked back to the anointing of David in Bethlehem of Judea (*1 Samuel 16*) and spoke of another ruler of the line of David coming to be a shepherd to his people (*Micah 5. 2-4*). Then towards the end of this period another prophet, whose ideas were ascribed to Isaiah, developed the idea that one day a Messiah, or Saviour, would come to redeem Israel from all her sins and put everything right. The crooked would be made straight and the rough places plain (*Isaiah 40. 1-5*). The language they all used was metaphorical, of course, its imagery was powerful and moving and it had a lasting effect.

Exile

But everything still went wrong. The two kingdoms were in a strategically significant zone, between Egypt to the southwest, Assyria in the northeast and Babylon in the east. The outcome of a complicated series of alliances and wars was that in about 700 BC the Assyrians took captive and deported into exile all the leaders of the northern Kingdom of Israel, and the people of that kingdom disappear from history, probably by inter-marriage with others living in the area. Their descendants are no doubt now scattered throughout Israel, Palestine, Lebanon, Syria, Iraq and beyond, though some people still believe that the ten lost tribes of Israel will turn up somewhere such as Central Asia.

A century later, in about 600 BC, the Babylonians similarly deported the leaders of the southern Kingdom of Judah. It is that exile that produced Psalm 137, with its beautiful and sad opening, 'By the waters of Babylon we sat down and wept, when we remembered thee, O Zion', and its bitter and vindictive ending written later by someone else commenting on the past and addressing the Babylonians: 'Blessed shall he be that taketh thy children and throweth them against the stones.'

At about this time all those who shared the religious heritage of the Children of Israel, and not just the tribe of Judah, come to be referred to as Jews to distinguish them from the Gentiles, or non-Jews. The term 'Israelite' falls into disuse and even today the citizens of the republic of Israel think of themselves as Jews rather than as Israelites. This deportation of the leading Jews to Babylon is the beginning of the great dispersion of Jews through the World. Many of them retained a sense of their national and religious identity. Whether abroad or at home Jews often had to practise their religion in a society ruled by others – whether Babylonians, Greeks or Romans. They clung to such things as observation of the Sabbath, annual feasts and circumcision as symbols of their national and religious identity, and, without access to the Temple, they began to gather for worship and teaching in synagogues, or meeting places.

The return from exile

While the leaders of the Jews were still in exile the Babylonian Empire was overthrown by the Persians. Some exiled Jews flourished at the court of the King of Persia, and about five hundred years before Christ they were allowed to return from exile to rebuild the temple in Jerusalem. It is at that time that there developed among them an increased zeal for exclusiveness. From now on they aimed to avoid intermarriage, and Jewish men were even told to put away their foreign wives (*Ezra 10.9-14*).

It is also at this time that Judaism became a religion centred on the Hebrew scriptures. Most religious writings from the Exile onwards are concerned to preserve the religious and cultural inheritance of the Jews and emphasise the need to keep themselves separate from the rest of the World. Ancient writings were carefully transcribed. The five books of Moses were gathered together in the form which has survived till the present day, and they include hundreds of detailed rules about how Jews should live and what they should and should not do. The words of the prophets of former times were recorded, and new religious ideas were often added.

The restored state of Judah was now effectively ruled by priests, and not everyone was happy with the new regime. One consequence was that at some time after the return from exile the Children of Israel divide into Jews, in the Land of Judah, and Samaritans, based on Samaria, the administrative centre in the northern area which had once been the kingdom of Israel, and which was halfway between Nazareth, Jesus's childhood home, even further North, and Bethlehem, his reputed birthplace in the land of Judah in the South. The Samaritans, who were on the whole the poorer people whose families had never gone into exile, kept to the five books of Moses, but accepted no other scriptures and had nothing to do with the Temple in Jerusalem. The Jews accepted a wider range of scriptures, were attached to the Temple as the central place of sacrifice, and regarded the Samaritans as backsliders.

Judaism

Eventually some of the writings even of mainstream Jews indicate a belief that other nations have a part to play in the purposes of their God. The story of *Ruth* is a polemic, however gently expressed, which points out that the great king David was descended from a Moabitess and suggests that inter-marriage was not an entirely bad thing. The story of *Jonah* makes the point that the mercy of God extends to other nations. The tension between exclusiveness and reaching out to all mankind was there long before the time of Jesus and St Paul.

The Jewish religion had moved a long way in the thousand years since Moses led the Children of Israel out of Egypt. It began as the religion of a people who entered into a covenant with a powerful tribal god who would support them if they kept faith with him and punish them if they did not. It developed step by step into the belief that there was only one God, who was the Creator of all things, all-powerful, just, loving and merciful, calling humankind to turn away from sin and love righteousness, requiring not burnt offerings but a humble and a contrite heart (*Psalm 51.16 and 17*), and reaching out beyond his Chosen People to all mankind. There is a sense in which the Jews had developed a genius for religion. Their religious ideas had developed beyond those of any of the other peoples of the Mediterranean world, and just as their god was a jealous god, so they were jealous of their religious heritage.

Greek philosophy

While the Jews had developed what looks like a communal genius for religion, the Greeks were developing a communal genius for philosophy, the love of wisdom. Some Jews had philosophical ideas, but it was their religion which was important in the development of the human consciousness. Some Greeks had religious ideas, but it is their philosophy which mattered. The Jews used two languages, classical Hebrew and Aramaic, both of which lacked abstract words, so their ideas are often expressed in striking visual imagery which should not be taken literally. The Greek language, on the other hand, is full of abstract words with which they tried to convey fine nuances of meaning. The two things eventually came together with interesting results.

While the Jews were codifying the Law and recording the words of the prophets, Greek philosophers were looking for that which was the source of everything. Perhaps it was the *logos*, which literally means 'word' but is probably best translated as 'universal wisdom.' They wanted to understand the nature of matter. Perhaps everything was made up of four elements: earth, air, fire and water. They wanted to understand the forces which generate change. Perhaps they were Love, which binds things together, and Strife, which pulls them apart.

Socrates, an Athenian who lived from 470 till 399 BC, asked awkward questions, challenged accepted wisdom and asserted that he knew nothing except that he knew nothing. He was condemned to death for corrupting the youth of the city with his ideas. He accepted the sentence and declined the opportunity to escape because it would set a bad example to the young. His teaching and his acceptance of his own judicial execution shine a light on the darkness of Athenian democracy, which is at least open to the accusation of being a form of tyrannical mob rule.

His pupil, Plato, following up some of the questions which Socrates had asked, came to the conclusion that there must be a world of *ideas* or *forms*, a 'real' world, behind the material world which we perceive with our senses. Behind all material things there is the immutable and eternal *idea* or *form* of the thing. A chair or a horse is a chair or a horse only in so far as it approximates to the eternal and unchanging *idea* of chair or horse. Plato illustrated this by suggesting that if cave dwellers were from birth bound, so that they could not look outwards towards the opening of the cave, and if they regularly saw shadows on the wall in front of them, they would believe that the shadows they saw were the only reality. If someone escaped, discovered the world outside and returned to tell them, they would not believe him and they would kill him. We, he suggested, with our limited perception, are to the real world much like those cave dwellers.

Plato's pupil, Aristotle, took this notion of a real world of *ideas* or *forms* a stage further. He decided that the *idea* of anything was the underlying reality within it, which was distinct from its external characteristics. To make that clear it is necessary to use English words derived from Latin. Beneath or *sub* that which is material, or stands out, is the 'substance', or underlying reality, of a thing. Over the years, of course, the common meaning of the word 'substance' has changed so much that it conveys the idea of something solid – almost the opposite of its original meaning. But what Aristotle was talking about was 'substance' as the insubstantial and underlying reality of a thing. That thing will also have various external characteristics or 'accidents': its colour, shape, texture, the noise it makes when struck, its brittleness or flexibility. But the 'substance' is in no way solid or, in the modern sense, substantial.

These ideas have a religious connection. Plato believed that all men have an immortal soul, which exists in the realm of ideas and is therefore unchanging – unlike the body which is subject to decay. Both he and Aristotle believed that there must be a transcendent God, and Aristotle believed that this transcendent God was the 'first mover', or Creator, of all things.

Hellenisation

The Greeks also developed a new, brutal and effective method of fighting in close formation, and during the fourth century BC Alexander the Great of Greece, whose tutor had at one time been Aristotle, defeated the Persian Empire and in the process conquered Palestine. His aim was not only conquest but also the dissemination of Greek culture through the world – or Hellenisation (*Hellas* is the Greek word for Greece). After Alexander's death in 323 BC his successors continued the policy of extending Greek cultural influence and the use of the Greek language, and this resulted in the need for Greek translations of the Jewish scriptures. Many were made, and one collection, known as the Septuagint because it was reputed to have been produced in 72 days by 72 translators, acquired a special authority. Some Jews were happy with these developments, so long as their religion was tolerated. Others were bitterly opposed, passionately defended their own practices, and regarded the translation of the scriptures into Greek as a sin.

In the first half of the second century before Christ a Greek ruler tried to destroy the Jewish religion. Antiochus IV, in a bid to bind his subjects together in a united Greek culture, tried to end circumcision and the observance of the Sabbath, banned and destroyed the books of the Law and set up altars to Greek gods. Many Jews, particularly 'the pious ones', or *Hasidim*, rose in rebellion and eventually, under Judas Maccabeus, the Hammer, won a series of victories and took Jerusalem. The Temple, where an altar to Zeus had been set up, was cleansed and rededicated to the God of Israel, something still celebrated annually by Jews at about Christmas-time in the feast of *Hannukah*.

The Roman occupation

The Jews won not only the religious liberty for which they had originally fought but also a short-lived political independence. It was not a success. They were by now not so much a holy people under God as a nation ruled by priests who required them in the name of God to obey innumerable rules regulating in detail their behaviour and their diet. They fought, conquered and tried to impose their own version of Judaism on the Samaritans in the North and on the Edomites, their neighbours in the South. They disagreed among themselves and politics was mixed with religion. A monarchy was established, but power came to be in the hands of a group known as the Sadducees, who were generally not only priests but also members of the aristocracy and often well disposed towards Greek culture. They were opposed by the Pharisees, who were in the tradition of the *Hasidim* and were passionately attached to scrupulous interpretation of and unswerving obedience to the Law. Eventually the ill-feeling between the two groups was so great that the Pharisees appealed for help to the Roman republic, whose power was now spreading all round the Mediterranean. In 63 BC the Roman general Pompey occupied Palestine and later incorporated it into the Roman province of Syria.

A generation later, after the chaos and civil wars following the assassination of Julius Caesar, the Roman Empire was established, with the Romans seeking to impose order throughout their empire and trying to get local rulers to do much of the work for them. About a quarter of a century after Caesar Augustus became the first Roman Emperor in 30 BC, the local ruler in Judea was a king called Herod, who was half Jewish and half Edomite. It was a society with a strong Jewish religious tradition, widespread Greek culture and Roman military occupation. Many people disliked Herod, disliked Greek culture, disliked the Romans and yearned for a saviour who would free them from foreign rule. Ideally that saviour would be the anointed one, the Messiah, of the house and lineage of David, who would also reconcile the Children of Israel with God.

Section 1
From Christ to Constantine
(from Jesus to the 330s)

Chapter 2

The Life and Ministry of Jesus

The Gospels

Most of what we know about Jesus is to be found in four accounts known as gospels – a word derived from the Old English word *godspell*, meaning 'good news.' They were all written some time in the first century after Jesus's birth, and they were all written in Greek. The name *Jesus* is the Greek version of *Joshua*, a Jewish name meaning 'The Lord saves.' The word *Christ* is the Greek version of the Jewish word *Messiah*, which means 'the Anointed One.'

For some years after the life of Jesus stories about him were passed on, as one person after another spoke of what he or she had heard. It is probable that the gospel of Mark, the first surviving written account of those stories, appeared in Rome during the reign of the Emperor Nero, in about 65 AD, in response to the accusations being put about that Christians had started the great fire of Rome of the previous year. It is direct and vigorous, and clearly written for non-Jews, or Gentiles. Although it starts with a quotation from the prophet Isaiah, there are hardly any other references in it to the Old Testament, and Mark explains Jewish customs and puts into Greek any expressions in Aramaic, the language used by Jesus and his followers. Mark writes simply, possibly on behalf of Jesus's follower, or apostle, Peter, with the aim of revealing Jesus to his readers as the promised *Messiah*, the Anointed One, the Son of God.

Another account was written perhaps fifteen years later. It is possible that its author, Luke, who wrote not only this gospel but also the Acts of the Apostles, was the doctor who had travelled with the apostle Paul spreading the good news of Jesus in Asia Minor. He was a Gentile and he was writing for a Gentile audience. He made use of Mark's gospel and other narratives which no longer exist, particularly one known to scholars as 'Q', from the German word *Quelle*, a source. He added material which he collected from others and he fitted together a beautifully written account, which emphasises Jesus's sympathy for all men and women and shows his sympathetic understanding extending to a Roman centurion and a Samaritan woman, to outcasts of society, to people who were ill or in distress, and to those who were seen by others as sinners.

The first gospel to be written for a specifically Jewish audience (it is also printed first in the Bible) is the account attributed to Matthew, the tax collector who was called by Jesus to be one of the twelve apostles. It was clearly written to persuade Jews that Jesus was the promised Messiah, it has frequent references to the Old Testament in it and it portrays the life and death of Jesus as the fulfilment of ancient prophecies. But it was not completed until some years after the Romans had destroyed Jerusalem in AD 70, and the fact that, like Luke, it makes frequent use of Mark and 'Q' seems to indicate that the author was not someone with direct knowledge of Jesus.

The fourth gospel was composed right at the end of the first century and is quite different from the other three. It is attributed to the apostle John, but uses the language of an educated Greek rather than that of a Galilean fisherman. It is entirely different in style from the other three and unlike them it includes none of the stories or parables which Jesus told. Instead, right at the beginning it uses the language of Greek philosophy to discuss the relationship between Jesus and God the Father, and goes on with descriptions of what Jesus did and said to deal with the great issues of Love and Faith and the sense in which Jesus can be seen as the Light of the World and the Way through which we can come to God.

The Virgin Birth

None of the gospels is a biography in the sense in which we understand the term. The first to be written, probably Mark's, makes no reference to Jesus's birth. Nor does John's. But Matthew begins by tracing the ancestry of Jesus back forty-two generations to Abraham, arranging his account in three groups of fourteen, ending with Joseph, and showing that Jesus was of the house and lineage of David. All he says about the birth is that while Mary was engaged to Joseph, she was found to be pregnant by the Holy Spirit and Joseph, who was a good man and did not want to see her disgraced, was going to break off the engagement quietly until he had a dream reassuring him *(Matthew 1, 18-20)*.

The tradition that Mary was still a virgin when Jesus was born developed early in the life of the church. Later there grew up a belief that she remained a virgin throughout her life. But Matthew appears to be unaware of that tradition when he says that Joseph 'had no intercourse with her until after her son was born', and Mark implies that she eventually had a large family. He describes how, when Jesus taught in the synagogue of his home town of Nazareth, some people said, 'Isn't this the carpenter, the son of Mary, the brother of James and Joseph and Judas and Simon, and are not his sisters here with us?' *(Mark 6, 3)*.

It is the first two chapters of Luke's gospel that give us the beautiful and fairly detailed Christmas story that is so widely known. The account raises some problems for the historian. There is, for example, no other evidence of a proclamation by Caesar Augustus of a general census, and even the choice of Bethlehem as the birthplace of Jesus may have been made to fit in with a prediction of the prophet Micah *(Micah 5.2)*. But that is not the important issue. Luke was proclaiming that something wonderful and unique had happened. An angel of the Lord, he says, appeared to shepherds bringing 'good tidings of great joy, which shall be to all people.' The angel told them of the birth of the Saviour, and suddenly there was with the angel a multitude of the heavenly host praising God and saying, 'Glory to God in the highest, and on earth peace, goodwill toward men.' *(Luke 2.8-14)* Whatever actually happened, the story of the birth of Jesus had, and still has, power to inspire and enthral.

Resurrection and Ascension

Similar considerations apply if one adopts a critical approach to the stories of the resurrection and the ascension. All of the gospels deal in some detail with the events leading up to the crucifixion of Jesus, but their treatment of what happened afterwards is more varied. The earliest manuscripts of Mark's gospel finish with three of his female followers fleeing from the empty tomb trembling and amazed. The last verses, which were added later, tell of his appearing to one of those three, Mary Magdalene, then 'in a different form' to two people out walking, and finally to the eleven apostles, telling them to proclaim the gospel throughout the world *(Mark 16.15)*. Matthew's and Luke's gospels are much the same, with Luke providing more detail: the two disciples to whom Jesus appeared on the road were walking to Emmaus and one of them was called Cleopas *(Luke 24.13-18)*. But by the time we get to St John's gospel, Jesus is appearing in a locked room *(John 20.26-7)*, inviting Thomas to touch him, and helping Peter to catch fish *(John 21.5-11)*. Christians understandably ask themselves if those stories should be taken literally or if they should be seen as a symbolic proclamation that Jesus lives on as the Messiah and Son of God.

The answer is not self-evident. Many Christians, when they proclaim in church what are known as the Apostles' Creed or the Nicene Creed, assume that they are giving public assent to a literal belief in the Virgin Birth and the Bodily Resurrection – and, indeed, the Ascension, which Mark and Luke mention very briefly *(Mark 16.19 and Luke 24.51)* and Matthew and John not at all. But it is also possible, and always has been possible, to take the view that what Jesus said, the way he taught, his impact on people, the way he lived his life and died, and what happened after his death, were so extraordinary, so brilliantly illuminating, and so continuing in their impact, that it is no wonder that his followers told stories about his life which, even if not literally true, were intended to convey something of his significance and have lasting value.

Healing and Miracles

Jesus is described as preparing for his ministry by spending forty days in the desert, just as the Children of Israel had spent forty years in the desert – in his case fasting and subject to a number of temptations. After that he returned to Galilee and taught in the synagogues, and at the same time acquired a reputation as a healer. The gospel writers are agreed on his remarkable gifts as a healer, but the stories develop with time. In Mark's gospel we see him driving out evil spirits and curing lepers and the blind, the deaf and the dumb. His motive was compassion for the individuals concerned, and he was anxious that his reputation should not rest on his miracles, even if they indicated that he was the Messiah and that the Kingdom of Heaven was near. By John's gospel he is raising Lazarus to life after he had been dead for some days *(John 11. 1-44)*.

Similarly we hear from Mark how he fed a great multitude when only five loaves and two small fishes seemed to be available *(Mark 6.35-44)*. By John's gospel he is turning water into wine *(John 2.1-11)*. The stories told by John are rich in symbolism, and the symbolic meaning may well have been more accessible at the end of the first century than it is at the beginning of the twenty-first. It is at least questionable whether it is necessary to take them all literally, and it is even possible that a literal interpretation is now more of an obstacle than an aid to faith. Some people may be turned away from faith in Jesus by the perception that they are expected to accept the raising of Lazarus and the turning of water into wine as things which actually happened rather than as stories signifying his life-giving and transforming power.

Teaching with authority

Jesus also acquired a reputation as a teacher. Luke particularly makes the point that his teaching had a ring of authority about it, and it is worth illustrating what that means. Those who came to hear him included not only ordinary people but also Pharisees, who were the religious puritans of their time, committed to scrupulous obedience to the Law, and some scribes, the technical experts in the Law, which by the time of Jesus had become extraordinarily detailed and complicated. Mark tells how one of the scribes who admired Jesus's teaching asked him, 'Which is the first commandment of all?' *(Mark 12, v. 28)*. Jesus did not reply with the first of the ten commandments of Moses: *I am the Lord thy God, which have brought thee out of the land of Egypt, out of the house of bondage. Thou shalt have no other gods before me. (Exodus 20, vv. 2 and 3)* Instead he selects verses 4 and 5 from Chapter 6 of Deuteronomy (though perhaps it should be mentioned that the numbering of verses did not become usual until many centuries later): *Hear, O Israel: The Lord thy God is one Lord, and thou shalt love the Lord thy God with all thy heart, with all thy soul, and with all thy might.* And then he comments, 'This is the first commandment, and the second is like, namely this: *Thou shalt love thy neighbour as thyself.'* And he adds: 'There is none other commandment greater than these.' What he describes as the second commandment is from the second half of verse 18 of chapter 19 of Leviticus. Clearly Jesus knew his way around the scriptures. He had the authority which comes from knowing his subject; and when the scribe says that Jesus is absolutely right and adds that to love God and one's neighbours, as Jesus suggests, is 'more than all burnt offerings and sacrifices', Jesus tells him, 'You are not far from the kingdom of God.'

Jesus's answer was based on the Hebrew scriptures. He puts two texts together in such a way as to breathe new life into them, and the second commandment, to love your neighbour as yourself, is based, rather significantly, on an assumption that you will love yourself. Jesus was thinking in terms of what is often called 'original sin', the idea that human beings are by their very nature self-centred, and what he was suggesting is that all human beings should seek ways of escaping their natural self-centredness and entering into a sympathetic understanding of others. Start by loving your brother, whom you have seen and eventually you may later come to love God, whom you have not seen. His followers understood the message and passed it on (*1 John 4. 20-21*).

It is worth noting that he did not ask anyone to love their neighbour more than themselves. He knew that he was already setting them a difficult task by suggesting that they should aim to love their neighbours as themselves. For it is not just a matter of treating those around you well. That is not enough. He required us to learn to love them.

Loving one's neighbour

But, of course, one has only got to hear an answer like that and someone will ask, 'What is love?' or indeed, 'Who is my neighbour?' Faced with that sort of question, Jesus would never provide a definition, or even give a direct answer. Instead he would tell a story. His stories are well known, but changed circumstances and familiarity have deprived some of them of their immediacy and impact. So perhaps it may be appropriate, even if presumptuous, to illustrate his approach with a modern story. During the *apartheid* era a black South African who worked in Johannesburg set off home to Soweto one evening and on his way was set about by thugs, beaten up and robbed. He lay by the side of the road for some hours, unconscious and in a pool of his own blood. No one came by until early in the morning when the first car that passed was driven by a white social worker on his way to a meeting. He saw the body lying there, but his meeting, on the rights of African workers, was important and he felt sure that someone else would be along soon. So he drove on. A few minutes later another car came by driven by a black priest on his way for an appointment with the bishop. He also saw the body but was anxious not to be late for his appointment and, similarly, knew that someone else was sure to be along in a short while. So he drove on. The third car that came by was a police car. Two white South African policemen got out. One turned the body over with his boot. Then they lifted him up, put him in the back of the car, took him to the nearest hostelry and told the hostel keeper to sluice him down, patch him up, put him to bed and give him something to eat. They gave him some money for his pains, and said they'd be back later to see how he was.

The question Jesus asked after a similar story was 'Who behaved as neighbour to the man who fell among thieves?' *(Luke 10.36)* We probably all know that in the original story the answer is the person we refer to as the Good Samaritan, and nowadays the term Samaritan is used for kindly and understanding people who can be relied on to listen to you at the end of a telephone line when you are in a state of suicidal despair. But the word 'Good' is not to be found in the original. In the time of Jesus Samaritans were assumed by Jews to be bad – those awful people from the area around Samaria who had intermarried with Gentiles, despised the Temple in Jerusalem and betrayed the faith of their fathers. The story was intended to upset normal expectations and did.

Paradox and ambiguity

It was characteristic of Jesus's teaching that it upset normal expectations. 'Love your enemies,' he said, 'Do good to those who hate you, bless those who curse you, pray for those who treat you badly. If someone hits you on one cheek, offer him the other one as well. If a man is taking away your coat, do not stop him from taking your shirt as well.' *(Luke 6.27-29)* Those are not rules, of course. They are an attempt to get people to look at things differently. Paradoxes and ambiguities abound in his teaching. But it is sound practical advice as well: 'Treat men exactly as you would like them to treat you. If you love those who love you, what credit is that to you? Even sinners love those who love them. Love your enemies. Do good, and lend without expecting to get anything back. Your reward will be wonderful and you will be children of the Most High. For He is good to the ungrateful and the wicked!' *(Luke 6.31-2 and 35)*. It is possible to imagine this being said with a twinkle in the eye. But that does not detract from its force. It may even strengthen it.

Even when Jesus makes a straightforward statement, he often says something else which appears to contradict it. At one time he suggests that a good tree will bear good fruit and a rotten tree bad fruit, and that you can tell the difference between them by the fruit *(Luke 6.43-4)*. But at another time he says, 'Judge not that ye be not judged.' *(Matthew 7.1)* Can he have it both ways? Of course he can, because the answer to these matters lies not in precise, clear-cut rules and definitions but in understanding. And understanding involves the acceptance of ambiguity, of paradox and of contradiction. At one time he calls Simon *Rocky*, or *Peter* (the French name *Pierre*, which also means a rock, conveys the point rather better). Peter is the rock on which Jesus will build *(Matthew 16.18)*. Shortly afterwards he calls him *Satan*, telling him to get out of his way, because he is looking at things in a human instead of a divine perspective *(Matthew 16.23)*. Both things were appropriate in context. There are dangers in taking either of them out of context.

It is also worth looking at the language Jesus uses when he speaks about the Kingdom of Heaven. For example, 'You ask what the Kingdom of Heaven is like. What illustration can I use? It is like a grain of mustard seed, which a man took and dropped in his own garden. It grew up into a tree and all the birds came and nested in its branches' *(Matthew 13. 31-2)*. Or on another occasion, when a Pharisee asks him when the Kingdom of God will come, he replies, 'The Kingdom of God never comes by watching for it. Men can't say, 'Look, here it is, or there it is. The Kingdom of God is within you' *(Luke 17.21)*. It is also, he suggested, 'among you' and 'near you' (Matthew 24. 33).

The clash with the Pharisees

His teaching brought him into conflict with the Pharisees. Although Jesus's standard answer when asked about how people should behave was that they should keep the Law, he saw the Law as a helpful guide to living well rather than as a burden to be borne, and he recognised that the most serious failing of many of the Pharisees was that they were self-righteous – sure that they were right about everything and pleased with their own behaviour, while lacking human sympathy and understanding.

When one of the Pharisees asked Jesus to a meal with him, a woman who was notorious in the town brought an alabaster flask of perfume and stood by Jesus crying, letting her tears fall on his feet, drying them with her hair, kissing them and anointing them with the perfume. The Pharisee thought to himself, 'If this man were really a prophet, he would know what sort of a person this woman is.' And Jesus said to him, 'You see this woman? I came into your house and you provided no water to wash my feet. But she has washed my feet with her tears and dried them with her hair. There was no warmth in your greeting, but she, from the moment I came in, has not stopped covering my feet with kisses. You gave me no oil for my head, but she has put perfume on my feet. That is why I tell you, Simon, that her sins, which are many, are forgiven; for she has shown me so much love.' The men at table with him didn't understand it, but said to each other, 'Who is this man, who even forgives sins?' *(Luke 7. 36-49)*

On another occasion a Pharisee who had invited Jesus to dinner was surprised that he did not wash before the meal and Jesus said to him 'You Pharisees are fond of cleaning the outside of your cups and dishes, but inside yourselves you are full of greed and wickedness! Have you no sense? Don't you realise that the One who made the outside is the maker of the inside as well? Far better to make the inside clean by doing good and you will find the outside things become clean as a matter of course. Alas for you Pharisees. You scrupulously give a tenth of every little piece of mint or rue or any other little herb, but you lose sight of the justice and the love of God. That's what you should be concerned with.' *(Luke 11.39-42)* That did not mean that lesser duties should be neglected. But Jesus was always more concerned with the spirit of the Law and with the ideals which lay behind it than with scrupulous adherence to detailed regulations.

One of the most powerful of all his stories was about two men going to the temple to pray. One was a Pharisee and the other a tax-collector working for the occupying Roman forces. The Pharisee was pleased with himself and in his mind ran over his virtues and good works, all of which was, no doubt, true. The tax-collector looked down at the ground and said, 'God, have mercy on me – a sinner.' And Jesus said, 'I assure you, it was this man who went home justified in God's eyes rather than the other.' *(Luke 18.10-14)* It was a novel and a very upsetting way of looking at things.

The end

It was not only the Pharisees whom Jesus offended. One of the Scribes said to him, 'Master, when you say things like this, you are insulting us as well.' And Jesus replied, 'Yes, and I do blame you. You pile up back-breaking burdens for men to bear, but you will not lift a finger to help them.' *(Luke 11. 45-6)* And he said to his disciples, while everybody was listening, 'Be on your guard against the Scribes who enjoy walking round in long robes and love having men bow to them in public, getting front seats in the synagogue and the best places at dinner parties – while all the time they are battening on widows' property and covering it up with long prayers. These are the men who are heading for the deepest damnation.' *(Mark 12.38-40)*

Not surprisingly the Scribes and the Chief Priests wanted to catch him out. So they sent spies into the crowd to get hold of something he might say which they could use to hand him over to the jurisdiction of the Roman governor. One of them asked Jesus whether or not it was right to pay taxes to Caesar. It was a clever question and they must have thought that, whatever he replied, they had caught him. But Jesus called for a coin, asked whose face was on it, and said, 'Well, give to Caesar what is Caesar's and give to God what is God's.' *(Mark 12.13-17)* It was an even more clever response, and it was also simple, practical and straightforward. But it made them all the more determined to find a pretext on which to have him arrested.

Jesus warned his disciples of what was about to happen and Matthew, Mark and Luke, but not John, all describe what is known as the Last Supper at the time of the Jewish feast of the Passover. According to the account given by Matthew, Jesus took bread, blessed it, and gave it to his disciples, saying, 'Take this and eat; this is my body.' *(Matthew 26.26)* Then he took a cup, gave thanks to God and gave it to them, saying, 'Drink from it, all of you. For this is my blood, the blood of the covenant, shed for many for the forgiveness of sins.' John instead gives an account of what Jesus told his disciples about his own relationship with the Father and describes how Jesus prayed to the Father both for his disciples and for all who would believe in him (*John 17*.). Each of the four gospel writers then gives his own account of how Jesus was betrayed by Judas Iscariot, arrested, accused, interrogated, crucified and buried.

The Jews had longed for a Messiah, but when he came they rejected him. They strewed palms in his way and shouted *Hosanna* when they thought he might be going to lead them to victory over the occupying army of the Roman Empire. But when he told them to love their enemies they called for his crucifixion. Actions like healing the lame on the Sabbath and giving the blind their sight were seen as offences, and, given a choice between saving a murderer or Jesus, they chose the murderer. The Roman governor, Pontius Pilate, 'conspired with the Gentiles and the peoples of Israel' (*Acts 4.28*) to have Jesus executed. So Jesus went to his death weighed down by the sin of mankind, grieving, but forgiving those who were crucifying him *(Luke 23.34)* and giving his life as 'a ransom for many' (*Matthew 20.28*) – an 'atonement', in order that we might be 'at one' with God.

The Roman centurion who presided over the execution saw what was done and then glorified God, saying, 'Certainly this was a righteous man' (*Luke 23. 47*).

Jesus's moral teaching

At this point it may be worth quoting a philosopher, Bryan Magee, who does not count himself a Christian, writing in the mid-1990s, after travelling in the Middle East and reading the New Testament in a new English translation, about his view of Jesus's teaching (*Confessions of a Philosopher, Ch.16, pp.292-3*) :

'What came through to me most strongly was the radically 'different' character of Jesus's moral teaching. So different is it, indeed, that it borders on the incomprehensible. Other moralists put forward rules of behaviour; other revolutionists in morals try to overthrow whatever are the existing rules and establish different ones in their stead; but Jesus is saying that rules, any rules, are not what morality is about. God, he says, is not in the business of awarding prizes to people who live in accordance with moral rules. You will not win any special favours from him by being virtuous, but are only too likely to find – to your great chagrin, no doubt, as well as your incomprehension – that he loves sinners just as much as he loves you. If this infringes your sense of justice you have not understood the situation. It is no use being good in the hope of getting a reward from God: this is pure self-seeking, and therefore a self-contradictory conception of morally admirable behaviour. Only if you are good when it is not rewarded is your behaviour morally admirable. But then there is indeed no reward: so the goodness has to be its own justification, regardless of consequences. God's loving you has nothing to do with your deserving it. He loves everybody, including the most undeserving, indeed he loves them as much as he loves you. Just as he loves the undeserving, so you also should love those who are undeserving of your love, including those who deserve it least, namely your enemies. Love is what matters, not deserving, and least of all rules. In fact, love matters above everything else. It is the ultimate reality, the true nature of existence, God. Perfect love is unconditional, and to unconditional love, deserving has ceased to matter or even have any significance. It is not that Jesus is against our living in accordance with rules. On the contrary, he recognises that rules are necessary wherever human beings live together, and he believes that they should be obeyed; but he sees them as arbitrary, superficial things that should be made subservient to human needs, not human needs made subservient to them. If we had enough love and concern for one another there would be no need for rules. We need them only because we are selfish. They are not, in themselves, good.'

Washing feet

That gets to the heart of the matter. Above all he has seen that Love is at the centre of Jesus's teaching, and he has also seen that the truth lies in contradictions and paradoxes and not in definitions. So it is appropriate to end with a story from John's gospel about Jesus's relationship with his disciples. Before the Jewish feast of the Passover 'Jesus, knowing that the Father had given all things into his hands, and that he was come from God, and went to God; he riseth from supper, and laid aside his garments; and took a towel, and girded himself. After that he poureth water into a basin, and began to wash the disciples' feet' *(John 13.3-50)*. It is both an anti-climax and a revelation of the nature of the God whom Christians worship.

It is worth considering why he did it. First, it was because their feet were dirty and needed washing. Secondly, it was a lesson. He was teaching by example: 'If I then, your Lord and Master, have washed your feet, you also ought to wash one another's feet.' Thirdly, it was a symbolic gesture that his mission was to wash humankind clean. What is more, when he physically washed the feet of his companions, who, like him, were free, Jewish and men, he stooped down and undertook work reserved for slaves, Gentiles and women. He identified himself with all humankind, particularly the poor, the despised and the oppressed. His action proclaimed that he was there for all who needed him. It is a revelation of the nature of the God whom Christians worship, and it is revealed through a paradox. Christians know that God is almighty, omniscient and eternal. But their Lord and Saviour, the Son of God, washes feet.

It was and is a moral and a theological revolution. Jesus's teaching was paradoxical, ambiguous and illuminating, and it throws moral responsibility back to the questioner. As a guide for how to live it is better to ask what Jesus would have done than appeal to principles. Principles are dangerous. An appeal to principle will always provoke an appeal to counter-principle. But Jesus had told his disciples that he was himself 'the way, the truth and the life' *(John 14.6)*. They saw him as the promised Messiah, the Son of God, and he had commanded them to preach repentance and the forgiveness of sins to all nations *(Luke 24.47)*. They had to decide what to do about it.

Chapter 3

The Early Church

The early Christians

We know very little of the early church. Christians were the *kyriaki*, the Lord's followers, from the Greek word *kyrie*, the Lord. It is from that that we get the word 'church'. They were also the *ekklesia*, those called forth to follow Christ. As it happens both those words came to apply in time to the buildings in which Christians met as well as to the congregations who met there, and just as the English word 'church' comes from *kyriaki*, so the French word 'église' comes from *ekklesia*. But the Christians of the early church had no thought of church buildings. Nor would they have imagined congregations dispersed through the world. They assumed that the Creation was relatively recent and that the Day of Judgement was imminent, so they had no reason to concern themselves with how the church should be organised. Nor did they engage in theological speculation about the nature of Jesus and his relationship with the Father. They were quite simply confident that he was the Messiah, the Anointed One foretold by Isaiah the prophet, and they believed that the Holy Spirit of God had come to them at the Feast of Pentecost (*Acts 2.1-4*), fifty days after the Passover meal which Jesus had shared with the twelve apostles, and which came to be called the Last Supper.

Christians joined the church through the rite of baptism, at which they were symbolically washed clean of evil, and which had been commended to them by Jesus (*Matthew 28.19*). They were also taught by Paul to regard it as dying to sin and rising to new life. They awaited Christ's return in glory to judge the living and the dead, and they met together regularly for an act of remembrance (*anamnesis*) and thanksgiving (*eucharistia*) at which they took bread and wine, consecrated it and then ate the bread and drank the wine in remembrance of how Christ's body and blood had been given for them on the cross. At a fairly early stage they made a practice of meeting on Sundays, either before going to work in the morning or when they got back in the evening, because that was the day on which the disciples had found the empty tomb. Both the washing with water in baptism and the taking of bread and wine in the eucharist were physical acts with spiritual significance. Each was what came to be called a sacrament – 'an outward and visible sign of inward invisible grace.'

From the beginning the Christian Faith centred on the proclamation of the crucified and risen Jesus. Faith was essentially a matter of trust. It was not a matter of belief in or of giving assent to intellectual propositions. It was far more a matter of trusting in Christ and seeking to follow him than of believing the right things about him – whatever the right things may be. Jesus had pointed to an ideal. 'You should' he said, 'be perfect, even as your father in heaven is perfect.' But he also knew that they would fall short of the ideal and he told his followers to preach repentance and the forgiveness of sins. He had proclaimed a way of living based on what was best in Jewish tradition. But at the same time he was offering a new moral perspective, a new way of looking at things. Rather than concentrating on meticulous adherence to the Law, Christians were expected to love God and their neighbours. Their faith in God the Father and in Jesus was expected to bear fruit in the way in which they lived.

Christianity and Judaism

In the early years the distinction between Christianity and Judaism was not entirely clear. Christians set out to proclaim Jesus's message of love, forgiveness and reconciliation. But one problem for the early church was that it was unclear whether Christianity was simply a form of Judaism or something new and dramatically different. The earliest Christians were Jews. Their religion, like other religions, had the function of binding people together and providing them with a shared ideology which was passed on from one generation to the next and underpinned the laws and customs of society. Their prophets had foretold a Messiah, and they saw Jesus as that Messiah.

On the other hand, Jesus had set out teachings which applied to all mankind and for all time. He had commanded the apostles to teach all peoples, baptise those who wished to follow his teaching, look after them and above all show them that all people needed to acknowledge their own guilt, try to put right whatever they had done wrong and seek and hope for forgiveness. The object was to transform the world. Understandably those Jews who did not see Jesus as the Messiah criticised Christians as an heretical sect which failed to keep strictly to the Mosaic Law, accepted Gentile converts, intermarried with Gentiles and had eventually even fallen away from the essential and central monotheism of Judaism with their talk of Father, Son and Holy Spirit.

Luke describes conflict with the Jewish authorities early in his account of the Acts of the Apostles. He tells the story of a lame man lying at the temple gate known as the Gate Beautiful in Jerusalem and asking Peter and John for alms. Peter replied, 'Silver and gold have I none, but such as I have I give thee. In the name of Jesus Christ of Nazareth rise up and walk' (*Acts 3.6*). And the man leapt up and walked and praised God. That evening Peter and John were arrested and the next day were brought before the high priest and asked, 'By what power, or by what name, have you done this?' Peter replied, 'You rulers of the people and elders of Israel....Be it known unto you all, and to all the people of Israel, that by the name of Jesus Christ of Nazareth, whom you crucified, and whom God raised from the dead, even by him does this man stand here before you whole.' And then he ended his explanation with a comment which is usually translated, 'There is no other name under heaven given among men by which we must be saved' (*Acts 4.12*).

31

When Peter spoke of the name of Jesus he was speaking of it as something which represented the whole personality and nature of Jesus, and it is worth appreciating that the Greek word *dei*, which can be translated as 'must', also means 'it is appropriate'. That makes particularly good sense here. For since 'Jesus' is the Greek form of the Jewish name 'Joshua', which means 'The Lord saves', what Peter was saying was that it is the one name by which it is appropriate that we should be saved, precisely because that is what it means. Understanding that alters the whole flavour of Peter's words. They are not a hard-line, exclusive statement by a member of the religious establishment that you have got to toe the official Christian line or be damned. They are a joyful affirmation by one of a persecuted minority of trust, or faith, in their crucified yet risen Lord. That was too much for the High Priest. So Peter and John were commanded not to teach in the name of Jesus.

The first martyr

They did, of course, and the number of disciples grew rapidly. It is difficult to be sure quite why the church grew so rapidly. No doubt people joined for a range of different reasons and, indeed, the motives of any individual were likely to be mixed. But probably the single thing which most attracted people to Christianity was the way Christians looked after each other. They cared for widows and orphans in distress, they tended the sick and visited prisoners, they offered hospitality to travellers and they gave alms to the poor. They tried to avoid violence and other forms of excess. They expected husbands to be loyal to their wives, and contrariwise. They believed in treating all men and women as equal in the eyes of God. They knew that they were passed from darkness into light because they loved the brethren (*1 John 3.14*). Whether male or female, Jew or Gentile, slave or freeman, they were 'all one in Christ Jesus' (*Galatians 3.28*). Christianity could be dismissed as a religion for slaves, and often was. But it was not only slaves who found it attractive. Nor was it just the widows and orphans, the elderly, the sick and the poor. Many Gentiles looked with admiration at Christian love in action, saw it as something divine and joined the *ekklesia*, those who felt called forth to follow Christ.

Having Gentiles join the church produced internal problems. For example, some of the Gentiles were soon dissatisfied because their widows were neglected in the distribution of alms. So the apostles appointed seven men 'of honest report' (all seven of them had Greek and not Jewish names) to look after such matters (*Acts 6.1-6*). One of them, Stephen, was the first Christian martyr. He came to the attention of the High Priest and was brought before the Council, where he accused the members of the Council of being 'stiff-necked and uncircumcised in heart and ears' and eventually, looking up into heaven, proclaimed, 'Behold, I see the heavens opened and the Son of Man standing at the right hand of God' (*Acts 7.56*). At that they seized him and stoned him to death. He died calling on the Lord Jesus to receive his spirit and saying, 'Lord, lay not this sin to their charge.'

Paul

A young Pharisee called Saul, who was there 'consenting unto his death', afterwards 'made havoc of the church', hauling many of the disciples off to prison. One consequence of this was that the church spread even further, because the disciples fled from Jerusalem to other towns, and before long Saul, 'breathing out threatenings and slaughter against the disciples of the Lord', obtained from the High Priest letters to the synagogues in Damascus and set off to destroy the Christian church there (*Acts 9.1-2*).

It was to be one of the most significant journeys in history. The story of Saul's conversion on the road to Damascus is well known. As a result of it he broke away from his training as a Pharisee, exchanged the proud and royal name of Saul for the new and humble name of Paul, which means 'Little' or 'Small', and set out to convert the world. He saw it as his mission to preach Christ and explain the significance of Jesus's death and resurrection to the Gentiles. The infrastructure of the Roman Empire, its roads and shipping routes, enabled him to travel relatively easily through Syria, Asia Minor and Greece and eventually to Rome; and whenever he came to a new town he would start by teaching in the synagogue. Rabbis, of course, expected their congregations to keep the Mosaic Law. But Paul was preaching a new covenant, under which Christians were set free from the Law and called to follow Christ. So after a while he would be driven from the synagogue and move somewhere else in the town. He would seek to build up the Christian community and later keep in touch by letters. He was preaching a gospel of love to all humankind and wanted Christians to avoid empty rites and ceremonies. But it was not easy to switch from the letter of the law, which kills, to the spirit which gives life (2 *Corinthians* 3.6). At Corinth, for example, the belief spread that all material things are evil and all that is immaterial is good. This led some to interpret the Pauline doctrine of freedom from the Law as a justification for lust and self-indulgence, and at the other extreme it led others into extremes of asceticism. It was to combat tendencies such as these that Paul wrote his letters to the Christian communities at Corinth, and similar problems were to recur over succeeding centuries.

Paul's achievement

One of Paul's greatest achievements was to establish equal status for Gentile and Jewish Christians. Inevitably there were disagreements about this issue. James, the brother of Jesus, emerged as the leader of the church in Jerusalem, and seems to have assumed that all Jesus's followers would be Jews and would keep the Mosaic Law. Peter, who led the church in Antioch, some three hundred miles to the North of Jerusalem, opened it to the Gentiles and apparently did not expect them to be circumcised or keep the traditional Jewish festivals, but did expect them to keep the Jewish food laws. Paul's view, that the Gentiles were not bound by the Mosaic Law but rather were called to follow Christ, went further. The Acts of the Apostles and Paul's letter to the Christians of Galatia both refer to a conference in Jerusalem of the leaders of the Christian Church (*Acts 15 and Galatians 2*). Fourteen years after Paul had first been to Jerusalem to meet Peter and James, he went there again for a meeting at which the leaders of the church settled a number of matters on which they had disagreed. There was a clash between traditionalists, who expected all male Gentile converts to be circumcised, and those led by Paul who thought in terms of a new covenant. James, 'the Lord's brother', Peter and John agreed with Paul's view, and James seems to have had the last word. At the same time James, Peter and John acknowledged that their mission was to the Jews while Paul's was to the Gentiles – though Peter may later have joined in spreading Christianity among the Gentiles and, like Paul, have suffered martyrdom at Rome.

A second and related achievement was to establish that it was faith, or trust, in God rather than good works which was essential for salvation. The conservative view was that the basis for salvation was obedience to God's commandments as set out in the Mosaic Law. Paul, on the other hand, argued that no one could acquire sufficient merit for salvation by obedience and good works. What was needed was for men to recognise their own sinfulness and seek the divine forgiveness which Jesus had promised. Once this right relationship with God was established, once Christians were at one with God, that should lead them on to perform 'good works.' But those works would be the fruit of salvation – not the means by which salvation was achieved. It was Paul who established this as a fundamental element of Christian teaching.

Paul's third great achievement, shared with the other apostles, notably Peter, was to develop a church in which all its members formed 'a chosen generation, a royal priesthood, an holy nation, a peculiar people'(1 Peter 2.9), unified in Christ and in love, and seeking to spread this loving communion to all mankind and throughout time. At first many Christians, including Paul, took the view that the end of the world was at hand and that Christ might at any moment return in glory. But Paul soon moved to the idea that Christ is, was, and ever will be present within the church. The truth embodied in Jesus's message about love and reconciliation, Paul suggested, did not depend on whether the world ended sooner or later. It was an eternal truth. The church continues in time, embraces all believers, and unites all Christians through the sacraments of baptism and the eucharist and through shared faith in the Lord.

Church organisation

The problem of time running on was a real one. So long as most, or even some, of the apostles were still alive, it was natural to turn to them for a decision over anything in dispute. Hence the conference in Jerusalem at which Peter, John, Paul and James the brother of Jesus had reached agreement on what should be required of Gentile converts. But one after another the apostles and other leaders of the early church died or were killed. Meanwhile Christian communities had spread as far as Rome and by the time the apostles had all died questions had arisen about how the church should organise itself and where people should turn for authority when decisions were needed. As Christians came to realise that the end of the world was not necessarily immediately at hand, they also realised that they needed some sort of organisation for the continuing church, and a form of ministry with bishops, priests and deacons gradually developed,

When a large group of Christians bought, or eventually constructed, a building to use as their meeting place, the leading member of the group would be their 'overseer' or *episcopos*, a word which we now translate into English as 'bishop.' Every sizeable Christian community had its own bishop. Some, like Timothy and Titus, were appointed by the apostles to continue their work. Most were chosen by the local community. Bishops were usually prominent citizens who would baptise converts, represent the church at meetings and join with other bishops in consecrating new bishops. They would seek to reach agreement on matters in dispute and would bring the answer back to the local congregation. Above all they presided over the weekly meetings of thanksgiving, the eucharist, in which Christians came together to worship God and remember the sacrifice of Jesus on the cross. Those who advised bishops, and shared in preaching and in celebrating the eucharist, were referred to as presbyters, or priests. Other leading members of the community, who helped in a range of different ways but did not celebrate the eucharist, were called deacons.

Ignatius, bishop of Antioch at the end of the first century, tried to resolve the problem of how the whole church should be

36

governed. He was the first person to use the phrase 'the catholic church.' *katholikos* was a Greek word meaning 'universal', from *kata*, 'according to', and *holos*, 'the whole.' Ignatius used it to make the point that he saw the Christian church as one, rather than as a collection of separate congregations, and he wrote a number of letters when on his way to martyrdom in Rome arguing for government of the church by local bishops. The fact that he did so is an indication that the matter was not yet settled, but even when it was, that did not resolve the problem of how to decide an issue if bishops disagreed with each other. For many practical purposes it made sense for bishops to exercise authority in their own areas but meet from time to time in conference to settle matters about which there was disagreement. But there was a danger that the church was setting up just the sort of authorities Jesus had objected to and clashed with, while at the same time shifting the emphasis from following his teaching and example to asserting what its members should believe about him.

Scriptural authority

The early Christians continued the Jewish tradition of studying the Hebrew scriptures which later came to be called the Old Testament. They read them in worship, they sang the psalms and they sought to understand the things concerning Jesus by reference to the prophets. But after the deaths of all those who had known either Jesus or the apostles, another source of authority came to be the writings which the apostles left behind them, and also those which were either authorised by them or attributed to them. Well into the second century there were Christians who had met at least one of the apostles, and it was understandable that teaching from such people (even if it was indirect experience) carried more weight than written texts. But bit by bit books were admitted to what came to be known as the New Testament if they conformed to the traditional and authoritative teaching of the church, and eventually the books of the New Testament came to be the touchstone by which the validity of Christian beliefs or teaching could be assessed.

The life and teaching of Jesus and the circumstances surrounding his crucifixion resulted during the first and second centuries AD in a range of writings about him and his teaching. First, and earlier than any of the gospels, there were letters by various Christian leaders dealing with particular problems and seeking to resolve them by explaining aspects of Jesus's teaching. Paul in particular wrote many letters to the Christian communities he had helped to establish. He was tackling immediate issues, and although there is no indication that he was intending to produce documents giving guidance to all future generations, much of what he wrote has had wide, lasting and valuable application. On the other hand, prejudice rather than understanding has sometimes resulted from failure to appreciate the context in which the letters were written.

Meanwhile the oral traditions of the words and life of Jesus were being replaced by the gospels of Matthew, Mark, which was seen as being authorised by Peter, and Luke, which was seen as being authorised by Paul. There were others which either have not survived or were repudiated as misleading. John's gospel took longer to gain acceptance, partly because it was written later and partly because it was so different from the other three. Its author, writing at the end of the century, was less concerned than the other gospel writers with telling the story of Jesus's life and ministry and more concerned with explaining its significance and with conveying the message that Christ and his spirit are living in us now and that his truth lives for ever. Another very different book, a poetic vision mixing hatred of the Roman tyrant with awe of God and a prediction of imminent judgement and destruction, was the so-called *Revelation* of another John, who was writing from the Roman penal colony on the island of Patmos, and that was also eventually accepted as part of the New Testament.

The New Testament

The gospels, *The Acts of the Apostles*, the various epistles and *The Book of Revelation* were no more a coherent body of writing in which everything fitted with everything else than were the Hebrew scriptures. They were written by a range of different people and for a range of different purposes and audiences, and some of them were mistakenly attributed to one of the leading figures in the church in order to give them authority. *The Letter to the Hebrews*, for example, was not written by Paul but by an unknown scholarly writer who was concerned to relate Christ's death, understood as sacrifice, to Jewish tradition and show how it should be seen as a fulfilment of earlier Jewish writings and history. That wish to connect with the Jewish past was not universal. In the second century another influential Christian writer, Marcion, believed that the important thing about Jesus's teaching was how entirely new it was – what a complete break from all that had gone before. Eventually he was excluded from the church in Rome because he wanted to get rid of the Hebrew scriptures altogether on the grounds that keeping them stressed continuity with the past, while what was needed was to stress what was new.

The outcome of these disagreements was that in the later part of the second century Christian communities considered which books gave reliable testimony of the things concerning Jesus and should be seen as authoritative. By the third century they had reached considerable, though not complete, agreement about which writings should be accepted. John's gospel had by now come to be accepted. *The Letter to the Hebrews* was accepted in the East but not until later in the West. *The Revelation of St. John the Divine* was accepted in the West but not until later in the East.

Once there was widespread agreement about which books constituted the New Testament, there was a gradual shift towards treating them as if they were not so much divinely inspired as divinely dictated, and eventually, in the largely illiterate society of what came to be the barbarian West, where the Bible was inaccessible to ordinary people, it was interpreted to them by priests. Down the ages Christians either read the Bible, or had it read to them, or had it interpreted to them. They sought the guidance of scripture, of the Church and of the Holy Spirit about issues of personal, social and political importance; and they varied, and still vary, about how far to accept the authority of the

Bible, the Church, or what they take to be the guidance of the Holy Spirit. A frequent danger has been the ascribing of authority to particular biblical texts in the manner of those Scribes whom Jesus condemned for their slavish adherence to details of the Mosaic Law. It is easy to forget that the scriptures were made for Man, not Man for the scriptures. It is even possible to be so attached to the authority of scriptural texts that it replaces devotion to the example and teaching of Jesus.

Christian apologetics

But whether authority was vested in bishops or in the scriptures or, indeed, in the operation of the Holy Spirit, the centre of Christian faith was always Jesus, whom Christians saw as the Word of God made flesh, and the central issue debated in the second century was the question of the relationship between Jesus and God the Father. In *The Acts of the Apostles*, a relatively early work, that relationship is confidently proclaimed as one in which Jesus is Lord and Christ to men (*Acts 2.36*) and also the Son of God (*Acts 3.26*). Then the widespread dissemination of Pauline teaching, in particular such assertions as that Jesus is 'the image of the invisible God' (*Colossians 1.15*), led to a more explicit view of his divine nature, and the gradual acceptance of the authority of John's gospel was accompanied by the belief that Jesus was both God and Man, and by an attempt to express the relationship between God the Father and God the Son in the language of Greek philosophy, as John does in the opening of his gospel.

It became increasingly necessary to explain Christian ideas as the Gospel spread through the Graeco-Roman world, and Christians had to justify their beliefs to converts, Jews and pagans alike – a task technically known as apologetics. One particularly attractive example of explaining the Christian way of life is the anonymous Letter to Diognetus of the mid-second century, in which the author describes how, wherever they live, Christians follow the customs of that country 'in dress, food and general manner of life', but are aware of a higher calling. 'They pass their life on earth, but they are citizens of heaven. They obey the established laws, but they outdo the laws in their own lives.'

The church flourished mainly in the eastern Mediterranean, but it soon spread to the West, and one of the earliest Christian theologians was the Greek bishop Irenaeus of Lyon in Gaul, who believed that bishops should agree on the teaching of the apostles as recorded in scripture and limit their teaching to that, which should form the basis for harmony among Christian thinkers. He himself compared the Son and the Holy Spirit to the two hands of God, but he never ventured into the question of how divinity and humanity could be united in the Son. We could, he believed, leave to God 'mysteries too great for us.'

Christology

Not everyone agreed. In the middle of the century Justin Martyr, a student of Greek philosophy who had been influenced by Plato's idea of a transcendent god, saw Christ's Incarnation as the supreme example of God immanent as distinct from God transcendent. Father and Son, he argued, are the same God, but the supreme, unknowable, transcendent God makes contact with the created order through the *logos*, the Word, which is divine reason. He had done this in the past by inspiring Jewish prophets and Greek philosophers. Thus Abraham and Socrates were in a sense pre-Christian Christians. Jesus is a light shining in darkness. In his person as God the Son he is separate from God the Father, but, suggested Justin, only as one torch lit from another is separate, though they both shine with the same light. They are two persons of one God. Jesus is a light lit from, and the same as, the one true light: light of light, true God of true God, of one substance with the Father. It is the beginning of systematic theology.

Tertullian, a layman writing in Carthage at the end of the second century, was the first person to write about these matters in Latin. But he also was influenced by Greek philosophy. He made use of Aristotle's distinction between the 'substance' of a thing (its inner or 'real' being) and its 'accidents' (or physical characteristics) to describe the Trinity as 'three persons in one substance' and Christ as 'two substances in one person.' It was a particularly ingenious and clever way of expressing the relationship between the three persons of the Trinity, and its influence was lasting.

Another of the great early Christian thinkers was Origen, who wrote in the East in the first half of the third century. He believed that the purpose of the scriptures was to raise Man from the world of the senses to the world of the spirit and convey eternal truth. It was the spiritual point of a story, not the factual content, which mattered, and he applied this approach even to the account of the Resurrection. In his theology he emphasised the separate reality of the Son from the Father, and he tried to solve the problems arising from that by stressing the identity of the incarnate Christ with the pre-existent *logos*.

A developing problem was that anyone who wrote anything about these issues was liable to be seen as a heretic – someone holding a personal opinion contrary to the commonly accepted teaching of the church. But the teaching of the church was far from clear. One person might stress the identity of God the Father with God the Son, thus tending to deny the manhood of Jesus. Another might emphasise their separateness, thus leading either to a denial of the divinity of Jesus or to a belief in two separate gods. The problem with all of this is that it owes more to Greek philosophy than to the visual imagery which Jesus so often used to aid understanding. It is a problem which went on causing difficulties down the centuries and continues to do so.

Chapter 4

The Spread of the Church through the Empire

Rome and polytheism

The Christian Church took root in a world in which the dominant power in the lands around the Mediterranean was Rome and the dominant culture, at least from Italy eastwards, was Greek. The Romans were polytheists, worshipping a range of gods, each of whom represented some aspect of life, or even death. They accepted the worship of many other deities, and it was commonly held that the success of the Romans in the world could be seen as a reward for this all-embracing piety. They were generally tolerant of almost any religious sect, but they drew the line at groups which undermined the stability of society, whether by weakening morality or by offering a challenge to constituted authority. The Jewish religion was difficult to tolerate. The Jews worshipped only one God, saw themselves as his chosen people and denied the validity of the worship of all other gods. The outcome was the sacking of the Temple by the Romans in 70 AD, and the total destruction of Jerusalem, the expulsion of the Jews from their homeland and their dispersal through the empire in 132 AD.

Christianity was open to the same objection. The trouble with Christians was that they objected to taking part in the cult of emperor-worship and often appeared hostile to and intolerant of the traditional religion of Roman society. On the other hand they were often worthy, well-behaved folk who paid their taxes and kept the law. Christians, of course, criticised Jews for their exclusiveness and argued that Christ was the Way which all men should follow. But they seemed pretty exclusive themselves, were suspected of strange and possibly vicious practices, such as eating human flesh and drinking blood, and were viewed by respectable Romans with more suspicion than were the Jews. Celsus, a Roman polytheist writing in the late first century, disliked Jews but was prepared to tolerate their strange practices since, although their religion was peculiar, it was, he pointed out, 'at least the custom of their fathers.' Christians, on the other hand, lacked the respectability which came from an ancient tradition. But after 132 AD the Jews no longer presented a threat, while Christians did. They were overtly critical of the polytheism of the Roman Empire, and as their numbers grew and increasing numbers of slaves joined them, they came to be seen by many in authority as a threat not only to the religion but also to the social fabric of society.

Persecution

For nearly three hundred years Christianity remained an illegal, minority religion in a predominantly polytheist society. Some emperors persecuted Christians. Others thought it more sensible to leave them in peace so long as they did not openly provoke trouble. Very often the extent of persecution depended on the zeal of local governors. As early as AD 44 King Herod Agrippa had the apostle James beheaded (*Acts 12.2*), and he went on to imprison Peter. Persecution itself was intermittent, but the threat of it was pervasive and the victims numerous. The island of Patmos, where the *Book of Revelation* was written, was a Roman penal colony. James, the Lord's brother, was stoned to death in Jerusalem in the reign of the Emperor Nero (AD 54-68). During the same reign Paul was executed in Rome – and very probably Peter as well. Justin Martyr, one of the first Christian theologians, was beheaded in Rome in the middle of the next century because he refused to sacrifice to pagan gods. Origen, whose father had died as a martyr at the beginning of the third century, and whose theology identified Christ with the pre-existent *logos*, was tortured to death in Syria in the middle of the century. But every phase of persecution was followed by a phase of expansion. A Stoic, such as the emperor Marcus Aurelius, might find distasteful the 'theatricality' with which some Christians sought martyrdom. But that same theatricality had a powerful appeal to many ordinary people who saw virtuous men and women sent to their deaths by a vindictive state.

There was no sudden change, but step by step Christianity spread through the empire. In the first and second centuries the question of whether Christians should or should not be persecuted was often a local matter. It could depend on the attitude of the local provincial governor, on the attitude of the church in that area, and on the interrelationship between them. But by the middle of the third century the Christian church was seen by a number of emperors as a threat to the stability of the state and successive attempts were made to eliminate it. In 248 AD, when Rome celebrated a thousand years from the foundation of the city, many Christians refused to join in, so two years later the Emperor Decius launched a persecution directed particularly at bishops. But the Christian church continued to spread, and early in the fourth century the Emperor Diocletian, who doubted the loyalty of Christians, was concerned that they were getting into senior positions in the army and in government, and therefore launched the period of vigorous persecution which lasted for ten years, from 303 till 313.

Consequences of Persecution

Persecution had a range of consequences. It resulted in the deaths of many who clung to their faith. It caused some to abandon their faith, either temporarily or permanently. Others tried to hide their faith or simply kept quiet about it. Yet others looked for ways of fitting in with the requirements of the state while retaining their faith. A bow of the head in public towards pagan gods or a pinch of incense on the altar of the emperor might be all that was needed. In the case of church leaders it might be necessary to hand over holy books, or what passed for holy books, to the authorities, to hand over the sacred vessels used for the eucharist, or other vessels which they might say had been used for that purpose. They might need to arrange to meet secretly instead of publicly. Tertullian, writing in North Africa in about AD 200, had suggested that the blood of martyrs was the seed of the church. But on the balance sheet of such matters there is always a loss column as well as a profit column. Martyrdom may have attracted some to the church. But it will have put others off – either straightforwardly from fear or from distaste for unreasonable fanaticism.

Evil breeds evil, and persecution had the effect of dividing the church against itself. The relatively rich and those in senior positions in society, even bishops, had more to lose and were more likely to seek compromise at a time of persecution. If they survived they could return to building up the work of the church once the persecution had died down. But those who held firm and faced martyrdom might find this attitude difficult to forgive, and even they divided into those who were rigorous and unforgiving and those who were more inclined to be merciful. There were real practical problems about what an appropriate response should be. How does one weigh the guilt of someone who offers incense under torture against that of someone who offers incense without any torture? What about someone who gets a friendly official to forge a certificate saying that he had offered incense when he had not in fact done so? What about someone who gets a pagan friend to do it for him as proxy, and thus avoids doing it directly himself?

There was probably a difference between the sort of person suited to be a leader of the church, such as a bishop, and the sort of person likely to be a martyr. Of course many distinguished bishops went to their deaths, as had the early apostles, and many ordinary folk no doubt apostatised. It nevertheless remains true that, whatever their merits, many martyrs were not of the stuff to be leaders of the church – and contrariwise. There would always be a tension in the church between these two elements. The martyr dying with a vision of the Holy City seems very different from a bishop finding a way of reaching accommodation with a local provincial governor by arranging for his congregation to meet discreetly in a private house and by handing over a few not particularly important books or some sacred vessels. The church may well need its share of martyrs and mystics and poets. But it is more likely that lawyers, administrators and politicians will be in positions of power and run the affairs of the church.

The Donatist Schism

One particularly sad consequence of the era of persecution was the so-called Donatist Schism. In the Eastern part of the empire, where persecution was extensive, it was accepted that it might be necessary at times to hand over sacred books and church plate to the authorities, though sacrifice to the emperor or to pagan gods was regarded as apostasy. In the West (and in the political geography of the time Carthage, in the area which is now Tunisia, was part of the West) persecution was briefer and many areas did not suffer at all, but where it did happen the divisions among Christians were bitter. In Carthage the authorities banned public worship. The bishop accepted that and tried to establish friendly relations with the lay power. When he was required to hand over sacred books, something which the bishop of Rome had already done, he managed to avoid doing so by letting them have some heretical volumes instead. But many of the local congregation regarded even that as a disgrace and an affront to the martyrs of the church who had died rather than apostatise. This group eventually established a separate schismatic church known as the Donatists, after their own bishop, Donatus. Those who had compromised with the lay power during the persecution continued in communion with Rome and the other churches north of the Mediterranean, while the Donatists, contemptuous of their softer, catholic co-religionists, with whom they lived side by side, developed as a separate community and continued to worship separately. It was not unlike the situation centuries later in Northern Ireland, where Protestants and Roman Catholics lived side by side but bitterly estranged from each other. The conflict between them was brutally ended when the Vandals invaded North Africa in the early fifth century and slaughtered indiscriminately both Donatists and Catholics.

Orthodoxy

Another effect of persecution was to produce a more closed and rigid approach to things. If the authorities outlawed particular books, rites or opinions, that could drive Christians into a greater attachment to those books, rites and opinions than might have been the case otherwise. From an early time there was a distaste for disagreement and a feeling that right-thinking persons generally ought to believe the same things. This produced a pressure towards orthodoxy, which means 'correct belief', from the Greek *orthos*, 'correct', and *doxa*, 'belief'. There had always been potential for disagreement over the relative weight to be given to the authority of church leaders, the scriptures, and the Holy Spirit. But that made it all the more desirable to decide on what was the 'correct teaching' on important matters. Thus the requirement for orthodoxy and intolerance of contrary opinions was partly the consequence of persecution.

But the requirement for conformity and orthodoxy could also have the effect that almost anyone who gave serious thought to theological issues was liable to be treated as a heretic. Justin's distinction between the transcendent Father and the immanent Son resulted in accusations that he was setting up two separate gods when what really mattered was to maintain the principle that God was One. But Justin had seen the problem that excessive emphasis on the unity, or Oneness, of God could result in a denial of the essential manhood or human nature of Jesus. Justin was one of the earliest scholars of distinction to encounter the problem that thinking and questioning can be seen by those in authority in the church as a dangerous and seditious challenge to orthodoxy. It is a problem which continues today.

Early in the third century Tertullian joined an extremist sect known as the Montanists. They believed that their leader, Montanus, was directly inspired by the Holy Spirit, they expected the imminent establishment of the New Jerusalem on a specific hill in Asia Minor, and they wanted a spiritual church guided by the Holy Spirit rather than what they saw as the rather worldly, inadequate and fallible church around them. They wanted a church of the perfect, which would exclude known sinners. Again, this was something which would keep recurring through the history of the church.

Origen was another scholar who fell out with the church authorities. His view that the Father and the Son were distinct realities, or *hypostases*, provoked strong opposition – so much so that the bishop of Alexandria objected when Origen was ordained as a presbyter by the bishop of Caesarea, and Origen had to leave Alexandria. Particularly in the West he was seen as treating Father, Son and Holy Spirit as separate beings, or even separate gods. His talk of the pre-existent *logos* was seen in the West as being too clever by half, and his views contributed to a developing division between East and West, because in the more intellectual East the conventional Western view now came to look both naive and barbaric, failing to distinguish the different persons of the Trinity.

All these speculations and disagreements were happening in a world in which the Christian Church was an illegal and often persecuted sect. Sadly it was possible for both parties to an internal church argument to go to their deaths divided from each other, but with the state officials who executed them seeing nothing to choose between them.

Authority

The wish of the church authorities to achieve conformity extended not only to matters of belief but also to matters of practice. Christians regularly celebrated the eucharist on Sundays, and from an early date it was specially celebrated at Easter. At first Easter was simply kept at the same date as the Jewish Passover – the fourteenth day of the Jewish month of *Nisan*. But that day was not necessarily a Sunday. So in Alexandria Christians took to celebrating it on the next Sunday after the Jewish Passover, which in practice meant the next Sunday after the first full moon after the vernal equinox. When the celebration of Easter was introduced among the Christians in Rome in the middle of the second century, they adopted the Alexandrian custom and towards the end of the century bishop Victor of Rome demanded that that

should be universal throughout Christendom. The churches of
Asia Minor objected. But the celebrating of Easter on a Sunday
came to be the normal practice. Those who kept to the old
practice of celebrating on the fourteenth day of *Nisan* came to be
stigmatised as Quartodeciman heretics. They continued as a
schismatic church, out of communion with the main body of
Christendom, for another six or seven hundred years until the
eighth century.

The exceptional authority which the bishop of Rome asserted
over this matter of the dating of Easter derived partly from the
fact that he was the bishop in what had been the chief city of
the empire and partly from the fact that he was the 'successor of
Peter and Paul'. The issue of the nature of his authority came up
again in the middle of the third century over the question of
whether or not there was a need for anyone who had been
baptised by schismatic clergy to be re-baptised on being received
into the orthodox church. The bishop of Carthage, with the
support of the bishops of the Greek East, who were anxious
to ensure correct belief, or orthodoxy, asserted that it was
necessary. The bishop of Rome took the view that it was not, and
for the first time appealed to the text, 'Thou art Peter, and upon
this rock I will build my church' (*Matthew 16.18*), as the reason
why his view should be accepted. It is the first clear clash between
'orthodoxy' and Petrine authority. That text came to be so crucial
in arguments over the issue of authority that eventually any
reference to Paul was dropped and the bishop of Rome referred
to himself as 'the successor of Peter.'

External influences

Meanwhile, among the mass of non-Christian people in the
Roman Empire, religious attitudes were changing in a way which
was ultimately to the advantage of Christianity. The idea of a
transcendent god was not exclusively Christian. All through the
Roman Empire there were local gods in the various different
provinces, and those provinces were ruled by provincial governors
who acted on behalf of the supreme authority of the emperor far
away. Just as the local governor could be seen as deputising for the

emperor, so the local gods could be seen as acting on behalf of a supreme transcendent god. That is, among educated people the climate of opinion was shifting in the second century towards monotheism. Then in the third century the yearning for a single supreme god came to be attached rather uncertainly to the sun. But if a more satisfactory idea of a single god could be found, the climate was right for the shift.

As Christianity spread through the Empire it inevitably came into contact with and was affected by a range of influences. For example, a sacred meal was one of the rites of the worship of the Persian god Mithras, and Egyptians would have been used to the image of the goddess Isis as a mother with a baby on her knee or suckling at her breast. Meanwhile, the intellectual background of educated Gentiles was likely to be the philosophy of Plato and Aristotle, who both believed in a transcendent God. It might also include the ideas of the Stoics, who taught the need to accept the inexorable workings of Fate. The language of all this Greek philosophy was very different from the pictorial language of the Jews, and much early theology was influenced by it. But as time went by another immensely important influence was the cult of the sun. In a range of ways it seemed to fit with Christianity. According to John's gospel Jesus had said, 'I am the light of the world' (*John 8.12*), apparently identifying himself with the sun, which provided humankind with both light and warmth. When early Christians prayed they turned to the East, to the rising sun. When they built churches they built them so that the congregation faced an eastern window through which would shine the rays of the morning sun. Once one had made the step to monotheism, the next step, from sun worship (the most popular form of monotheism in the second century) to Christianity, was a fairly easy one. Old Testament prophets had spoken of the coming of the 'sun of righteousness.' Clement of Alexandria at the end of the second century spoke of Christ driving his chariot across the sky like the sun god. The fact that Christians worshipped on Sunday and turned to the East to pray associated them with sun worship. And by about 300 AD Christians had taken over the traditional birthday of the sun god, 25th December, as the day for celebrating the birth of Jesus. That is the time of year, just after the winter solstice, when the sun is in a sense re-born as the days start to get longer and the nights shorter.

Constantine

Meanwhile the powerful emperor Diocletian, who ruled from 284 until 305 AD, had tried to improve the government of the empire by new arrangements which separated the East from the West. In 306, when the emperor in the West, Constantius, died, his son, Constantine, was proclaimed emperor by his troops at York. Both Constantius and Constantine worshipped the Unconquered Sun, but there was clearly some Christian influence in the family, for Constantine's half-sister was named Anastasia after the Resurrection (the Greek word for resurrection is *anastasis*). Constantine was first of all a soldier and then an emperor, and it is a mistake to attribute clearly thought out religious and theological ideas to him. It may be that there was no clear distinction in his mind between the one God whom Christians worshipped and the god of the sun. Indeed, once one thinks in terms of the god of the sun rather than of the sun itself, the problem starts to go away.

By 312 AD Constantine had established his authority in the Western half of the empire and on his way to victory had fought and won a battle after having a vision of a cross inscribed in Greek with the words 'by this sign conquer' across the mid-day sun. Note the juxtaposition of the sun and the cross. The following year, at Milan, he and his colleague who was ruling in the East agreed on a policy of religious freedom for all and the restoration to Christians of all property confiscated in the years of the Diocletian persecution, i.e. since 303. In 316 he decreed that criminals should not be branded on the face 'because man is made in God's image', and in 321 he sought to establish Sunday as a universal day of rest, giving his reason as respect for the sun. As it happens the Christian practice of giving a particular significance to one day in seven derived from ancient Jewish practice, though the Christian Sunday is, of course, at a different time from the Jewish Sabbath. It was clearly well established by the time Paul wrote his first letter to the Christians at Corinth. But during the next century the idea was spreading through the ancient world that each day was presided over by what they thought of as the seven planets, and Christians saw it as symbolic that the Lord's day was the day presided over by most important so-called planet, the sun. Thus Christianity and paganism combined to establish a seven-day week, with Sunday as the day of worship and of rest.

The religious toleration proclaimed in the Edict of Milan continued throughout Constantine's reign. He saw himself as a Christian, while still reverencing the sun, and he saw it as part of his duty to keep the church united, so he intervened in the Donatist controversy and tried unsuccessfully to settle it. In 321 he established his authority over the eastern part of the empire and was now seeking to re-establish the unity of the empire. For it to be successful and prosperous he wanted a religion or ideology which would unite rather than divide. In 324, by which time he was sole Emperor, he decided to travel to the East and be baptised in the Jordan. But by the time he arrived he found the churches of the East bitterly divided about the teaching of an Alexandrian presbyter, or priest, called Arius, who had a large popular following in Alexandria and who had been excommunicated by his bishop because he asserted that Jesus, the incarnate Son of God, could not be one with the pre-existent *logos*, the Word, which was the first cause of creation.

The Council of Nicaea (325)

Constantine delayed his baptism and the following year, 325, summoned a general council of the church at Nicaea on the coast of Asia Minor in order to settle a whole range of problems by discussion and agreement. At the opening of the conference Constantine urged the bishops to seek unity and peace. They did and they achieved a lot. Constantine agreed to a measure of tax exemption for the church to help it with its work of caring for the poor. Some schismatics in Egypt were reconciled to the church. The bishops agreed numerous canons, or rules and regulations by which the church was to be governed. They agreed on how to calculate the date of Easter, though that left the Quartodecimans unreconciled. They made arrangements for the future appointment of bishops: although the local community could still chose its own bishop, the neighbouring bishops now needed to agree to the appointment before consecrating him. They established the general principle that when differences arose among local bishops, the bishop of the main city of the province, the metropolis, should have the power of veto. Thus the bishop of the town where the secular administration of the empire was exercised became the metropolitan archbishop. They recognised that two bishoprics already exercised a jurisdiction even wider than the province in which they were situated. They were Rome in the West and Antioch in the East. Now the Council gave similar jurisdiction over all Egypt and Libya to the Bishop of Alexandria, and at the same time affirmed that special honour attached to the see of Jerusalem, which was not even a provincial capital. It was the first step towards the creation of the five great patriarchates of Rome, Constantinople, Alexandria, Antioch and Jerusalem – though it was another ten years before Constantinople was built and raised to that position.

It was a remarkable achievement and it is a measure of the extent to which the centre of gravity of both the church and the empire was already in the eastern Mediterranean that almost all of about 220 bishops who attended were Greek and only four or five, together with two priests sent by bishop Silvester of Rome, came from the Latin West. Perhaps the most important of all the achievements of the Council is that all except two of the bishops present agreed on a creed, or statement of faith, to be used at baptisms. Their aim was to leave no room for Arianism, and the consequence is that the Nicene Creed has a brief reference at the beginning to 'God the Father All-sovereign, maker of all things visible and invisible', and later a somewhat perfunctory mention of the Holy Spirit, while most of it is a detailed attempt to find an acceptable way of expressing the nature of Christ. In particular it asserted that the Son was *homoousion toi patri* (i.e. of the same substance as the Father), and therefore substantially one even though distinct in existence. That assumes that the Aristotelian notion of 'substance' is a universally acceptable way of looking at things, but at the same time it was sufficiently ambiguous to be interpreted in two different ways. On the one hand it can be seen as asserting a rather general identity, thus leaving room for distinguishing sharply between the different persons of the Father and the Son. On the other hand it can be seen as asserting a sufficiently specific identity of Father and Son as to rule out any possibility of seeing them as two gods. No doubt this element of ambiguity helps to explain the overwhelming majority in favour of the formula.

Church and State

Constantine did not seek to make Christianity the only religion of the empire, but he clearly favoured it. In 335, when he built his new capital city, Constantinople, at Byzantium, on the shore of the Bosphorus, looking across to Asia Minor, Christian clergy conducted the dedication ceremonies and at this point Constantinople became one of the patriarchates – understandably, because while Rome had long been the capital of the empire in the West, Constantinople was now the capital in the East and could be seen as the Second Rome.

Constantine provided it with two Christian churches, but he also placed a statue of the sun god in the forum. Then on his deathbed in 337 AD he was at last baptised. He had put it off until he was dying, but that was not unusual at the time. Baptism washed you clean of sin, so it seemed sensible to put it off until near death to reduce the danger of sinning subsequently. He had transformed both the empire and the church. God seemed to have given victory and imperial power to him in order that he might embrace the Church of Christ, which could then spread through the empire and even the *oikumene*. That Greek word, which originally meant 'the whole inhabited world', came to be used to mean the universal Christian church, whose members trusted that it would one day embrace 'the whole inhabited world' reconciled to God.

There remained questions about the extent and nature of the emperor's authority in matters to do with the church. In the East his authority was generally accepted, though with the proviso that it was essential that the emperor should be 'orthodox' in his beliefs. The West was more inclined to question it. But however one views imperial authority, Constantine's conversion transformed relations between church and state. In the relatively recent past Christians had been seen as subversive. Even when Jesus's teaching was well understood, it could still look dangerous. For example, the requirement to love one's enemy could be seen as so impracticable as to be damaging to the social fabric, while at the same time the adoption of such principles could result in a feeble response to barbarian invasions. Now the emperor was directly involved in the development of the church and the church was involved in politics.

It was, of course, possible to take the view that God was working out his will in history as the church flourished under Constantine and his successors. But it was also possible to take the contrary view that the church had moved in the wrong direction when it associated itself with imperial power. It made itself vulnerable to being used for human purposes, as the agent of imperial policy, when perhaps it could and should have carried on separately, influencing but not assimilated by the state. With hindsight that is an understandable opinion. At the time few looked at things that way. To most Christians the conversion of Constantine was unequivocally a cause for rejoicing.

Section 2
Christendom and the Roman Empire
(the 330s to 660s)

Chapter 5

The Official Church of the Empire

The church under Constantine

For three hundred years Christianity had been an illegal sect in a pagan empire. Then under the Emperor Constantine the Christian church was accepted and it became possible to look forward to an ideal world in which the empire became a sort of heaven on earth. Christ had come on earth for the salvation of mankind, and within the bounds of the empire the opportunity for salvation was there for all. God ruled in heaven. The emperor ruled on earth. Although Christianity had not yet been proclaimed as the official religion of the empire, Bishop Eusebius of Caesarea, writing at the court of the Emperor Constantine, already saw the Christian empire as the earthly image of the heavenly kingdom, with the emperor as God's representative on earth.

The Christian church had developed within the Greek, or Hellenistic, culture which was already well established long before Christianity. It expressed its theology in the language of Greek philosophy and many of its practices were partly inherited from and influenced by Roman traditions. Constantine described himself as 'bishop of external things', and he also kept the pagan title *pontifex maximus*, 'the most high priest', which had been held by his predecessors.

In some ways the church had less freedom under a Christian emperor than it had had under a pagan ruler. Traditionally a bishop had been freely elected, or chosen (the Latin word for 'chosen' is *electus*) by the people, though the agreement of the neighbouring bishops was also needed, since it was they who consecrated him. Now the emperor began to intervene or exercise influence in episcopal elections. But that could seem a small price to pay for his favour, especially if one looked back to the relatively recent past. A generation earlier, at the end of the third century, there had certainly been some Christians in positions of influence in the government and the army. But in worldly terms it had been a serious disadvantage for it to be known that one was a Christian, and it was precisely because the Emperor Diocletian was concerned about the possibly subversive influence of Christians in positions of influence that he had launched the ferocious persecution which lasted a decade from 303 onwards. Now, as a consequence of Constantine's embracing of the church, it was an advantage in society and in the affairs of state to be a Christian.

The Arian heresy

On matters of doctrine the emperor needed to take account of the general will of the church. An emperor could not require heresy to be accepted as orthodoxy. But it was not yet clear what was heretical and what was not. In the early fourth century an Alexandrian presbyter, or priest, called Arius had made an attempt to express the relationship of Father and Son in a way which would make sense to an educated public by emphasising the divinity of the Father and the manhood of the Son, and avoiding formulas which presented the Son as divine and existing from all eternity, since that was something which many people found difficult either to understand or to accept. The controversy arising from that dominated the history of the Christian Church in the East during most of the fourth century. Bishops were appointed and deposed according to what view they took on this issue and opinion swung sometimes one way and sometimes the other, depending partly on the persuasiveness of arguments and partly on political and even military considerations. Arianism remained popular and persuasive, and the effect of the Council of Nicaea, which Constantine had summoned and presided over in 325, twelve years before he was himself baptised, seems to have been to intensify the controversy rather than settle it.

St. Athanasius

Things came to a head as the consequence of the election in 328 of a young man in his early thirties called Athanasius to the see, or patriarchate, of Alexandria. Three years earlier, as a deacon, he had attended the Council of Nicaea with his bishop. He was then, and he remained, passionately opposed to anything which smacked of Arianism. So strongly was he attached to the contrary position that in practice he was out of sympathy with the views of most of his colleagues in the East. The outcome was that he was formally excommunicated and fled to the West, where he was welcomed into communion at Rome by bishop Julius, thus increasing the possibility of a division between East and West. Already the empire was at times divided between East and West. Here was the first sign of a similar division in the church. The controversy raged for the next thirty years, with theological issues and linguistic problems getting inextricably intermingled with issues of ecclesiastical authority and imperial politics.

It seemed to many bishops that it would be sensible to draw up a creed which would be deliberately worded in such a way as to include or comprehend as many views as possible, avoid unscriptural words and avoiding commenting on those things which God had not revealed clearly. The Emperor Constantius II, Constantine's son, approved of this approach. It was not in the interest of the empire for Christians to be engaged in vehement dissension, and it suited him to have a formula in which the Son was described as 'like' the Father (*homoiousion toi patri*) without commenting on the nature of the likeness. But Athanasius, restored to his position as Patriarch of Alexandria in 346, saw that approach as so comprehensive that it tolerated something he believed to be fundamentally false and incompatible with the truth that the Son was of the same substance as the Father (*homoousion toi patri*). The little letter 'i' in *homoiousion* made all the difference to the meaning, and the conflict continued.

Upheaval and uncertainty

The middle years of the fourth century were a time of both political and religious upheaval and uncertainty. Athanasius was driven out again, this time by military force, in 356 and was replaced by an Arian. Then in 359 Constantius II proclaimed the Arian form of Christianity as the official religion of the empire, and after his death in 361 Constantine's nephew Julian, known to history as Julian the Apostate, tried to revive paganism, the ancient religion of the *pagani*, which originally means the people who lived in the countryside rather than in the towns. He was unsuccessful, if only because he was killed in 363, just eighteen months after coming to the throne, while campaigning against the Persians. Divine Providence appeared to have disposed of him conveniently, and in the event he was the last pagan emperor.

But all problems were not over. There was warfare with the Persians in the East and with the Goths in the North, and at the same time internal conflict within the empire which was usually mixed up with religious issues. Before long two brothers, great grandsons of Constantine divided the empire between them. Valentinian I, who held religious views which included what eventually came to be accepted as the orthodox view of the Trinity, ruled in the West. His brother Valens, who was an Arian, ruled in the East. But just as paganism met its end as the official religion of the empire with the death of Julian in 363, so Arianism came to an end as the official religion of the empire with the death of Valens in battle against the Goths in 378.

Theodosius the Great (379 – 395)

Between 379 and 392, and after protracted fighting in the West, Theodosius the Great, the son-in-law of Valentinian I, reunited the empire under his own rule, with profound consequences for the church. While Constantine had made the first important move towards accepting Christianity in the empire, and while his son, Constantius II, had proclaimed the Arian version of Christianity as the official religion of the empire, it was not until the reign of Theodosius that the Trinitarian version of Christianity was established as orthodoxy and as the official religion of the empire. Theodosius then issued edicts against paganism and made it illegal for people to maintain the shrines of their traditional household gods. Pagan temples were either destroyed or turned into churches. It became illegal to offer animal sacrifices or wine or incense to the gods. Meanwhile Christians, as members of the catholic, or universal, church, were expected to be orthodox in their beliefs, and heretics were punished.

Church and state were now one, and under divinely ordained imperial authority the catholic and orthodox church helped to maintain a society which was Roman, Christian and civilised. The emperor was the supreme power in the empire, but the effective functioning of the state required him to work in partnership with the patriarch of Constantinople, who soon became the chief officer of state, taking precedence over everyone except the emperor himself. The emperor appointed the patriarch, though usually after taking advice from the Holy Synod, the local council of bishops, which met regularly to deal with a range of ecclesiastical matters, and if he wanted the patriarch deposed, he could usually get the synod to do so. But ideally they co-operated. Church councils were presided over by the emperor, and the church adopted an organisational structure in which bishoprics were grouped within imperial provinces, and the bishop of the metropolis, or chief town, of the province was an archbishop. It was almost as if the church was a particularly important office of state for religious affairs. The Roman Empire, Christendom and civilisation were co-terminous. Beyond their bounds lay paganism, barbarism and darkness.

Establishment

The Christian church had been established in the empire in three stages. During the first three centuries it spread through its virtues and despite persecution. Through much of the fourth century it flourished and grew under imperial favour and patronage. From the last two decades of that century onwards it was established in power by imperial legislation, able in turn to persecute first pagans and then its own dissidents. Christian mobs now ran riot in one city after another, destroying pagan temples and purging idols, and in 384, in the West at Trier, there was the first state execution of a Christian heretic, Priscillian.

One can look at the first phase, when it struggled into birth, with admiration, at the second phase, when it flourished and grew, with understanding, and at the third stage, when it was dominant, with concern. Christians had gone from victims to executioners and persecutors within one century. But it may help with understanding that if one appreciates that the Christian martyrs of the Diocletian persecution did not die for religious toleration and freedom. They died because they were sure they were right and could not and would not deny their faith. Once Christians were in a position of power they were still sure that they were right. But now they were the oppressors instead of the oppressed.

The consequences of establishment

Since Christianity was the official church of the empire it could be to the advantage of anyone seeking advancement in worldly terms to become a member of that church. If you wanted political power or promotion in the civil service, it no longer paid to be a pagan, and by the early fifth century Christianity was strongly established throughout the empire. Most town-dwellers counted themselves as Christians. So did most of those living in the countryside in the East, and even in the countryside in the West Christianity was making strong progress.

By the end of the fourth century local churches had acquired substantial lands. The position of bishop became one to which leading members of society would aspire, and every bishop was expected to look after the secular interests of the people of his diocese as well as their spiritual welfare. The question was already being raised of whether one could serve both God and Mammon. Was it possible to render to Caesar the things that were Caesar's and to God the things that were God's? Could the church retain its independence as it became an established institution of society? Could it retain its moral integrity? Did it still exist for those reasons for which it had been created?

As Christianity came to be part of the accepted and expected way of life of the Roman world, it became increasingly difficult to see how Christians differed so very much from other citizens. Indeed the other citizens were Christians. They might still take part in the traditional Roman festivals. They might live much the same social and cultural life as they had before Christianity became the official religion of the empire. But they were nevertheless members of the *oikumene*, the universal Christian world. Over the years they gradually replaced their household gods with statues or pictures of saints. They attended the weekly eucharist. They worshipped God the Father, the Creator of all things, God the Son, who was of one substance with the Father, and God the Holy Ghost, who proceeded from the Father, and they proclaimed that belief in a creed which had been drafted at the Council of Nicaea in 325 and was then modified and agreed as the official teaching of the church at a further Council called by the emperor to meet at Constantinople in 381.

Almost all members of the ruling class were Christians, and one effect of this was a change in the social status of the higher clergy. Callistus, who had been bishop of Rome from 217 until 222, had been an emancipated slave. Such an appointment was no longer likely. Increasingly, from the fourth century onwards, church leaders came from families with high status in lay society. They would normally wear the cope and other vestments of a Roman aristocrat, and that is still the outer clothing worn by many bishops and priests when celebrating the eucharist seventeen hundred years later.

Episcopal authority

The office of bishop, which had begun to develop late in the first century, came to be important, and bishops were increasingly seen as the living symbols of the life of the church. *Ubi episcopus, ibi ecclesia*, it was said: 'Where there is a bishop, there is the church.' Then, in response to the need to maintain unity a theory of 'apostolic succession' was developed, which vested authority in the leaders of those churches which could trace their origins back to one of the apostles, and that in turn led to a requirement for all bishops to be consecrated by others who were already in the line of 'apostolic succession.'

The emphasis on episcopal authority was not particularly related to Rome, and Christ's commission to the apostles was not widely regarded in areas far from Rome as an assertion of Peter's pre-eminence. After all, St Mark had described how Jesus had gathered the apostles together after they had been arguing about who should be greatest, and said to them, 'If any man desire to be first, the same shall be last of all, and servant of all' (*Mark 9. 35*). It is an attitude which does not fit well with assertions of primacy, still less supremacy. So the general assumption was of a need to seek agreement rather than rule by authority, and by the middle of the third century it was becoming usual for bishops from neighbouring towns to meet each other regularly in synods at which they sought to resolve any issue of current importance.

Among those bishops some were particularly influential, and an outstanding example in the late fourth century was St Ambrose, Bishop of Milan, which was then the administrative centre of the western part of the empire. He had been the governor of the province in which Milan was situated, and in 374 was chosen as bishop. For more than twenty years, until his death in 397, Ambrose was the leading churchman of the West. His influence even reached into the eastern limits of the empire. In 388, when some Christians burned a synagogue at Callinicum on the Euphrates and the Emperor Theodosius ordered the local bishop to recompense the victims out of church funds, Ambrose, with what now looks like disgraceful anti-Semitism, protested and refused to allow the eucharist to be celebrated until the emperor revoked the order. Theodosius gave in. But the pre-eminence of Milan was short-lived. Increasingly it was no more than a frontier outpost of an empire whose centre was Constantinople, and when military operations against the barbarians required it, the emperor moved his headquarters in the West to Trier or Ravenna rather than to Milan.

The martyrs

By now the Roman Empire and the Christian Church had in a sense taken each other captive, and both were taken by surprise. The Empire and the Church transformed each other, and for neither was the transition easy. Above all the Christian Church was no longer a persecuted minority. It was the party of power. Some Christians relished their new-found dominance and rejoiced at the opportunity to build heaven on earth. Others were profoundly uncomfortable with the new world they found themselves in.

Now that the church was privileged and prosperous, Christians would sometimes look back with a sense of guilt or nostalgia at the heroes and heroines of the church, the martyrs who had died in the times of persecution. They remembered them with reverence, and they conscientiously commemorated the anniversary of the death of any local martyr, so that very often we know the particular day on which a martyr died, but not the year in which it happened. At first Christians had prayed for the souls of the faithful departed and saw the martyrs as numbered among the communion of saints, which embraced both the living and the dead. Next they established an annual act of remembrance (or *anamnesis*) in which past and present were mingled so that the past was made active in the present. Before long, instead of praying for the souls of the martyrs, they were praying to them, asking them to intercede in heaven for those still living on earth. The next step (and it was a practice which became increasingly common) was to dig up the bones of martyrs and re-house these precious relics under the altar in a church.

It had long been part of the Christian tradition that God was in all things. God the Father was the source of all created things. God the Holy Spirit moved through all creation. With the building of churches, and particularly with the development of a cult of the martyrs, God came to be seen as particularly present in holy buildings. Quite how such changes in attitude come about is not something about which one can be confident, but it may have something to do with the inheritance of a pagan culture in which gods were associated with temples which had been dedicated to them. It may also be that, as Christianity became a mass religion, it seemed desirable to worship in a manner and in places which made that worship more readily accessible to all. The church was adapting to the world around it. As it became acceptable, even required, for all citizens to be Christians, the church increasingly found itself conforming to such characteristics of Roman society as the subordinate position of women.

The search for perfection

This still left for those who felt themselves to be in some sense true rather than nominal Christians the problem, or question, of how far they were any different from anyone else? Could they live in the world but avoid being of the world? Or was it necessary to withdraw from the world in order to strive to live a life of perfection. By choosing a life of poverty or sexual abstinence or the subjugation of one's own will to rules, or perhaps all three, might it be possible with the help of God's grace, to achieve a conversion or change of life to make one worthy of the Kingdom of Heaven?

This, of course, was a contradiction of the view that the universal Christian church, the *oikumene*, within the *imperium romanum*, was a sort of model of heaven on earth. It implied that the officially Christian society of the empire was so far from that model that the route to salvation lay in withdrawing from the world to seek perfection elsewhere. That attitude, however understandable and even admirable it might be, carried with it a danger which has recurred throughout the history of the Christian church. The danger lies in seeking to establish a church of the perfect, an elite who would keep themselves pure and unspotted from the world and look down with contempt on their fellows. It was a danger that was recognised, and many who withdrew from the world consciously sought to avoid falling into that trap. The problem lay in finding a way to cultivate a genuine humility rather than an appearance of humility which could become a particularly offensive expression of the sin of pride.

The idea of the desirability of withdrawing from the world and avoiding all forms of self-indulgence had another important consequence. The view developed that virginity and celibacy were more virtuous than married life, and that in turn led to the suggestion that bishops, priests and deacons should not marry. This was an approach which carried with it the danger of creating a priestly elite separated by their way of life from ordinary people, and an attempt at the Council of Nicaea in 325 to establish a general practice of clerical celibacy was defeated. But as the century went by the idea took hold in Rome, and in 385 Bishop Siricius of Rome declared that all bishops, priests and deacons should be unmarried and should avoid all sexual intercourse.

It was a rule which was difficult to enforce in towns and impossible to enforce in the countryside, but it remained an ideal in the West and had the effect for centuries of generating guilt and secrecy about sexual matters, causing the wives of clergy to be referred to euphemistically as housekeepers or hearth-girls, and resulting in clergy children being treated in law as illegitimate. It also had the important and positive practical consequence that bishoprics and parishes could never be inherited by the male heir of the incumbent, because the clergy necessarily had no legitimate children.

Monasticism

In the East some Christians sought to retreat from the world and live either alone or in a religious community where they might join with others in a life of prayer and worship. Already in the early fourth century an Egyptian called Anthony had given up all property and retreated to struggle with devils in the desert. A number followed his example, and such men, who separated themselves off from the world to pray, were known as *monachoi*, or solitaries. From that we get the word 'monk', which rather peculiarly and paradoxically came eventually to mean people who lived in a community. Another Egyptian, known to history as St. Pachomius, is thought to have been the first person to gather a number of solitaries, or hermits, together to try to lead a communal life under a rule. He established a community on the Nile in which men under rigid discipline engaged in manual labour.

That example was widely followed. The community in which monks lived was known as a *coenobium*, from the Greek *koinobion*, meaning 'communal life'. Groups of men would live under the authority of an elected abbot, a word deriving from the Aramaic *Abba*, meaning father, and similarly groups of women would live under the authority of an abbess. In each case they met together regularly through the day for prayer and worship, they ate their meals together, they slept in a common dormitory, and they worked in the fields and at a range of crafts in order to be self-sufficient.

St. Basil, who lived in the middle of the fourth century as a hermit in Egypt, then as a monk in Asia Minor and became the bishop of Caesarea in 370, founded a number of monasteries and wrote rules for them, establishing a tradition of monastic life which has been followed ever since in the East. The monasteries of this tradition were communities of laymen who came together to live an orderly life under the authority of an abbot, owning all things in common, and above all engaging in prayer and worship. They worked in the fields and at other forms of manual labour in order to keep themselves. Some worked at copying the scriptures, but that was seen as an essentially manual or mechanical activity rather than as scholarship. They might offer hospitality to travellers, and they frequently engaged in charitable work. But that was not the reason for their existence. It was a by-product. They were there to pray, to worship God, to change or convert their own lives, save their own souls and, where appropriate, offer spiritual guidance to others.

There remained the problem that there were still no widely known and generally accepted orderly arrangements either for hermits or for members of religious communities – still less for those ascetics who wandered from place to place. There were also practical problems, such as the need to protect communities of women who chose to withdraw from the world. That particular problem could be solved by having an associated monastery nearby, with both houses ruled by an abbess. But at first most bishops viewed any development such as this with suspicion of the possibility of sexual misdemeanours, and consequently with disfavour. In the fourth and fifth centuries the inclination to retreat from the world was more widespread in the East than in the West, where monasticism developed later and in different circumstances. At first it was seen as a problem, but the church gradually came to accept it and before long the monasteries of the East were providing the training and education of the church's leaders. In the East parish priests were usually married, but bishops were unmarried, so the route to a bishopric in the East lay through being a celibate monk, not a married parish priest. In the West particularly talented monks sometimes became bishops, but most bishops were members of the ruling class, often related to and appointed by the local ruler.

The conversion of the barbarians

While some Christians retreated from the world within the empire, others sought to preach the good news of Christ to the barbarian peoples beyond the bounds of the empire. One of the earliest and most successful of these missionaries was a Visigoth called Ulfilas. The name is an affectionate diminutive meaning 'Little Wolf'. Although his father was a Visigoth, his mother was the daughter of Greeks from Cappadocia who had been taken captive by the Goths. He was born early in the fourth century, in about 311, came to Constantinople as a young man, and when he was thirty was consecrated as bishop of the Goths. But at that time orthodox Trinitarian theology had not yet been settled, and the Christianity which Ulfilas proclaimed so successfully to the Goths was essentially Arian rather than what later came to be accepted as orthodox. He worked among the Goths for forty years until his death, made a Gothic alphabet and translated most of the Bible into Gothic. (The bible he wrote can still be seen in the university library at Upsala.) So successful was he that the Goths in turn provided most of the missionaries who converted the other Germanic tribes which were invading the empire. Consequently it was an Arian form of Christianity which characterised the worship not only of the Visigoths and

Ostrogoths but also that of the Vandals, the Burgundians, the Lombards and the Suevi.

Most of the barbarians who flooded across Europe into the empire in the fourth, fifth and sixth centuries came not to destroy Rome but because they wanted a share in what it had to offer. Part of what it had to offer was Christianity, and the barbarians generally were happy to accept it. If the first version of Christianity they encountered was Arian, they accepted that. It might be somewhat modified by their own customs, but they were unlikely to give much, if any, thought to the theological arguments which raged among Christians who had grown up in an essentially Greek culture. This had the peculiar effect that Arianism, which had begun as an intellectual eastern solution to a difficult theological problem, came to look like a simple-minded barbarian view. By the middle of the fifth century there is a sense in which the Catholic, or Orthodox, position was associated with the idea of the Roman Empire, while Arianism was associated with barbarism. It also had the effect that Christianity, instead of being a uniting force, bringing Roman and barbarian together, was for some time to be an additional cause of conflict because of disagreement about the doctrine of the Trinity.

Chapter 6

The Search for Orthodoxy

Trinitarian theology

The Christians of the early church acknowledged Jesus as their Lord and Saviour, knew that they should follow his teaching and example, and believed that the Holy Spirit was working in them. Once the church was the official church of the empire there was an increasing concern with understanding the nature of the relationship between Jesus and God the Father and the nature of the relationship between them and the Holy Spirit. The view which is particularly associated with the presbyter Arius emphasised the divinity of God the Father and the manhood of the Son and also recognised the importance of the Holy Spirit which came from the Father. The contrary and conflicting view emphasised the unified nature of a God of three persons, Father, Son and Holy Spirit, who were co-eternal and co-equal. That is the position which came to be described as Trinitarian.

This Trinitarian position eventually triumphed in Christian theology over the Arian view, which was anathematized as heresy. In the early fourth century the difference between the two positions was nothing like as clear as it later appeared to be, and much depended on the language being used, but the issue generated passionate debate and the theological issues came to be inextricably mixed with politics.

Ecumenical councils

The Emperor Theodosius the Great made it clear from the start of his reign in 379 that he wanted church unity throughout the empire. He expected the whole church to accept the creed hammered out at Nicaea in 325 and he expected the churches of the East and the West to be in communion with each other. He saw himself, as emperor, as the champion of orthodoxy. So shortly after becoming emperor he summoned the second great ecumenical council of the church to meet at Constantinople in 381. The word *ecumenical*, like *catholic*, means 'universal'. But the two words have come to have quite different overtones. The first, *ecumenical*, now suggests a universality in which those with differing opinions engage in discussion. The latter, *catholic*, suggests a universality in which a supreme monarchical authority rules the whole. But that distinction would not have been clear in the fourth century. It might even have seemed the other way round.

One apparent advantage of becoming the official church of the empire was that leaders of that church could now meet in council from time to time to seek agreement on matters of doctrine and organisation. A precedent had been set by the conference at Jerusalem, described both in *The Acts of the Apostles* (*Acts 15.1-30*) and in Paul's letter to the Christians of Galatia (*Galatians 2.1-10*), for church leaders to meet together to discuss difficulties and seek to resolve problems. But there was no opportunity for another such conference, or council, until Constantine summoned the bishops of the empire to meet together at Nicaea in 325. From now on it was the emperor who summoned general councils of the church and usually it was the emperor who decided what was to be discussed. Either he or his representative presided over the council, and he confirmed its decisions, proclaimed them as law and then enforced them.

Nicaea was the first of a series of seven ecumenical councils which took place over a period of just over five hundred years with the principal object of defining orthodox doctrine, or correct belief. They all met either at or relatively near Constantinople, the furthest away being Ephesus, half way down the West coast of Asia Minor. At Nicaea the most important achievement was agreement on a creed which asserted that Christ was 'of one substance with the Father.' Then the First Council of Constantinople, which met in 381, went further in defining the relationship between the three persons of the Trinity. The next three, which met from the late fourth until the middle of the sixth century, successively at Ephesus (431), Chalcedon (451), and for the second time at Constantinople (553), tried to define the nature of Jesus as both God and man. The last two were the Third Council of Constantinople in 681 and the Second Council of Nicaea in 787.

The good thing about councils was that they enabled the church to reach a consensus, or at least a majority view, not only on matters of doctrine, but also on issues of how the church should be run, and once they had reached a consensus they could expect imperial authority to uphold orthodox teaching throughout the church. The problem with them was that they tended to deal with issues about which there was disagreement. There is, after all, not much point in discussing something when everyone is agreed. The process of discussion tended to heighten the disagreements instead of resolving them. So after the council was over it was all too easy to be left with a discontented minority, whether over the calculation of the date of Easter or over how to express the relationship between God the Father and God the Son. In a world in which orthodoxy was backed by the power of the state there was little room for dissent. The emperor wanted church unity and expected to use his authority to enforce it. Those who maintained a minority view found themselves stigmatised as heretics, choosing their own ideas instead of orthodoxy, or as schismatics, in that they were cut off from communion with the catholic church. History was written to favour the victors.

The First Council of Constantinople (381)

The centre of theological interest in the fourth century was first of all the nature of the relationship between God the Father and God the Son, secondarily the relationship to each other of the three persons of the Trinity, and finally the question of how one should express the nature of those relationships. The issue of the relationship of Father and Son was of such consuming importance that any consideration of the position of the Holy Spirit seems to have been secondary. Given the origins of Christianity in monotheistic Judaism, it was the relationship of Father and Son which mattered most. The assertion at Nicaea in 325 that Christ was *homoousion* ('one in essence' or 'of one substance') with the Father, left open the possibility of distinguishing quite sharply between the different persons of Father and Son. Many in the East did just that, for they were influenced by the theology developed at Antioch, where the humanity of Jesus was stressed and where people still spoke Syriac, a language close to the Aramaic of Jesus and the apostles. Others, influenced by the Greek-language tradition established by St. Athanasius at Alexandria, emphasised the unity of the Father and the Son. An attempt was made to reconcile the two opposing positions and to find an acceptable way of expressing the relationship.

Athanasius had died in 374 during the reign of the Arian emperor Valens; and by the time the Council of Constantinople met in 381, summoned by Theodosius the Great, most of the eastern bishops were sympathetic to a view of the relationship of the persons of the Trinity which was expressed by speaking of three *hypostases*. But when *hypostases* was translated into Latin as *substantiae* (substances), this view looked to Westerners suspiciously like a belief in three separate gods. In the more intellectual and sophisticated East the western view looked like a naïve assumption that Father, Son and Holy Ghost were really the same, with three different names being used to describe different aspects of the same being. In the West it looked as if the bishops in the East were abandoning monotheism. Detailed consideration of theological issues in open council was in danger of splitting the church.

Nevertheless the council settled the issue as far as the main body of Christendom was concerned. It reaffirmed the Nicene Creed, though with slightly different wording. Above all it confirmed that the Son was 'one in essence with the Father' and it is this creed agreed at Constantinople which is commonly known as the Nicene Creed. A new article declared that the Holy Spirit, 'who with the Father and Son together is worshipped and glorified', was equal to the other two persons of the Trinity, and it was asserted that the Son was 'begotten of his Father', while the Holy Spirit 'proceeds from the Father.' These assertions do not relate to the begetting of the infant Jesus or to the coming of the Holy Spirit to mankind. Both refer to the nature of the Trinity, one person of which was 'begotten of his Father before all worlds', and another of which was the 'Lord and giver of life, who proceeds from the Father.'

Papal primacy

Another issue dealt with at the First Council of Constantinople had to do with the issue of authority within the church. Constantinople was now the capital of the empire, so the council agreed that 'the bishop of Constantinople shall have rank after the bishop of Rome because it is New Rome.' Both Alexandria and Rome resented this. Alexandria had long seen itself as the second city of the Empire and felt demoted. Rome disliked it because, although the declaration accepted the primacy of Rome, it implied that that primacy rested on the status of Rome as the former imperial capital rather than on the special pre-eminence of the bishop of Rome as the successor of St. Peter.

Constantinople and the other patriarchates all recognised the primacy of Rome. But primacy is not the same thing as supremacy. The patriarchs of the East saw the bishop of Rome as first among equals, *primus inter pares*, or, to use a Greek term derived from the theatre, the *koruphaios*, leader of the chorus. The assumption, of course, is that the chorus will speak with one voice. But in this case the *koruphaios* believed that in the case of any dispute he should have the last word. The patriarchs of the East, on the other hand, saw each other, and the bishop of Rome as well, as autonomous, working each in his own area of jurisdiction in consultation with other bishops. The local synod, or council, was seen as the normal and natural way of reaching decisions, and occasionally they met in an ecumenical, or universal, council, under the authority of the emperor, God's ordained representative on earth. This was not a view acceptable to the bishop of Rome. In the end this differing view over authority in the church was even more of a threat to unity than differences over theological issues such as the relationships of the persons of the Trinity or the extent to which Jesus should be seen as human or divine.

The continuing Donatist Schism

Yet another important division in the church was rooted in the history of persecution. In North Africa the Donatists still clung to the idea of their own church as an elite of the chosen living in the midst of a corrupt society. They looked back to the time when, they believed, Catholics had weakly collaborated with the authorities during the Diocletian persecution of 303 till 313 by handing over sacred books and church plate, and they saw the Catholics as being in communion with and in succession from the guilty men. The Catholic majority disputed the facts and also pointed out that, while they were in communion with the churches outside Africa, the Donatists were not, so they were, and the Donatists were not, part of the universal church. The Catholics seem to have accepted the ideal of a godly Roman Empire, whose rulers would stamp out heresy and protect the faithful, while the church acted as leaven within the state, transforming its political and social life by the ideals proclaimed by Christ. They regarded the Donatists as both heretical and schismatic.

Clearly reconciliation was difficult so long as the two sides maintained these attitudes to each other, and the two communities lived alongside each other with mutual dislike or contempt, punctuated by occasional incidents which kept the antagonism alive, but on the whole managing to co-exist without serious violence. The antagonism ran deep, yet the divisions which appeared on the surface were largely superficial and even trivial and related to the way men interpreted the facts. What was needed was a willingness on both sides to forgive and seek reconciliation.

St Augustine (354 – 430)

Then in 395, when the Donatist schism had already lasted for eighty-five years, St. Augustine became bishop of Hippo, near Carthage, in the part of North Africa which is now Tunisia. He had been born in 354, in the period between the death of Constantine and the accession of Theodosius, in what is now Algeria. He was educated in Carthage, the centre of Latin literary culture, and his ability led to a career as a professor of Rhetoric, first at Carthage, then briefly at Rome and finally at Milan, where he heard the sermons of St Ambrose. He was converted to Christianity, was baptised in 387 and the following year returned to Africa. He founded an ascetic society and exercised his mind on understanding and explaining the Bible and on seeking to understand God, his own nature, the nature of Man, and the relationship of Man to God. At that time Latin or Western theology was relatively primitive or immature by comparison with the thinking which had gone on in the East, and Augustine was the first really important Western theologian writing in Latin since Tertullian. His *Confessions*, in which he grappled with these problems, was published in 397, two years after he became bishop of Hippo and proved to be one of the most influential books of all time.

But the immediate task facing him when he became bishop of Hippo, other than the normal pastoral work of a bishop, was to find a way of ending the Donatist schism. At first he opposed the idea of the use of force to ensure conformity. He believed that persuasion and reconciliation were preferable to force as a way of achieving anything, and he hoped to get men on both sides to seek reconciliation and find a way out of the conflict. But it was not possible. The attempt to reach an accommodation revealed two fundamental issues on which it was impossible to get agreement.

The first of these issues was related to the nature of the church. The Donatists' view was that the church is a holy and exclusive community whose members should and could keep themselves pure and do no wrong. The contrary Catholic view was of a church made up of sinners as well as saints. It was up to God to winnow the harvest at the Last Judgement and separate the wheat from the chaff. It was not for Man to judge.

The second issue concerned the validity of the sacraments. The Donatists took the view that the validity of the sacraments depended on the sanctity or standing of the minister administering them. The Catholic view, expressed by Bishop Stephen of Rome in the middle of the third century, was that the validity of the sacraments is independent of any merit or virtue of the minister. They are valid by virtue of what is done by an authorised person, such as a bishop or priest, regardless of the worthiness of that person. The fundamentally different positions of the Donatists and the Catholics on these two issues made an accommodation impossible.

The problem came to a head at a conference presided over by an imperial commissioner in Carthage in 411. The following year the Emperor Honorius, who was ruling in the West, issued an imperial edict condemning Donatism. By that time Augustine had come round to the view that force could be justified. Ideally Love brought men to God. But Fear could do so also, and so long as the motive for punishing someone was to bring him to repentance, it was always possible that punishment might do more good than an attempt at persuasion. It is an understandable viewpoint, but Augustine's justification of the use of force against the Donatists was a dangerous argument in a world in which the secular power was issuing edicts against heresy and paganism. It could be used as a justification for taking action against any group which did not conform to the orthodox teachings of the church. In this case it was also ineffective.

The City of God

Augustine had failed in the immediate task of achieving reconciliation with the Donatists. But he left behind him a massive legacy to religious thought, some of it in the area of Trinitarian theology, but most particularly in the area of his views on Man's relationship with God. In his book, *The City of God*, he challenged the view that the Christian empire could be seen as the earthly image of the heavenly kingdom. Augustine saw all human society as part of a fallen and necessarily corrupt world, while the City of God was something divine and entirely different.

His views on the contrast between the fallen world of Man and the divine City of God are closely related to his teaching on original sin and on divine grace. He put forward a view of original sin in which the reproductive act is seen as the means by which sinfulness is transmitted from one generation to the next, so that babies are necessarily already corrupted by sin when they are born. They are therefore in need of divine grace, and that is something which may be freely given by God and is in no way dependent on any human act or choice. God has predetermined before the beginning of time who will and who will not be saved. His grace, when offered, is irresistible. When it is not offered it is inaccessible. Man, in fact, says St Augustine, is in no way the agent of his own salvation. He is entirely dependent on the grace of God. God, who is almighty and omniscient and the creator of all things, will offer redemption to those whom He elects and not to those whom He does not elect.

This Augustinian view of original sin, predestination and divine grace is a hard and extreme position which has gone on down the centuries having an appeal to those who want hard and extreme solutions to theological problems. Its strength is that it is based on an acknowledgement of the might, majesty, power and dominion of God. Its weaknesses are that it is harsh and that it appears to destroy the concept of Free Will and even the idea that human beings have some responsibility for the way they live their own lives. For good or ill it is an approach which has been immensely influential, and Augustine's fatalist and determinist approach, apparently combining despair of all things human with faith in God, has continued to influence Christian thinking ever afterwards.

It was while St Augustine was bishop of Hippo that the Goths crossed the Danube, and while they invaded Italy the Vandals swept into Gaul in 407 and into Spain in 409. The conference which met in Carthage in 411 with the aim of settling the Donatist schism took place the year after Alaric and the Goths sacked Rome, and St Augustine wrote *The City of God* as a meditation on that destruction of Rome, which had been the greatest city in the world and had now fallen to the Goths. Christians needed to put their trust in the heavenly kingdom, not in the works of Man. 'The greatest city in the world has fallen in ruins', wrote St Augustine, 'but the City of God endureth for ever.' He completed *The City of God* in 427. In 429 the Vandals crossed into Africa, slaughtered Donatists and Catholics alike, and in 430 they besieged Hippo. Augustine died that summer shortly before they took the town.

The Council of Ephesus (431)

The news of St Augustine's death had not yet reached Constantinople by the following year when the Emperor Theodosius II invited him to the ecumenical council held at Ephesus to consider whether or not Christ was 'of one being with the Father.' This was now the main issue exercising the minds of theologians in the East. Once the Council of Constantinople had stated authoritatively the orthodox position on the Trinity, theological speculation had moved to more detailed consideration of the nature of Christ. Could he be both God and Man? If he was both, could he be one person?

The problem came to a head when in 428 a monk from Antioch, Nestorius, became the bishop, or patriarch, of Constantinople. Nestorius followed the Antiochene tradition, which emphasised Christ's humanity and insisted that he was a man like any other man, except for his perfection as the Messiah and Son of God. Nestorius particularly disliked having the term *Theotokos*, God-bearer, applied to Mary (though he was happy with *Christotokos* or Christbearer) and he caused offence by asserting that 'God is not a baby two or three months old.' The patriarch Cyril of Alexandria saw his position as dangerously heretical and believed that it was important to stress the unity of Christ's person as God and Man combined. It was while this controversy was raging that Theodosius II in 431 summoned the bishops of Christendom to Ephesus for a council.

The council began with Cyril of Alexandria excommunicating Nestorius. Then the patriarch of Antioch arrived and deposed Cyril. Next legates from Rome arrived and supported Cyril. Nestorius gave up and asked to return to his monastery in Antioch, and the declaration which emerged from the council followed Cyril's belief. Jesus was a single and undivided person, who was both God and Man at the same time. To see him simply as an ideal man, whose essential humanity was somehow infused with the divine, was to err into heresy. Mary was *Theotokos*, God-bearer, or Mother of God – a God who had existed from the beginning of all things. That is, she bore in her womb a baby who was the creator of all things and had existed before his incarnation and before time as the Word, the *logos*.

It was a ruling which the churches of the East, beyond the borders of the Roman empire, could not accept, and it resulted in lasting schism. The Church of the East survived for centuries, cut off from communion with the main body of Christendom, because it believed in the essential humanity of Jesus and because it could not accept an orthodox definition which, in any case, was revised twenty years later. It flourished for centuries, and by the thirteenth century had spread as far as China. Since then persecution has almost entirely destroyed it and it is very largely forgotten.

The Council of Chalcedon (451)

The problem of how to express the nature of Jesus would not go away, even within the bounds of the empire. Ephesus had been a triumph for the Alexandrian emphasis on the unity of Christ's person as God and Man combined, but the price was lasting schism with the Church of the East. Yet even among those who did not go into schism there were many who remained attached to the Antiochene Christology. They could not and would not get away from the point that, even if Jesus was both God and Man, there had to be some difference between his Godhead and his Manhood, or else one would be saying that God and Man are the same thing.

In 450, when Theodosius II died, his elder sister, Pulcheria, seized power and took a soldier called Marcian as her consort.

He summoned a council to meet at Chalcedon in 451. One issue which it dealt with was the establishment of Jerusalem as one of the independent patriarchates, coming in precedence fifth after Rome, Constantinople, Alexandria and Antioch. But the main task of the council was to find a way of accommodating the Antiochene Christological view, with its emphasis on the essential humanity of Jesus, with orthodoxy. Eventually the council produced a formula which was intended to do that.

It is worth quoting the relevant passage in full. Its inaccessibility when read for the first time need not be a concern. It is worth getting the feel of it. Jesus Christ was, 'at once complete in Godhead and complete in manhood, truly God and truly man, consisting also of a reasonable soul and body; of one substance (*homoousion*) with the Father as regards his Godhead, and at the same time of one substance with us as regards his manhood; like us in all respects, apart from sin; as regards his Godhead, begotten of the Father before the ages, but yet as regards his manhood begotten, for us men and for our salvation, of Mary the Virgin, the God-bearer (*Theotokos*); one and the same Christ, Son, Lord, Only-begotten, recognised in two natures, without confusion, without change, without division, without separation; the distinction of natures being in no way annulled by the union, but rather the characteristics of each nature being preserved and coming together to form one person and subsistence (*hypostasis*), not as parted or separated into two persons, but one and the same Son and Only-begotten God the Word (*logos*), Lord Jesus Christ.'

What would Jesus have made of that? The complexity of the language is a measure of the desperate attempt to find some way of agreeing. The Council of Ephesus in 431 had failed to get genuine agreement and led to schism between those who were orthodox and the Church of the East, which emphasised the humanity of Jesus. Now the revised definition at the Council of Chalcedon in 451 led to schism between the orthodox and the Christians of Egypt and Syria, who were condemned as *monophysites* because they emphasised (and still in the Coptic Church and the churches of Abyssinia, Armenia and Syria continue to assert) the essential unity of Jesus's nature. However the nature of Jesus was defined, the definition was going to offend some one. The tragedy of this is that they all agreed that Christ was both truly human and truly divine, but they could not agree on how to express it.

The Second Council of Constantinople (553)

The quarrelling and the discussions went on. This was partly because theologians were genuinely struggling with the attempt to express the nature of Christ as accurately as possible and believed that they ought to be able to get the right answer. It was also because the central authorities wanted reconciliation with the Egyptians and the Syrians. In 553, after another hundred years, another council, this time at Constantinople, was called by the Emperor Justinian. It tried to restate what had been declared at Chalcedon in 451 in language which would have been acceptable at Ephesus twenty years earlier, in 431. But no amount of linguistic juggling could satisfy the disputing parties and the schism continued. The Church of the East had been out of communion with the main body of the church since Ephesus because it was seen to emphasise excessively Christ's humanity at the expense of his divinity. The Coptic Orthodox Church of Egypt and the Syrian Orthodox Church had been out of communion with the main body of the church since Chalcedon because they were seen as monophysites, emphasising excessively the essential unity of Jesus's nature. The schism hardened and in practice the monophysite cause became the banner of Egyptian and Syrian opposition to central imperial authority.

The establishment of the church as an official and integral part of the empire had made it possible for conscientious and well-intentioned people, in particular the bishops, to meet together in the ecumenical councils to discuss matters they considered important and seek to reach agreement. But the one rule of general application about such meetings is that they lead to bitter disagreement and division. People will unite and support each other against an external enemy. Without an external enemy they have the luxury of being able to fight among themselves. The leaders of the church proved to be no different from others in this respect.

What is more, the bishops who engaged in these discussions were virtually officers of state in an empire which required religious conformity, and one consequence of their search for an orthodox and agreed theology was that the bishops were increasingly out of touch with ordinary people. The more they acted as leading figures in an imperial institution, the less did they seem like the leaders of a Christian community open to Jew and Gentile, slave and freeman, male and female (*Galatians 3.28*). It could easily appear as if they saw it as more important for Christians to give assent to specific intellectual propositions about the nature of Christ or the nature his relationship with the Father, than to live a life seeking to follow him. It was not the best way to make Christianity attractive to, for example, the people of Arabia.

Chapter 7

Christianity, Barbarism and Islam

The decline of Rome

The second century AD had been the Golden Age of the Roman Empire. Edward Gibbon, in the third chapter of his *History of the Decline and Fall of the Roman Empire*, wrote that 'If a man were called to fix the period in the history of the world, during which the condition of the human race was most happy and prosperous, he would, without hesitation, name that which elapsed from the death of Domitian to the accession of Commodus' – i.e. 96 AD to 180 AD. For the last eighty-two of those years the empire was ruled by just four great emperors: Trajan, Hadrian, Antoninus Pius and Marcus Aurelius.

The third century, by contrast, was a difficult time for the Roman Empire. Until the accession of Diocletian in 284 it was ruled for an average of about three years each by twenty-six emperors, few of whom have any claim to distinction. Most came to power by the sword. Most died by the sword. The threat from invading barbarians was continuous, and at the same time the empire was beset by economic problems. The constitutional arrangements set up by Caesar Augustus were no longer suited to the running of a vast empire, and the centre of power shifted to wherever the current emperor was able to maintain the support of the army.

The wholesale reorganisation of Diocletian's reign (284 – 305) had included early on, in 286, the transfer of the seat of government from Rome to Milan in the North of Italy, which was strategically better-placed than Rome for facing the barbarian threat. But that was an inadequate response. The centre of gravity of the empire had shifted east, and by the end of the reign of Constantine the Great in 337 the new capital of the empire was Constantinople, built on the site of the old settlement of Byzantium. The whole empire was divided into provinces, each ruled by a provincial governor, and in the metropolis, or principal town, of each province there was an archbishop. The more densely populated East, with its numerous and prosperous towns, was well adapted for economic and military survival. It either kept the barbarians outside the borders of the empire or assimilated them. The West was far more vulnerable.

The barbarian invasions

The principally agricultural economy of the West proved to be inadequate to support the armed forces necessary for defence, and the barbarian tribes swarmed into the Western provinces of the empire in numbers too large to be defeated by the Roman legions. The barbarians took over Western Europe, Roman administration collapsed and the principal human link between the invaders and all things Roman was often the local bishop. There were no longer any Roman provincial governors, but there was still an archbishop in the principal town of each province, and within each province there were several dioceses, each with its own bishop. So the barbarians learnt about Roman culture from the leaders of the Christian church, and through much of the West the bishops were influential with their new political masters.

At first the Christian church did not feel that it had much to learn from the barbarians. But inevitably, as it engaged in the process of converting the barbarians, it was changed by them. The Christianity which was preached to the barbarian world was concerned with how people should live and with personal and social relationships rather than with what one should believe about the nature of Christ or about the correct terminology for expressing his relationship with the Father. Christian ideas gradually influenced and modified the customs of the barbarian people, but the barbarians' customs were the laws which held society together, and Christianity was in turn influenced by them. Bit by bit, as the West was lost to the empire, things Roman mattered less. In the East the interrelationship between the Graeco-Roman civilisation and Christianity was central to the way a Christian society developed. In the West the interrelationship which mattered was between Christianity and Barbarism.

With pagan barbarian tribes the process of conversion was not usually a matter of spreading Christianity from one person to another. What mattered was to convert the king, or war leader. Once he was converted, then the whole people could be baptised, and that could be followed by the long, slow process of Christianising society. The fact that many of the barbarian tribes were not pagan, however, but had already been converted to Arian Christianity resulted in their conversion to Trinitarian, or orthodox, Christianity taking significantly longer and being far more difficult than the conversion of pagan tribes.

The task was vast. Early in the fifth century Arian Goths were invading Italy, Arian Vandals were sweeping through Gaul and Spain into Africa, and pagan Franks were invading Gaul. At the same time the Roman legions in Britain, which had been a province of the Roman Empire for three and a half centuries, were withdrawn in a vain attempt to save Rome from the Goths. Pagan Angles and Saxons invaded, usually led by war-leaders who traced their ancestry back to the god Woden. Catholic Christianity was in retreat.

Papal claims

The most important of all the bishops who met and negotiated with the barbarian leaders in the absence of Roman officials was the bishop of Rome. The pre-eminence of the Roman bishopric rested partly on the fact that Rome was the former capital of the whole empire; and now that there was no longer an emperor in Rome, the bishop of Rome inherited some aspects of imperial authority. His authority in the church also rested on an association with St Peter. In AD 170, about a hundred years after Paul is known to have been executed in the persecution instigated by the

Emperor Nero, there is the first record of a tradition that Peter was also at Rome and was executed at the same time. If we add the story of Jesus telling Simon that his name was now Peter, or Rocky, 'and on this rock I will build my church' (*Matthew 16.18*), we have the making of claims to authority which were to grow ever greater in succeeding centuries.

By the early third century Peter's tomb was being venerated. Already in the time of Bishop Callistus (217-222) he was being listed as the first bishop of Rome. In the middle of the third century a bishop of Rome, when disagreeing with the bishop of Carthage, quoted the Petrine text as a reason why his own view should be accepted. Then, more than a hundred years later, in the time of Bishop Damasus (366-384), that text was adopted as a scriptural justification for a general claim to Rome's primacy throughout Christendom. Damasus particularly felt the need to assert himself because he had only acquired the bishopric when his own supporters had massacred his rival's supporters at the time of his election. But his insecurity was also the consequence of a decline in the eminence of the bishopric produced by a decline in the importance of the city of Rome, and he was sufficiently unimportant not to be invited to the Council of Constantinople called by Theodosius the Great in 381. Damasus made up for it by adopting the plural form when writing to his fellow bishops at the council, addressing them as sons rather than brothers, and at the same time he explicitly claimed the prerogatives of St Peter exclusively for Rome.

This, of course, was not an attitude which could be accepted in the East. Nor was it even generally accepted in the West, where St Ambrose, who was bishop of Milan at the time, took the view of St Peter that he had 'a primacy of faith not of rank.' It seems probable that the stimulus for Rome to assert itself was occasioned by the rise in importance of both Constantinople in the East and Milan in the West. Paradoxically it was the decline of Rome as a city that led to its bishops feeling the need to make greater claims about their own authority.

It had long been customary for Christians to use the Greek *pappas* or the Latin *papa* when addressing their bishop. They were words implying a mixture of respect and affection which children used when addressing their father, and bishops would sometimes address their metropolitan superior, the archbishop of the province, in that way. From the time of Damasus's successor, Siricius (384-399), bishops of Rome sought to have the term generally applied to themselves. It was a slow process. In the fifth century African bishops were still addressing the archbishop, or primate, of Carthage as *papa*, because he was their metropolitan superior. They did not address the bishop of Rome in that way. But in the sixth century Rome began to assert an exclusive claim to the use of the word, and increasingly the bishop of Rome was known through western Christendom as *papa* – the Pope.

Theory and reality

The gap between papal theories of authority and the reality of the political situation grew ever wider as the political situation worsened and the theoretical claims grew. Early in the fifth century Pope Innocent I (401 – 417) asserted that decisions of the pope applied to 'all the churches of the world.' But it was during his pontificate, in 410, that the Goths under Alaric sacked Rome. In the middle of the century Pope Leo I (440 – 461) asserted that the papacy had a *plenitudo potestatis*, or 'fullness of power', and he adopted the title *pontifex maximus*, 'the most high priest', which Theodosius the Great had abandoned. But by then most of the West was in the hands of barbarians who were Arian heretics and the effective authority of the pope in both religious and secular affairs extended no further than central and southern Italy.

Not surprisingly the Council of Chalcedon of 451 decided that Constantinople should now enjoy 'the same primacy' in the East as Rome in the West. But when Pope Leo I wrote to the council, he made it clear that what he wrote was not open to discussion and that it had to be accepted as a Petrine utterance. The Greek bishops did accept it, but they made it clear that that was because they considered it to conform to orthodox doctrine, not because of papal authority. Leo in turn accepted the Council of Chalcedon's doctrinal definition because, as he saw it, he had himself ratified it.

Twenty-five years later, in 476, a barbarian general called Odoacer, who commanded Roman forces, deposed the last Roman Emperor in the West, Romulus Augustulus, and made himself 'king' of Italy, ruling until he was killed and replaced by the Ostrogoth Theodoric the Great, who ruled Italy from 493 until 526. Both Odoacer and Theodoric were Arian heretics, but they took the pope under their protection. Meanwhile, in 482 the Emperor Zeno, with the approval of the patriarch of Constantinople but without summoning an ecumenical council, published a document known as the *Henotikon* in which he tried to find a compromise in the controversy about the relationship between Christ's Godhead and his Manhood by avoiding any reference to 'one nature' or 'two natures.' The pope reacted in 484 not just by repudiating the document but also by excommunicating the patriarch and the emperor. This produced a schism between the Orthodox church of the imperial East and the Catholic church of the barbarian West which lasted more than thirty years, until 518. By then the patriarch of Constantinople was claiming authority over the universal church, and rather peculiarly a pope in schism with most of Christendom retained his authority in Rome and central Italy because he had the protection of an Arian king. The division between East and West seemed to be hardening.

The Emperor Justinian (527 – 565)

But neither the political nor the religious division between East and West was final. In 527, the year after the death of the Ostrogothic king Theodoric, the Emperor Justinian came to the throne in Constantinople, the capital of the eastern and more densely populated part of the empire, which, with its greater economic resources, had survived the barbarian invasions. He saw it as his mission to restore the ancient boundaries of the empire, and now appeared to have the opportunity. He would drive out the barbarians from the West and uphold orthodoxy throughout the empire, which would once again be the same as the Christian *oikumene* – the universal church. The idea of one united Christian empire had survived.

Justinian ruled for thirty-eight years, from 527 until 565. He conquered the Vandal kingdom in North Africa and then went on to conquer Sicily, Italy and the South of Spain. He put down rebellion at home in Constantinople and built the magnificent church of the Holy Wisdom, the *Hagia Sophia*, in place of a rather smaller church which had stood since the fourth century and been destroyed in a riot. He codified the law in a manner which reflected the influence of Christian ideas, and he established the authority of the emperor over all matters to do with the beliefs, organisation and practices of the church on a scale unsurpassed before or since. He imprisoned, deposed and appointed popes in order to ensure conformity with his own theological ideas, and at his death in 565 he left the empire financially exhausted.

Justinian had intended his work to be the start of a new era. In practice his reign was the last time in history when the Mediterranean was an inland lake of one world power. That power was intended to be both the Christian *oikumene* and the *imperium romanum*, the Roman Empire. But the Christian church had spread way beyond the bounds of the empire both in the East and in the West, and the empire lacked the resources to maintain its power even over the areas Justinian had reconquered. Within three years of his death another barbarian people, the Lombards, had invaded much of Italy, and soon afterwards the Visigoths reconquered southern Spain. Something was salvaged both in Italy and North Africa, but the universal Christian empire around the Mediterranean, ruled autocratically by a divinely appointed emperor in Constantinople, had gone for ever.

St Benedict

The West remained vulnerable to further barbarian raids and occupation. In the East the political solution to the barbarian threat had been greater centralisation of imperial power and military reorganisation. In the West the solution was to break up into very small self-contained economic units. The ancient world of interdependent cities linked throughout the empire by roads and ships was disappearing. In its place there developed self-sufficient economic units which might be no larger than an agricultural estate. At the same time the break-down of civilisation as it had been known for generations caused more and more men to wish to withdraw from a world collapsing under barbarian attack. So one of the most important developments in the West as a reaction to the uncertainties of the sixth century was the spread of monasticism. Monasteries were particularly well adjusted to the difficult circumstances of the time. Each one was largely self-sufficient. A monastery might be entirely destroyed by a barbarian raid. But if it avoided that fate it could, if necessary, survive by itself.

In 480, four years after Odoacer had deposed Romulus Augustulus, the last Roman emperor in the West, an Italian called Benedict was born in central Italy. In 529, a century and a half after the death of St Basil, who had done so much to develop monasticism in the East, Benedict, after some early experimenting with the monastic life, founded the monastery of Monte Cassino under his own direction in South Italy. He died there in about 550, at the time when the forces of the Emperor Justinian were fighting to recover Italy from the Ostrogoths. Benedict lived at just the time when the old Roman order was crumbling and being replaced by the new order established by the barbarian kingdoms. He looked back to the past, came to terms with present reality and planned for a new and very different future. Monte Cassino was a microcosm of the world, and in these years of political and social chaos in Western Europe it was a microcosm socially as well as economically. People from all strata of society, most of them young laymen rather than clergy, ex-slaves as well as nobility, could be instructed in the fundamental virtues expected of someone wishing to follow Christ. As monks they lived a communal, regular and simple life, under obedience to their abbot, in an enclosed community to which they were committed for life.

In 577, a quarter of a century after Benedict's death, Monte Cassino was destroyed by Lombard invaders and the monks were scattered. It was restored nearly a hundred and fifty years later in 717, and then, more than a millennium after that, it was destroyed again in 1943 as Anglo-American and Polish forces fought their way north against another wave of Germanic barbarians who had swarmed over Europe in the middle of the twentieth century. Monte Cassino was restored yet again after the Second World War and it still flourishes as a Benedictine monastery.

The Rule of St Benedict

While Benedict was abbot of Monte Cassino he wrote a 'little rule for beginners', which, as *The Rule of St. Benedict,* came to be the standard handbook in the West for groups of laymen leading a religious life in a community – a mixture of spiritual guidance and practical advice on how to run a religious community. The rule was simple and practical and required of those who retreated from the world into the cloister that they should give up all individual, though not communal, possessions, be obedient to a religious superior, remain permanently in one monastery, and seek conversion of life. The day was divided into three main parts. They were expected to engage in communal worship and prayer, which was thought of as the *opus Dei,* or the work of God. Time was set aside for *lectio divina,* or spiritual reading, which overlapped into private prayer and contemplation. Finally, a considerable part of the day was spent on the *opus manum,* or manual work, which included both work in the fields and those various crafts and administrative tasks which enabled the monastery to function effectively. But above all the purpose of the monastery was for the monks to worship God and live in such a way as would lead them to heaven.

The routine of monastic life was communal, disciplined and regular, and it insisted on 'stability.' That is, monks should not go from one religious house to another seeking perfection, but instead should bind themselves to remain in one monastery throughout their lives, obedient to its abbot. Benedict avoided extremes of austerity. He believed that monks should have warm clothes and sufficient food and sleep. The Rule, he said, included 'nothing harsh or rigorous.' It is above all practical, simple and orderly. It is also gentle and humane in its tone. An abbot is expected to consult his monks before making a decision and he is expected to prefer 'mercy to justice.' Over the centuries the nature of a monastic community inevitably changed. The form of worship developed and more and more monks came to be priests. But the pattern laid down by St Benedict survived as the model of communal religious life in the West for more than half a millennium. When eventually new and different religious orders were founded Benedictinism continued to be important for another thousand years.

There was no central organising body at the head of the Benedictine movement. Each monastery was independent. The one thing they had in common, and also the one unchanging thing down the centuries, was *The Rule of St Benedict*, a portion of which was read out every day, so that all monks down the ages were intimately acquainted with it. It had a profound, civilising and Christianising effect on generations of monks and eventually, since neither monks nor monasteries could be cut off completely from the rest of society, it had a civilising and Christianising effect on society as a whole.

Gregory the Great

An outstanding example of the influence of the Benedictine tradition on an individual and of his influence in the world is the life of Gregory the Great. He was born in about 540 AD, in the middle of the reign of the Emperor Justinian, a member of an aristocratic Roman family. In 573, while still a young man, he was appointed Prefect of the City – the chief civil administrator. Shortly afterwards he used his family wealth to found a monastery in Rome and a number of others on his family's estates in Sicily. He entered the monastery he had founded in Rome in 575, but four years later was appointed to be the papal agent in Constantinople, where he did not much like the civilised and intellectual East. His sympathies were back in the West and he returned to his monastery in 585. Five years later he was the first monk to be elected pope – the title by which the bishop of Rome was now generally known, and remained pope from 590 until his death in 604.

Back in 588 the patriarch of Constantinople had taken the title of 'ecumenical patriarch', or 'universal bishop.' Gregory, once he was pope, protested, but characteristically he did so with monastic humility. He did not assert the authority of Rome, but instead argued that no one could claim universal authority. It was not that he had abandoned Rome's claim to primacy. It was rather that he saw it as inappropriate to assert it arrogantly, so instead of asserting Rome's primacy, still less supremacy, he described himself as *servus servorum Dei*, 'the servant of the servants of God.' He also understood that at that time any claim by Rome to universal authority in the church could only be theoretical. The crucial issue facing the papacy was not rivalry with Constantinople over the leadership of the church but rather the struggle to survive in the face of succeeding waves of barbarian attacks.

In 592, two years after Gregory became pope, the Lombards were devastating northern Italy. There was little that the emperor could do from Constantinople to support or protect the Italian provinces, and in practice Gregory had to run the Roman duchy, paying its troops and negotiating with the invaders, as well as seeking to convert the Arian Lombards to Catholicism. Gregory was not aiming to carve out a separate temporal principality, independent of the Roman Empire. He remained loyal to the emperor in Constantinople not just in principle but also in practice as far as that was possible. But it was becoming increasingly clear that the empire could only expect to hold on to the eastern provinces. The West had fallen to the barbarian tribes, and the one leader of the church in the West with at least theoretical authority reaching far beyond a province or an archdiocese was the pope, who was by now not only the bishop of Rome but also in some measure the temporal ruler of central Italy. It was difficult to the point of impossible to maintain the fiction of one universal church in a Christian empire. The East was still an empire. The West was not.

Christendom divided

Gregory the Great negotiated with the Lombards when they swarmed into Italy, and he tried to establish good relations with them. Similarly he tried to establish good relations with both the Visigoths and the Franks. The Lombards and the Visigoths were eventually converted from Arianism to Catholicism. The Franks, who had never encountered the Arian version of Christianity, had already been converted to Catholicism, and their king, Clovis, had been baptised, together with three thousand of his men, on Christmas Day 498. A century later, in 596, Gregory sent one of the monks from his own monastery in Rome, Augustine, to convert the pagan Angles and Saxons who had settled in Britain. By the middle of the seventh century the Lombards ruled Italy, the Franks and Burgundians ruled Gaul, the Visigoths and the Suevi ruled Spain and the Angles and Saxons ruled Britain. All of them were Christians, and all were now Catholic, or Trinitarian, Christians rather than Arian heretics. They all acknowledged the authority of St Peter, and they saw the Pope as St Peter's representative on earth. The West had become a different world from the surviving Roman Empire in the East.

In the nineteenth century it became customary for historians to refer to the Roman Empire in the East as the Byzantine Empire, after the name of the site where Constantinople had been founded, and that empire, whether one calls it Roman or Byzantine, with its base of power in Asia Minor, proved remarkably resilient for another eight hundred years. In the early seventh century, with resources stretched almost to breaking-point, it managed to defeat barbarian invaders in the Balkans. At the same time it engaged in a long drawn out war in the East against the Persian Empire, and in 628 AD it broke the power of the Persians. But while the church in the West engaged vigorously in missionary activity, the Eastern church failed to reach out similarly to the pagan Arab peoples on its borders. This was partly because of the assumption that Christianity was characteristic of the empire, while beyond lay darkness, and partly because the nearest people in the empire to the Arabs were the monophysites of Egypt and Syria, who were seen as heretics by the central imperial authority and consequently became bitterly opposed to imperial rule. The result of the failure of the church to reach out beyond them to the Arabs with the good news of the Kingdom was dramatic and lasting.

Muhammad and Islam

628, the year in which the Byzantine Empire broke the power of the Persian Empire, was also the year when an Arab mystic, Muhammad, rode into Mecca in the West of Arabia at the head of 10,000 followers to establish the holiest shrine of the new religion which he had already proclaimed in the town of Medina, further north, in 622. The religion was *Islam*, or surrender to God, and its followers were Muslims. The word *Muslim* comes from the same root as *Islam*; Muslims were people who had surrendered themselves to God, and *Islam* is said to rest on five pillars which constitute the requirements made of all Muslims. They are expected to confess their faith regularly with the words, 'There is no God but Allah, and Muhammad is his prophet.' They need to pray facing Mecca at five set times each day. They should give alms to the poor. They are expected to fast from dawn till dusk in the month of *Ramadan*. They are expected to make a pilgrimage to Mecca at least once in their lifetime.

Muhammad wanted social, economic and political equality for both men and women, and in some ways his teaching was remarkably similar to that of Jesus. He taught that all Muslims were brothers and sisters and should treat each other with love and compassion. He was entirely opposed to paganism, but he was sympathetic to both Judaism and Christianity, which he saw as natural precursors of Islam, and he was sympathetic to their adherents, the People of the Book. Twenty years after his death in 632, his teaching had been gathered together in the Holy Book, the *Qur'an*, and its message welded the Arab world together in religious and political unity and released its immense latent energy.

One significant difference in the teaching of Muhammad from that of Jesus is that Muhammad believed in the use of force to spread the faith. Jesus rode into Jerusalem on a donkey. Muhammad rode into Mecca in 628 on a camel at the head of an armed force, and on his death the Arabs burst out of their homelands to conquer the world. The Persian Empire, already defeated by the Byzantines, was overrun. In 634 the Caliph Omar

(Caliphs were the successors, or deputies, of the prophet) led the Arabs into Byzantine territory. Syria and Egypt, where many of the monophysites welcomed the Arabs as liberators, fell in rapid succession. The patriarchates of Alexandria, Antioch and Jerusalem were all in the hands of the Arabs, and as the century went by the Arabs overran all North Africa and even besieged Constantinople itself.

The division of Christendom

During the reign of the Emperor Theodosius the Great from 379 until 395 it had been possible to see the Roman Empire as roughly co-terminous with the Christian *oikumene*. During the reign of the Emperor Justinian from 527 until 565 it was still possible to think of the distinction between *catholic* and *orthodox* as a linguistic one. But by the mid-seventh century the whole of the West was irrevocably lost to the empire and such imperial power as was still exercised in Rome was wielded by the pope. Much of the East was under Muslim rule, and barbarian Serbs, Croats and Bulgars were migrating into the Balkans. In 663 the Emperor Constans II visited Rome on his way to set up his military headquarters at Syracuse in Sicily. But East and West were now increasingly cut off from each other and it would be seven hundred years before another Byzantine emperor visited Rome.

Section 3
Christendom Divided
(the 660s to 1000 AD)

Chapter 8

Catholic West and Orthodox East

From Theodosius to Justinian

By the end of the fourth century, in the reign of Theodosius the Great (379-395), Christianity had been established as the official religion of the Roman Empire. The great ecumenical councils of Nicaea in 325 and Constantinople in 381 had established the orthodox doctrine of the Trinity. The next three ecumenical councils, Ephesus in 431, Chalcedon in 451 and the Second Council of Constantinople in 553 had apparently settled the Christological conflict about the relationship between the humanity and the divinity of Christ, but they had also produced enduring schisms with those who did not accept the orthodox formula.

As a result of the church now having an official position in society there was on the one hand a rise in both the social status and the administrative responsibilities of bishops and on the other a retreat from the world by many Christians into religious communities. Barbarian tribes, many of which had been converted to Arian Christianity, had invaded and conquered the West, and Christendom came to look very different in the West from the East. In Constantinople emperors ruled as

God's representative on earth, with the co-operation of orthodox patriarchs and bishops. In the West the principal religious authority was the pope in Rome. He and the other bishops of the West were faced not only with converting the pagan tribes to Christianity but also with converting their Arian conquerors to Catholicism.

The Emperor Justinian's attempt from Constantinople in the middle of the seventh century to reassert imperial authority in the West as well as in the East was followed by renewed barbarian advances in the West and then by the rise of Islam and the Arab conquests in the East. The period from these Arab conquests of the seventh century until the end of the millennium produced a division of Christendom into two main parts, with a Byzantine emperor and an orthodox patriarch of Constantinople in the East and a Germanic emperor and a catholic pope in the West.

The impact of the Arabs

In the half-century after Muhammad's death in 632 the Muslims conquered Persia, Arabia, the Middle East and North Africa. They developed sea power and in the years from 674 onwards even blockaded Constantinople. But after four years, in 678, the Byzantine fleet defeated them. The Byzantine Empire had been reduced to not much more than Constantinople itself, the territories of the patriarchate of Constantinople in Asia Minor and the Balkans, Sicily and some land in the south of Italy and in the Crimea. But this massive diminution of the empire had two great advantages. First of all the forces of the empire could concentrate on the defence of the homeland. Secondly, with the patriarchates of Alexandria, Antioch and Jerusalem under Muslim rule, Constantinople was in a better position than in the past to determine orthodoxy without having to take so much trouble to accommodate the theological positions adopted in Alexandria or Antioch. The Emperor Theodosius the Great at the end of the fourth century had wanted to establish an empire which was united both politically and ecclesiastically. One and a half centuries later Justinian had the same aim. Strangely enough that aim was now easier to achieve – and it was easier precisely because the empire was smaller. Economically, politically, militarily and ecclesiastically it was more cohesive than it had ever been before.

One relatively short term effect of the loss to Islam of so much land which had been Christian for centuries was to draw old Rome and new Rome closer together. At the same time the loss of the other patriarchates made it easier for the patriarch of Constantinople to seek an understanding and accommodation with Rome. However much pope and patriarch may have differed in their attitudes to authority and in the ways in which they expressed their theological opinions, in the seventh century they always thought of Christendom as being one. Now there was all the more reason to unite against the common enemy.

The Third Council of Constantinople (681)

Throughout the late seventh and early eighth centuries there was a great influx into the West of Christians from Syria and Greece, especially from the territories conquered by the Arabs. Rome became far more ecumenical than it had been, and the history of the late seventh century provides several illustrations of the unity of Christendom. Whereas nearly all the popes in the hundred years up to the middle of the seventh century were Romans, in the next hundred years most were either Syrian or Greek. In 663 the Byzantine emperor, Constans II, visited Rome and was accepted as the supreme ruler. In 668 Pope Vitalian sent a Greek-speaking monk from Asia Minor, Theodore of Tarsus, to be archbishop of Canterbury in the former province of Britain, which was now divided into a variety of Angle, Saxon and Jutish kingdoms, and where the mission sent by Gregory the Great was increasingly bearing fuit.

But the most striking illustration of the unity of Christendom is to be found in the Third Council of Constantinople of 681, the sixth of the seven great ecumenical councils in the five centuries between 300 and 800 AD. It was summoned by the Emperor Constantine IV specifically to condemn as heretical the teaching known as monothelitism, which involved asserting that Christ had only one will. Pope Agatho sent legates to the council and they joined in condemning monothelitism and proclaiming the existence in Christ of two wills, one human and one divine. It also involved them in condemning as heretical the views of four patriarchs of Constantinople and one pope, Honorius I.

At the time it could have been a really important step towards cementing the unity of the church, because the main issue liable to divide East and West was the issue of the nature of Roman primacy. If it was possible for just one pope to have erred, then it looked as if it should be possible to reach agreement on the basis of Roman primacy combined with the possibility of Roman fallibility. Although that agreement was never reached, for the moment there was a sense of unity, the pope continued to rule the area around Rome as an official of the emperor, and in 710 a pope who was significantly called Constantine visited Constantinople and was received with honour.

East and West go their own ways

Only a few years later, in about 726, a dispute began between the papacy and the empire over the rather squalid issue of the pope avoiding paying taxes to the emperor. That dispute was then transformed by a controversy in the East about the proper place of icons, or images, in worship; and it carried on for the next sixty years. In 730 the Emperor Leo III sent Pope Gregory II an order not to place pictures of martyrs and angels in churches. This gave the pope the opportunity to turn the dispute from one in which he was not rendering to Caesar the things which were Caesar's into one in which he, as St Peter's successor, was entitled to make decisions on how to render to God the things that were God's. He was not going to be dictated to in that area by the emperor. Thus one effect in the West of what is called the iconoclast controversy was that it gave the pope an excuse, or justification, for breaking free from the authority of the Byzantine emperor. If the emperor was an iconoclast, a destroyer of religious images, the pope could feel justified in denying his authority; and, at the time, there seemed to be nothing to fear from the power of the emperor. The threats from the Arabs in the East and from the Bulgars and the Serbs in the Balkans kept the forces of

Byzantium fully occupied and at the same time created new barriers between Rome and the East.

At that time the Byzantine Empire still held the South of Italy, Sicily and that part of the Dalmatian coast which had traditionally been in the Western Empire and under the jurisdiction of Rome. In 732 the Emperor Leo III transferred the dioceses in those areas to the jurisdiction of the patriarch of Constantinople. From his point of view it was simpler to have all the empire under the ecclesiastical jurisdiction of one patriarch. But Rome was bitterly offended, especially as it also lost the valuable revenues of its former estates in South Italy and Sicily. Both things were a source of friction for the next century. Add that to the fact that Leo III and his son and successor, Constantine V, were iconoclasts, and thus seen by Rome as heretical, and the breach between Rome and Constantinople, instead of healing, widened. When the papacy's lands came under threat from the ambitions of the Lombard kings in the middle of the eighth century, it was no longer either natural or practical to look for support to the emperor in Constantinople.

In 754 the Emperor Constantine V held a church council at which iconoclasm was adopted and claimed to be in accordance with orthodox traditions. From this time onwards, even though iconoclasm was condemned in the East only thirty-three years later, no popes came from the East for the next three hundred years. The overwhelming majority of popes until the middle of the eleventh century were Italians, and nearly three-quarters came from Rome itself. Meanwhile there developed many differences of practice between the Latin and Greek churches. For example, the Greeks excommunicated anyone who failed to receive communion on three successive Sundays; the Romans did not. The Greeks were prepared to accept widows as nuns; in the West there was at least some question about whether or not that was proper. Greek monks did not keep slaves; Western monasteries often did.

The East and West were not torn apart. There were no differences other than the Roman claim of papal supremacy which could not have been resolved as a result of regular contact.

But the Catholic West and the Orthodox East were drifting apart. No Byzantine emperor visited Rome until John V Palaeologus came in the fourteenth century to ask for help to fight off the Ottoman Turks. The agreement at the Third Council of Constantinople was soon forgotten, though it remained a potential cause of embarrassment centuries later whenever the idea of papal infallibility was discussed. No pope visited Constantinople again until 1967, when Paul VI visited the Patriarch Athenagoras.

Western vulnerability

The tendency for East and West to develop separately does not really begin until the eighth century. It might have been expected to have begun much earlier, with the ending of the Roman Empire in the West. But the deposition of Romulus Augustulus in 476 had not involved a significant change. After all, the barbarians had been hammering at the borders of the empire three hundred years earlier when Marcus Aurelius was fighting them, and many things carried on in much the same way for the next two or three hundred years after the barbarian tribes had taken over in the West. The barbarians entered into the inheritance of Rome. But the long-term effects of the Arab conquests in the eighth century eventually cut them off from the material and intellectual heartland of the empire in the East.

The Muslim world, like Byzantium, was richer, both materially and intellectually, than the barbarian West. It dominated not only the Middle East and the North African coast but increasingly the Mediterranean as well, and by the eighth century Muslim power reached far enough to control both Spain and Sicily. As a consequence of the spread of Islam, from around 700 AD till the mid-eleventh century, the barbarian and Latin West was more or less cut off from Byzantium, where the old Roman Empire continued for a thousand years after its destruction in the West. Trade between Western Europe and the East broke down. Syrian traders were no longer bringing silk to the courts of barbarian kings in the West and papyrus to monasteries in the North.

It was already centuries since Rome had been the capital of a great empire. Understandably, as it declined to become merely the principal town of a local community, its bishops came from local families. But despite this provincialism and the relative poverty (materially and intellectually) of the West generally, the papacy made increasing claims about its own supremacy and authority. The patriarchs of Constantinople were not so much inclined to argue against these claims as to view them with irritation or pained embarrassment. But in the West they came to be increasingly accepted – at least in theory if not always in practice.

The Franks defeat the Arabs

In 717 the Arabs besieged Constantinople again, but again the Byzantines defeated them and they had to raise the siege in 719. But by then, at the other end of the Mediterranean, the Arabs had conquered Spain and Portugal, and in 721 they crossed the Pyrenees and moved northwards through Gaul until they reached the valley of the Loire. Western Europe was threatened with being overrun and needed to find a way of checking and driving back the Arab advance. The solution was found by the Franks. They could only do it with heavily armed and armoured fighting men, seated on heavy horses and able to fight while keeping their seat in the saddle by means of one of the most important technological developments of all time, the stirrup. The economic cost of equipping these heavily armed horsemen with all the latest military technology such as chainmail was immense. So was the social cost. It transformed the social structure of Western Europe into one in which mounted men on horseback, or knights, ruled peasants, whose labour maintained the knights. It was the only way to halt the Arab advance, and in 732 at the battle of Poitiers the Frankish leader, Charles Martel, and his knights defeated the Arabs.

The Christian Church was involved in two ways. First, it unwillingly provided much of the wealth on which Frankish military power was based. Both bishoprics and monasteries had acquired vast lands and wealth over the preceding centuries. Now they lost a lot of it to feed and equip the knights and horses who defended them. They wanted the defence but resented the despoliation of their endowments which made it possible. Secondly the church provided rather more willingly the ideology for which the Frankish knights fought. The war against the Arabs was not just a territorial defensive war. What made it worth fighting was that they were defending Christendom from what they perceived to be the forces of darkness. The victory could only be achieved at the expense of church property, but the victory, once won, was a victory for the Christian Church.

The alliance of the Papacy and the Franks

The Franks saw themselves as the defenders of Catholic Christianity, and they supported the pope through both secular and ecclesiastical difficulties. 732, the year of the battle of Poitiers, was also the year in which the Emperor Leo III had transferred the dioceses of South Italy, Sicily and the northern part of the Dalmatian coast to the jurisdiction of the patriarch of Constantinople. The Franks encouraged the pope to free himself from allegiance to the emperor in the East, and in 753, twenty-one years after the battle of Poitiers, when the Lombards were threatening papal lands in central Italy and an iconoclast emperor, Constantine V (741 – 775), was on the throne on Constantinople, Pope Stephen II set out to cross the Alps and make contact with and agree an alliance with the Franks.

Any one who has driven over the Alps on modern roads can see what an extraordinary undertaking that was – and all the more so because the pope started his journey in November. He met the Frankish king, Pepin, and agreed the alliance. In practice this meant that power in Italy would be shared between them. The Frankish king was replacing the Byzantine Emperor as the lay authority in the West. In place of the long-established imperial authority in the East to whom all bishops and patriarchs were subordinate, the principal lay authority in the West was now a Frankish king who was the ally of the pope.

The pope had taken a step of immense political significance. Not merely was he neglecting his duty to pay taxes to the emperor. Not merely was he asserting his own authority against the emperor's in matters ecclesiastical. He was explicitly denying the authority of the Byzantine emperor in Italy, and he was asserting independent political authority for himself. It was the first time in history that a pope had done so. He was moving towards claiming the authority to make and break emperors.

The Donation of Constantine

It was probably at about the time that Pope Stephen II broke with the East and crossed the Alps to build an alliance with the Franks that a document was produced to justify the breach with the Eastern Emperor and to demonstrate to the Frankish king that the pope had the right to invite him to take over lands which were formerly part of the empire. The document, though written in the second half of the eighth century, purports to be a letter from the Emperor Constantine to Pope Sylvester I, written on 30th March 315, in which, among much else, the emperor grants the pope pre-eminence over all other churches, including the patriarchates of Alexandria, Antioch, Constantinople (which had not yet been built) and Jerusalem (which was not yet a patriarchate). At the same time it transfers to the pope imperial authority in the western provinces of the empire. The pope is portrayed as the 'universal bishop', St Peter's deputy on earth, and also temporal lord of the West, by gift of the emperor.

The Second Council of Nicaea (787)

The East, of course, was still the intellectual centre of Christendom. It was in Constantinople rather than Rome that learned men would argue over issues of logic and seek to hammer out definitions which would form the canon of orthodox belief, and in 787 there was another council of the church – again at Nicaea. This Council of Nicaea was the seventh and last of the universally acknowledged ecumenical councils of the undivided church. The patriarch of Constantinople presided over it. The pope sent legates to it. And it drew up a definition of the place of images in Christian worship which was approved by emperor and papal legate alike. Essentially iconoclasm was renounced as heretical, and this marks the end, at least for the moment, of the iconoclast controversy which had begun about sixty years earlier. It could perhaps, if things had gone differently later, have been seen as the moment of reconciliation when East and West were able to put aside their differences and reach agreement in a spirit of co-operation.

But the Frankish king, now Charlemagne, the son of Pepin and grandson of Charles Martel, the victor of Poitiers, was offended that the West had been underrepresented at the council, objected to its decisions, and launched a bitter attack both on the decisions and on the 'filthy pond of hell' from which they came. He was warning the East not to think it could dictate to the West. He was warning the pope to beware of fraternising with the enemy.

The Greeks saw it as absurd that an illiterate barbarian king in the West should presume to dictate doctrine to a learned emperor and to the bishops of the East. To them the ultimate arbiter of doctrinal matters was an orthodox emperor guided by the advice of the gathered bishops of the Christian Church, led in their discussions by the patriarchs – though in practice that meant led by the patriarch of Constantinople, since three of the patriarchs were now living within the jurisdiction of Islam and the pope was cut off from civilisation in the barbarian West, where men did not even speak Greek and could not hope to engage in intelligent and rational discourse at a higher level about theological issues. The pope also had no wish to have doctrine dictated by a Frankish king who could not read any language, let alone Greek or even Latin. But in his view ultimate authority on theological matters lay with himself – not with an ecumenical council of bishops, still less with an Eastern emperor. The gap between East and West was now very wide.

The *filioque* clause

It got wider. In 381 the Council of Constantinople had produced the definitive statement of Christian belief generally known as the Nicene Creed because it was based on what had been discussed at Nicaea in 325. That creed proclaimed that the Holy Spirit proceeded 'from the Father.' In the West, where there were many Arians who did not think of the Son as co-equal and consubstantial with the Father, it was possible to interpret that as an affirmation of the inferiority of the Son.

108

This was an issue St Augustine had tackled not long after the Council of Constantinople, and like many theologians in the East who had written about this before him, he was anxious to combat Arianism and assert the essential unity of the Trinity. His own particular approach to this was to emphasise that the Holy Spirit proceeded from both the Father and the Son. The so-called Athanasian Creed, which was produced in Western Europe in the second half of the fifth century and attributed to St Athanasius, perhaps to give it authority, was strongly influenced by Augustinian Trinitarian doctrine. What is more, the practice of adding the clause 'and from the Son' to Western creeds can be traced back to Augustine's teaching. In Latin it is expressed by the one word *filioque*, which means 'and from the Son'. The first part, *filio*, means 'from the Son'. The last three letters, '*que*', are a Latin suffix added to the second word of a pair to give the meaning 'and'. The Nicene Creed, as agreed at the Council of Constantinople of 381, had asserted a belief in the Holy Spirit, 'which proceeds from the Father', so by implication the Holy Spirit did not proceed from the Son as well. But that seemed to Augustine to be playing into the hands of the Arians. Hence his insistence that the Holy Spirit proceeded from both the Father and the Son, and hence the gradual inclusion in western creeds of the word *filioque* and eventually even its insertion into the Nicene Creed. It was to cause trouble on a quite disproportionate scale.

Interference with the Nicene Creed

It was probably someone in Spain who at some time in the seventh century inserted *filioque* into the Nicene Creed to make the point that the Holy Spirit proceeded not only from the Father but also necessarily from the co-equal and consubstantial Son. Greek theologians were later prepared to accept the idea of the procession of the Holy Ghost from the Father through the Son. They found the preposition 'through' more acceptable than the conjunction 'and'; and they were inclined to see the intellectual origins of the *filioque* clause in the fact that the Westerners were using Latin, a relatively unsophisticated language by comparison with Greek, and one far less suited to expressing the subtleties of Trinitarian theology.

Far more important than the question of whether or not it was theologically acceptable to express the procession of the Holy Spirit as being from the Son as well as from the Father was the question of the authority by which a clause should be inserted into the Creed. The explanation of the spread of the *filioque* clause is that men who had been in Spain combating the Arian heresy persuaded Charlemagne to include it in the creed used in the royal chapel, and once it was established there it spread throughout the Carolingian Empire. Pope Leo III (not to be confused with the iconoclast emperor Leo III) appreciated the problem of tampering with the creed and advised Charlemagne to drop the clause. But its use spread throughout Western Europe until it was used almost everywhere except in the papal chapel in Rome. In the light of the subsequent controversy about the intrusion of the *filioque* clause into the creed, it is worth noting that it was not a papal decision which brought it into use. It came about by custom and practice in a West cut off from the East, and it was custom and practice endorsed by a powerful Frankish king against the advice of the pope.

The coronation of Charlemagne

On Christmas Day 800 that same Frankish king was crowned as emperor by Pope Leo III. It was an action with long-term consequences for relations between East and West. First, it was a betrayal of the imperial ideal, for there was still an emperor, or at least an empress, in Constantinople, even if it was now about half a century since the pope had acknowledged imperial authority. Secondly, it was a betrayal of the unity of Christendom, for that had always depended on the authority of the emperor, under whom bishops from all over Christendom could meet in council at Nicaea or Chalcedon or Constantinople to thrash out an agreed formula – even if those formulae usually resulted in driving a disappointed and disapproving minority into schism. Thirdly, it was the source of frequent conflict between pope and emperor in the West in the coming centuries.

The coronation of Charlemagne marks a virtually irrevocable breach between the papacy on the one hand and the Byzantine emperor and the patriarch of Constantinople on the other. That had not yet happened in the last years of the eighth century. The political unity of Christendom had been eroded by the schisms following on from the Councils of Ephesus and Chalcedon, weakened by the barbarian invasions in the West and shaken by the spread of Islam. But it was not destroyed until the pope showed how entirely he had shaken off the authority of the Byzantine emperor by setting up a barbarian Frankish king as his own western emperor on Christmas Day of 800. Before that there was no rent in the seamless garment of Christ which could not perhaps be cobbled together. Now the papal action in establishing a western emperor had combined with the Muslim occupation of Alexandria, Antioch and Jerusalem to produce a clear and relatively simple structure for a divided Christendom, with an eastern emperor and an orthodox patriarch in Constantinople and a western emperor and a catholic pope in Rome.

The imperial ideal in the West

In the event Charlemagne's empire was of relatively short duration. Within thirty years of his death in 814 it had been divided among his descendants, and through most of the ninth century Western Europe was vulnerable to attack by a range of enemies: Muslims by sea from the South, Vikings by sea from the North and Magyars on horseback from the East. While the Byzantine Empire maintained a gold-based currency and paid for a powerful imperial army, trade in the West broke down internally as well as externally and defence became a local matter dependent on maintaining groups of heavily armed horsemen.

The idea and ideal of Rome, the consciousness that Rome represented something of value handed down from the past, was strongly associated with the papacy in those last centuries of the first millennium. From all over Western Christendom men wrote to Rome for advice and guidance. Many appealed to Rome as the final arbiter of justice. Some felt a need to visit the former imperial city and carried home accounts of its grandeur.

The idea of a western empire was lying dormant, but before the end of the millennium it would be revived, with emperors in the West seeing their own position as analogous to that of the Byzantine Emperor in relation to the patriarch of Constantinople, with the pope as their right-hand man in matters ecclesiastical. They would eventually take the view that it was the right and even the duty of the emperor to ensure that papal elections conformed to imperial wishes. Meanwhile the popes were in practice setting up their own authority to challenge that of the emperor. They had aspirations to untrammelled power as the successors of St Peter and were seeking not only to secure their spiritual authority but their temporal authority as well, with the emperor as the pope's lay executive officer. As early as Christmas Day 800 Leo III and Charlemagne were setting the scene for the clash between papal and imperial authority in the High Middle Ages and for the clash between papal and princely authority at the time of the Reformation.

Chapter 9

Iconoclasm in Byzantium

The resilience of Byzantium

Byzantium was remarkably resilient for a thousand years after the Roman Empire had collapsed in the West. Roman political ideas, Greek culture, Christian faith and a stable gold-based currency combined to produce a civilisation capable of adapting to changing circumstances and surviving. Just as Diocletian and Constantine had needed to reorganise the administrative and military structures established by Caesar Augustus three hundred years earlier, similarly in the seventh century another wholesale reorganisation of the empire was needed. At the heart of it lay the grouping of the provinces of Asia Minor into military zones and the establishment of an effective army and navy to cope with the Bulgars in the Balkans and the Arabs to the south-east and at sea.

The Byzantine Empire was a consciously religious society in which followers of Christ who were particularly venerated were thought of as saints, and those who had died for their faith were revered as martyrs. The army was encouraged to think of itself as defending Christendom from the infidel. It began and ended each day with a religious service and its battlecry was 'The Cross has conquered.' Meanwhile the coastal regions of the empire provided for and maintained a powerful navy, and although the Arabs developed naval power as early as the seventh century, the Byzantines still retained maritime supremacy.

As early as 628 the Byzantines had defeated the Persians in the East and at the same time they managed to retain control of the Balkans, while assimilating some of the Slav invaders into the empire as smallholders, soldiers, and converts to Christianity. They defended the homeland from the Arab invasion which was launched after the death of Muhammad in 632, and near the end of the century, in 678, they defeated the Arabs at sea, bringing the first siege of Constantinople to an end after four years. Forty years later, in 718, a year after the Arabs besieged Constantinople again, the forces of Byzantium yet again defeated the Arab threat.

The Syrian emperors

In 717, just before the second Arab siege of Constantinople began, a powerful general who had made his reputation commanding armies in the East became emperor as Leo III. His own origins were in the north of Syria, and he and his son, Constantine V, ruled Byzantium for nearly sixty years until 775, making effective use of their military skill and resources and also of their diplomatic skill and subtlety to consolidate the strength of the empire. The Byzantine economy remained strong. Trade continued not only with the East but also with the North, through Byzantine territory in the Crimea, and with the West through their lands in South Italy. They already had an effective legal system derived from Justinian. They now extended the administrative and military structure which had proved so effective in Asia Minor into other parts of the empire. But most important of all for the future history of Byzantium, they saw it as their duty to protect and, where necessary, reform the church.

The place of icons in worship

A problem which became important in the reign of Leo III was the question of whether or not pictures of the saints and of Christ could properly be used in Christian worship. Throughout the Christian church, and particularly in the Byzantine East, pictures of Christ and of the saints were widely used in worship. They were not thought of as being merely pictures. They were what the

Greeks called icons, and were seen as symbols of that which they represented. As a consequence they were treated with veneration. They were seldom pictures of events, though St George was traditionally represented slaying the dragon. Most commonly they were head-on representations, usually with paint on wood, of the face or figure of Christ or one of the saints.

Just as a saint might be thought to be particularly present in a church dedicated to him (or her), especially if the church preserved some relics, similarly the saint was thought to be in some sense present in the icon. It was seen as a link between this world and the next. A person might pray for help to a saint using the medium of the icon to transmit the prayer. By touching the icon the person might be healed of some mental, emotional or physical affliction; healing grace was thought to be transmitted through the icon.

Eastern opposition to icons

But there was a long and powerful tradition in the East of opposition to the use of statues or pictures in worship. It had been common in the pagan world, but once the ancient Jews had formulated the idea that God was spirit and should be worshipped in spirit, statues and pictures of gods become objectionable. No statue or picture of God could possibly represent that which was unknowable and inaccessible, holy and separated by that holiness from the material world. The Jewish tradition was forcibly expressed in the second commandment, which Christians accepted: *Thou shalt not make unto thee any graven image, or any likeness of any thing that is in heaven above or that is in the earth beneath, or that is in the water under the earth. Thou shalt not bow down thyself to them, not serve them, for I the Lord thy God am a jealous God.* Jews eventually objected not only to any graphical representation of the God whom they worshipped, but also to the graphical representation of anyone or anything else believed to be a god, since they believed there was only one God and thus whoever or whatever was represented must necessarily be a false god. Muslims went further and objected to the graphical representation of any living creature. Consequently their mosques were decorated with intricate geometric and other patterns but not with pictures of people or animals.

Understandably Jews accused Christians of idolatry when they saw pictures of Christ or of the saints in churches, and as early as the seventh century a bishop in Cyprus replied to that accusation by declaring about the cross and pictures of the saints that 'they are not our gods, but opened books to remind us of God.' But in a part of the world where people felt the force of Jewish and Muslim opinion it was understandable that many Christians began to question the appropriateness of using icons in worship, and by the early eighth century the use of icons both in churches and elsewhere was being seriously challenged. The case for icons can easily, and mistakenly, seem to us a mixture of aesthetic and educational arguments. Ideally a church should look attractive rather than drab, and icons provided decoration. Ideally a church should aid worship, and icons, by representing Christ or the saints, might help people to understand their faith and worship God. But that was not the reason for icons. The Muslims decorated their mosques lavishly without depicting any living creature. Christians in the West used pictures as a means to tell a story. The Greeks did neither. The icons were not intended as decorations, Nor did they tell a story. They were used as objects of devotion.

Leo III's iconoclast policy

The further East one went, the more there was opposition to the use of icons. At the same time the army was less sympathetic to the use of icons than were civilians. The Emperor Leo III, who came from as far east as Syria and whose whole career had been as a soldier, shared the distaste for icons. He was also, as emperor, inclined to assert his authority over the church as much as over every other aspect of Byzantine life. In the event it was nearly ten years before he took action over icons. When he first came to the throne he was faced with the second Arab siege of Constantinople, and after overcoming that there were innumerable military, administrative, organisational and legal tasks to tackle. But in 726, when he was well established in power, he made a start on removing

116

icons. He began at home and gave orders to pull down the great icon of Christ standing over the bronze gates of the imperial palace in Constantinople, facing the church of the Holy Wisdom, the *Hagia Sophia*. The immediate result was a riot in which the crowd killed the imperial official organising the work of destruction. A more significant outcome was the revolt of one of the provinces in Greece. The revolt was put down, but the fact that it had happened was an indication that a policy of iconoclasm, or the destruction of icons, was going to divide rather than unite the empire,

Leo III was undeterred. He made his preparations and in 730 gave orders banning all religious imagery other than the cross. The orders applied throughout the empire. Icons were either to be destroyed or covered in whitewash. Vestments embroidered with images were to be burnt. The relics of saints and martyrs in shrines all over the empire were to be destroyed. The patriarch of Constantinople refused to comply with the order, so Leo had him deposed and replaced by another patriarch who was willing to do as he was told. When Leo's instructions reached Pope Gregory II in Rome, Gregory also refused to obey and Leo tried, unsuccessfully, to have him arrested.

The case for iconoclasm

The iconoclast controversy was not at all a matter of aesthetic taste. Nor was it a simple matter of a clash between an authoritarian emperor and the leaders of the church. Iconoclasm was the continuation of the Christological controversy by other means. The argument about the nature of Christ had gone on for centuries. The Council of Ephesus in 431 had emphasised the unity of his divine and human natures. The Council of Chalcedon in 451 had allowed for rather more of a distinction between the divine and human natures. The councils of Constantinople in 553 and 681 had looked for a compromise. But disagreement and arguments continued, and the iconoclasts, while accepting the Chalcedonian formula on the nature of Christ, were uncomfortable with many of the practices which had developed in the church and which appeared to conflict with the second commandment of the Law of Moses.

We do not have any of the documents putting the iconoclast case, because the second council of Nicaea of 787, the seventh and last of the great ecumenical councils of the early church, not only declared against iconoclasm but also ordered the destruction of all iconoclast writings. We have to construct their case from the answers of their opponents.

They appear to have taken the view that it is impossible to portray the divine and, since Christ was divine, it must be impossible to portray him. The veneration of icons of the Virgin Mary and of other saints, and the adoration of the relics of martyrs, were also objectionable, and lavishly decorated liturgical vestments and pictures of angels were all part of this drift away from recognition of the truth that God is spirit and that He only should be worshipped. But most important of all was the point that the divinity of Christ precluded any attempt to portray him. To attempt to do so was positively blasphemous.

The iconodule case

There was a real theological problem about this objection to icons. After all, the saints were human, not gods, so why should they not be represented, so long as it was clear that they were not being worshipped? What is more, if Jesus, the Word made flesh, really was a true man, then in principle it should be possible to represent him pictorially as much as any other man. If one denies the possibility of producing a pictorial representation of Jesus (the question of how accurate it may or may not be is irrelevant), one is denying his humanity.

The case in favour of icons was most eloquently and powerfully put by a theologian known as John of Damascus. The Emperor Leo III would not tolerate the publication of the case in favour of icons within the bounds of the empire. But John lived in Damascus and worked as an official of the Moslem ruler, the Caliph Abdul Malek, as his father had before him. So ironically it was in Damascus, where no pictorial decorations were permitted in Islamic mosques, that the case in favour of icons was most effectively set out. John of Damascus, living under the protection of the Caliph, was free to publish his views on the use of pictorial imagery within the Christian religion. His main point was that it was essential to be able to depict Jesus, since Jesus was a man like any other man, except that he never sinned. To suggest on theological grounds that it was wrong to depict him was not only a denial of his humanity but also eventually a denial of the doctrine of the Incarnation. John also pointed out that it was God who had given artists their talent and that wood and paint are part of divine creation. To forbid the use of that talent for a good purpose and to forbid the use of wood and paint, also for a good purpose, was to denigrate God's creation.

Iconoclasm triumphant

The iconoclasts were not convinced, and Constantine V, who succeeded his father in 741 at the age of 23 and reigned for the next thirty-four years, pursued an even more determined iconoclast policy. He took his time, because he appreciated that so profound a change in the religious life of the empire could only be achieved with the support of the leaders of the church. So as episcopal sees fell vacant he appointed iconoclasts to fill them, and he created new bishoprics and appointed iconoclasts to them as well. Every attempt was made to persuade or convert church leaders from the iconodule position of venerating icons to iconoclasm. Iconodules who had the courage to speak out were arrested and silenced. At last Constantine V was ready to act decisively and in 754 he held a church council. The patriarch of Constantinople had just died, the pope was not present, and nor were the patriarchs of Alexandria, Antioch and Jerusalem. The pope and the oriental patriarchs did not even send representatives. But the 338 bishops who did attend adopted the principles of iconoclasm unanimously and asserted that it was in accordance with orthodox traditions. Then Constantine V appointed a new patriarch of Constantinople, and after that the decrees of the council were promulgated. The display of icons of Christ, of the Virgin Mary and of the saints was condemned, the chief protagonists of the iconodule position, including John of Damascus, were excommunicated, and Constantine V was proclaimed as the equal of the apostles.

With the authority of what he saw as an ecumenical council behind him, Constantine set out to destroy the iconodules. He persecuted them relentlessly. The opposition to his policy centred on monasteries, so before long the persecution of the iconodules had become persecution of monks generally. Monastic property was confiscated. Monasteries were converted into army barracks or used for other secular purposes. Monks were required to abandon the monastic life, and even to demonstrate that they had done so by getting married.

One thing led to another and eventually Constantine went far beyond the decrees of 754. No one was any longer to be venerated as a saint and eventually the cult of the Virgin Mary, the Mother of God, was banned. That decision is a measure of the extent of the revolution in the life of the church which Constantine V was seeking to bring about. It was a direct assault on the popular piety which had gradually developed in the previous three centuries.

The cult of the Virgin Mary

The Council of Ephesus in 431 had approved the idea of Mary as *Theotokos*, or God-bearer, and in 553 the Second Council of Constantinople had declared that she was 'ever-virgin.' That was in line with the view which by then was common that virginity was more virtuous than married life. But it is a necessary consequence of the pious belief that Mary must have continued as a virgin throughout her life that she cannot have had any children other than Jesus. As a consequence James, 'the Lord's brother', who had led the early church in Jerusalem, was relegated to being a kinsman, or a brother only in a metaphorical sense.

Mary met the need for a female element in the worship of the divine, and she came to be an idealisation of virtues seen as combining goodness with femininity: gentleness, simplicity, affection, maternal love, purity and humility. It takes us quite a long way from the assertive young woman in St Luke's Gospel who proclaims in the *Magnificat*, 'He hath shewed strength with his arm; he hath scattered the proud in the imagination of their hearts. He hath put down the mighty from their seats, and exalted them of low degree. He hath filled the hungry with good things; and the rich he hath sent empty away'(*Luke 1.51-53*).

Devotion to Mary inspired numerous works of art ranging from grand portrayals of her as the Mother of God and All-holy to pictures of her as a young mother with her child. Popular devotion also led to a range of feast-days associated with Mary: her birthday, which was unknown; the day of the Annunciation by the Angel Gabriel, which understandably was fixed just nine months before Christmas Day; the feast of Purification, after childbirth; and the feast of Dormition, when, it was comforting to believe, she did not so much die as fall asleep. That idea eventually spread to the West, where similarly people did not like to think of Mary dying, and in typically Western fashion a pious belief from the East was given a literal meaning, so that many Westerners came to believe that Mary, instead of dying, was physically taken up into heaven. The culmination of this tradition was the proclamation by Pope Pius XII in 1950 of the Doctrine of the Bodily Assumption of the Blessed Virgin Mary.

The restoration of the icons

Constantine V died in 775. His son, Leo IV, was a moderate man, and although iconoclasm remained the official policy of the empire, the attacks on the cult of the Virgin Mary and on monasticism came to an end. He married an iconodule wife, the Empress Irene, and after his early death she planned for and arranged the restoration of the icons. In 787, at the seventh ecumenical council at Nicaea, iconoclasm was renounced as heretical. It broke out again early in the ninth century at a time when a number of military defeats produced a yearning to get back to the military successes and even the ecclesiastical policies of Constantine V. But it was never a threat on the same scale as before and orthodoxy was restored again at a church council in 843. At the same time a clear distinction was drawn between the worship which is due to God alone and the veneration which may properly be accorded to created objects.

The victory of the iconodules made the use of icons an even more entrenched and essential part of Orthodoxy. The eventual defeat of the policies of the iconoclast emperors brought to an end a long drawn out crisis in the relationship between Church and State within the Byzantine Empire. It was possible to see the rule of Theodosius the Great in the late fourth century and that of Justinian in the late sixth century as 'Caesaropapism' – a system of government in which the supreme lay authority, the emperor, was also the supreme religious authority. But that is misleading. Even Justinian was not seen, and did not see himself, as having theological infallibility by virtue of his office. Rather he had an obligation to preserve orthodoxy. The iconoclast emperors, Leo III and Constantine V, were seen as failing in that duty, and after the iconoclast period imperial art and literature made of point of depicting emperors as servants of God anxious to preserve orthodoxy, and it avoided imperial triumphalism.

The Byzantine emperor was still seen as God's representative on earth. But he needed to be crowned by the patriarch of Constantinople, and after the iconoclast controversy it became customary for the emperor, before he was crowned, to sign a profession of faith, accepting the Nicene Creed and the decisions of the ecumenical councils. The church was under the care of the emperor, but the emperor had to be orthodox in his beliefs and practice. He could not impose his own theological will. His duty was to uphold orthodoxy, not to determine it.

The emperor and the patriarch were both essential to the proper functioning of the Byzantine state, in which secular and ecclesiastical authority were integrated and at best worked together in harmony. While the emperor had religious responsibilities, which included ensuring orthodoxy and an appropriate liturgy, the patriarch was involved in civil administration. Bishop Eusebius of Caesarea, writing in the reign of Constantine, the first Christian emperor, had written of the emperor as the living icon of Christ, and had set out the nature of the emperor's authority in the church. He had a duty to regulate the universal Christian empire so that it should be a reflection on earth of the heavenly kingdom above. He did not decide what was orthodox, but he was the defender of the orthodoxy determined in ecumenical councils. Of course the emperor was important, but in the last resort he could not overrule the faith agreed by a large body of bishops gathered together in council.

The Festival of Orthodoxy

The Greek Church was conscious of an unbroken heritage reaching back to the apostles. The earliest Christian communities were established in the Greek-speaking world. The New Testament was written in Greek. The very name by which their Lord and Saviour was known, Jesus Christ, rather than Joshua the Messiah, was Greek. It was understandable, indeed perfectly proper, that those living beyond the bounds of Greek civilisation should worship in their own languages, Gothic, Latin, Armenian, or later Russian. But Latin, like Gothic, was seen as a relatively barbarian language in which it was difficult to express theological ideas in anything other than a simple form. Greek was the language of orthodoxy, and it was the task of the Greek Church to maintain the faith of the apostles and pass it on in a pure form from one generation to the next.

The great ecumenical councils of the church had established the essentials of Christian belief. Nicaea and Constantinople had settled the issue of the relationship between the persons of the Trinity. All of the others had been concerned with establishing the orthodox position on the issue of the relationship between the divinity and the humanity of Christ. Even the decision of the Second Council of Nicaea in 787 to uphold the veneration of icons was really a decision on a Christological issue, upholding the humanity of Christ. So in 843, with the final defeat of iconoclasm, the Greek Church established an annual 'feast of orthodoxy' to remind itself of its sacred duty to maintain the purity and the fullness of the faith it had inherited from the apostles.

The conversion of the Bulgars

Once Byzantium emerged from the iconoclast controversy it underwent a period of revival and renewal which came to be known as the Golden Age of Byzantium and is seen as lasting from 843 until the next millennium. This Golden Age bore fruit in successful missionary activity among the Bulgars and Slavs in the Balkans and beyond. The Bulgars had invaded imperial territory in 756 and that precipitated some years of fighting in which Constantine V was brilliantly successful. He utterly defeated them in 763. The only problem with the victory was that it was so total and humiliating that it made enemies of the Bulgars for generations, and a century of diplomacy and missionary activity was needed before Boris I of Bulgaria, in the mid-ninth century, indicated that he was interested in adopting Christianity and corresponded both with the Patriarch Photius of Constantinople and Pope Nicholas I.

This was a time when relations between East and West were particularly strained. In 863 Pope Nicholas I declared the Patriarch Photius of Constantinople deposed because he disapproved of the manner of his appointment. But despite that Boris of Bulgaria was baptised the following year into the Orthodox Church. Byzantium was closer than Rome and was richer and more powerful than the disintegrating Frankish Empire. Meanwhile the Byzantine emperor and the patriarch were more irritated than awed by the presumption of the pope in deposing the patriarch, and in 867 a synod in Constantinople excommunicated Pope Nicholas I and condemned the Western use of the *filioque* clause in the creed as heretical.

An important element in the conversion of the Bulgars had been the decision by the emperor to send two state officials who were brothers into the Balkans as missionaries. One of them, who took the name Cyril when he became a monk, invented a Slavonic alphabet in order to be able to translate the Bible into Slavonic. The eventual outcome was the Cyrillic alphabet, still used in Russian and most other Slav languages today, and the development of Old Church Slavonic, which came to be the most used language of the liturgy after Greek and Latin, as well as the foundation of a Slav culture. The Greeks were also more sympathetic than the Latins to the use of the vernacular, and this policy of encouraging the use of the vernacular combined with the power and proximity of Byzantium to produce the conversion of the Bulgars. The papacy had also wanted to allow the use of the vernacular in worship, but the Frankish kings from Charlemagne onwards would not allow it. They saw Latin as the language of religion and insisted on its use in the liturgy. Just as it was the Frankish kings rather than the pope who decided on the policy of including the *filioque* clause in the Creed, so it was they rather than the pope who decided on the policy of using Latin in the Western liturgy which continued into the twentieth century.

The conversion of the Russians

Even more important than the conversion of the Bulgars was the conversion of the Russians. In the middle of the tenth century the Princess Olga of the early Russian state of Kiev was converted to Christianity and visited Constantinople, where she was well received. Two generations later her grandson Vladimir, Prince of Kiev, appears to have wanted an ideology or religion to weld his people together, and the story is told that he sent envoys to find out about both Christianity and Islam. The envoys were unimpressed by either Islam or Western Catholicism. But they visited the great church of the Holy Wisdom, the *Hagia Sophia*, in Constantinople, where they saw the celebration of the eucharist, and it was as if heaven and earth were merged. Never had they seen such splendour and beauty. They reported back to Vladimir and one of the boyars, or Russian noblemen, added the clinching Russian argument that 'it was the faith of your grandmother Olga.' So in 998 AD Vladimir opted for Orthodox Christianity as the religion of his people.

An alternative explanation of the conversion of Russia is that it was in 989 that Russia sent a contingent of six thousand fighting men, the Varangian Guard, to help the Byzantine Emperor Basil II in a military campaign against a force of rebels. The Varangian Guard crushed the rebels and as a reward for his assistance and as a symbol of future co-operation Vladimir was given the sister of Basil II in marriage and promised in return to adopt Christianity. The Varangian Guard remained in the service of the emperor as a sort of Byzantine Foreign Legion, which later attracted many Vikings to serve as mercenaries and had a great influx of Anglo-Saxons after their defeat by the Normans in 1066.

In 1240 Kiev was conquered by the Tartars, and the Russians were subject to the Khanate of the Golden Horde until 1480. By then, when the power of the Tartars had faded enough for Ivan III, the Russian ruler, to stop paying tribute to the Great Khan, the Turks had, in 1453, taken Constantinople and at last destroyed the Byzantine Empire, Ivan III had married the niece of the last Byzantine emperor, and he had taken the title of Tsar, implying imperial authority. Then a century later, in 1589, Moscow became the sixth patriarchate of the world. Since four of the others, Constantinople, Alexandria, Antioch and Jerusalem, were all within the borders of Islam, and since Rome was in schism in the West, it now became possible to see Moscow as the Third Rome.

Chapter 10

The Golden Age in the West

Colonisation and conversion

In the late seventh century Western Europe was still a society of barbarian tribes, each with its own customs. Some were pagan but many were Christian, and increasingly they were Catholic rather than Arian. In the centuries from the barbarian invasions until the end of the first millennium the foundations of the Western church were laid and a pattern for Christian life and worship was established. The history of the West was entirely different from the history of the Byzantine East. Byzantium remained the conscious successor of the Christian Roman Empire and remained a unified, civilised and centralised empire. In the West the influence of the Roman Empire had faded and it was the interrelationship between Barbarism and Christianity which would determine the future.

Much of the history of the West is the history of colonisation as well as of conquest. As Christendom pushed out its boundaries, forests were cleared, land was drained and churches were built. The Rhine was the eastern boundary of the Franks in the eighth century and also the eastern boundary of Christendom. But it was also a trade route. Beyond the Rhine were pagan Saxons and Frisians, who were a threat to trade on the river. In the short run they had to be fought. In the long run they had to be converted. One of the greatest successes of the Frankish king, Charlemagne, at the end of the eighth century was that he defeated and then converted the Saxons. Success only shifted the problem further East. In the next century the border of Christendom lay on the Elbe, and beyond that were pagan Slavs and Bohemians. They also had to be fought and eventually converted. Beyond them were Magyars, while to the North were the Vikings and to the South the Muslims, or Saracens. There was no end to the problems and no end to the opportunities.

Imperial, papal and royal authority

Theoretically both imperial and papal authority were important, and very probably, in so far as anyone thought about such things, they were unquestioned. But the single most important thing to appreciate about imperial and papal authority at this time is that they did not impinge directly or consciously on the lives of most people. By the eighth century the emperor in Constantinople exerted no effective authority in the West, and so remote was his authority at the end of the century that on Christmas Day 800 Pope Leo III had crowned Charlemagne as emperor and done homage to him, becoming his vassal and accepting him as his lord. It was both the first and last time that a pope ever did homage to an emperor. At the same time papal claims to ecclesiastical authority were extensive, and with the loss of Carthage in North Africa to the Muslims early in the eighth century Rome had become virtually the only great centre of spiritual authority in the West. But the last pope of any significance for nearly two centuries was Nicholas I (858 – 867), who tried to depose the Patriarch Photius of Constantinople and in return was excommunicated in a synod presided over by the Byzantine emperor.

Royal authority was more immediately important than either papal or imperial authority. Throughout this period Western Christendom was perpetually under threat from external enemies. The ideal solution was to convert them and bring them within the bounds of Christendom. But in practice it was often necessary to fight. Society was geared to doing that and had no (or few) inhibitions about it. In this context the Old Testament was more relevant than the New. It provided numerous illustrations of how the Chosen People, led by judges or kings chosen by God, fought their enemies and smote them hip and thigh. The leadership of western society in the last centuries of the first millennium was in the hands of fighting men, and Christianity had to adapt to a world led by barbarian war leaders. War-leaders were known as kings and were usually the leaders of a people rather than rulers of a place. Traditionally a king was descended from one of the old pagan gods such as Woden, was of fighting age, and preferably had been designated by his predecessor and acclaimed by the great men of the kingdom. Now he was seen as chosen by God, consecrated with holy oil, and anointed by a bishop to act as God's deputy, just as Solomon had been anointed king by Zadok the Priest and Nathan the Prophet (*1.Kings 1.34-39*). He was a law-giver, caring for his people, and had both religious and moral responsibilities.

The unity of society

In the light of subsequent history it is perhaps natural to think in terms of a distinction between Church and State. But it is a mistake to do so at this time. Barbarian tribes had always expected the whole community to keep to the customs of the tribe, and once those customs embraced Christian worship, everyone would be expected to accept that. Lay and ecclesiastical society were one. Alter one and you altered the other. Society was identified with the church, and all life, law and learning, much literature and even government and warfare operated within the context of a Christian framework.

There was also an assumption that everyone was part of a Christian community which reached out in space throughout Christendom and back in time to communion with all the saints of the early centuries of the first millennium. Therein lies the origin and explanation of infant baptism. Babies, so vulnerable to death in infancy, were baptised as soon as they were born to ensure that they did not suffer the pains of hell, and also to welcome them into the Christian Church and into a society whose members were all Christians.

The significant division of society was not so much between the lay and the ecclesiastical as between the ruling class who did the fighting, and the peasants, who tilled the fields. That distinction applied as much in the church as in other aspects of life. Church leaders, the bishops and the abbots of important monasteries, naturally came from the ruling class and shared in the tasks of government, for which they were well equipped by virtue of their education. Important men could hold both lay and ecclesiastical positions. Thus in the tenth century Bruno, brother of the Saxon king, Otto I, who was crowned as Roman Emperor in 962, held at the same time both the position of Duke of Lorraine and that of Archbishop of Cologne. Similarly in the eleventh century Odo, half-brother of William I of England, was Bishop of Bayeux from 1049, at the age of seventeen, and Earl of Kent from 1067. Village clergy, on the other hand, were usually peasants from the same background as their flock.

Bishops

Bishops were important throughout this period. Work which had previously been done by Roman aristocrats and administrators was now commonly done by bishops. In a united Christian society it seemed natural that those with the skills of reading and writing (unlike fighting men, such as the king and the leading laymen) should undertake the administration of the kingdom. So bishops exercised a range of different functions – as local administrators, as spiritual leaders and sometimes as missionaries. Not only did they care for the poor, the sick and the elderly, but they also repaired fortifications, built bridges, ensured the water supply, and sometimes held their lands in return for providing the king with fighting men.

Kings expected to appoint them, and clerks who proved particularly effective as administrators in the royal household were promoted to be bishops. At this time royal appointment of bishops was not only accepted by the papacy; it was approved and even insisted on. Pope John X early in the tenth century insisted that no bishop should be consecrated 'without an order of the king.' Kings were God's anointed and the assumption was that they would protect Holy Church from its enemies. Bishops in the West generally looked to Rome as the ultimate source of spiritual authority, saw themselves as being in some sense the subordinates, or servants, of the papacy and expected to co-operate in the work of the successor of St Peter. But they also saw themselves as loyal subjects and servants of their king, and expected to co-operate with him in the task of running a Christian society.

The conversion of Britain

Although the pope had no direct influence in most of Western Europe, his indirect influence could be considerable. One striking example is the conversion of the English. After the departure of the Roman legions from Britain early in the fifth century and the invasion of various Angle and Saxon peoples, Christianity survived only in the Celtic fringes of Britain and Ireland. It was entirely cut off from developments on the continent and inevitably developed in its own way and with its own customs. The Celts calculated the date of Easter differently from the way it was calculated at Rome and Celtic monks cut their hair in a different way from the Benedictine monks of the continent.

At the end of the sixth century Pope Gregory the Great sent to Britain a monk called Augustine together with some companions. They had been given the task of converting the peoples there, and in the long run the mission was a great success. But it took time. In each of the Angle and Saxon kingdoms the king had to be converted first. Then Christianity had to be disseminated among the people. Sometimes the movement progressed smoothly. Sometimes there were setbacks. Meanwhile the Celtic church was missionising with renewed vigour. Eventually there was the problem of how Celtic and Roman Christianity could co-exist. In the event that issue was settled in 664 largely in favour of Rome at the Synod of Whitby, where King Oswy of Northumbria was persuaded that the representatives of Rome were speaking with the authority of St Peter, who held the keys to the kingdom of heaven. It was a powerful argument, and the Celtic Christians, who saw themselves as the representatives of St Columba, could not match it. Four years later papal influence was felt again when

Pope Vitalian took advantage of the death in Rome of the archbishop-elect of Canterbury to appoint to the vacant see a monk from Asia Minor, Theodore of Tarsus. It turned out to be an inspired appointment. Theodore made use of the best elements of Celtic and Roman Christianity and reorganised the English church. Bede, writing a generation later, said that Theodore was the first archbishop whom the whole *ecclesia Anglicana*, or English church, obeyed willingly.

There are three really important points to appreciate about the conversion of the English people. The first is that papal intervention, when it happened, was a strategic decision followed by genuine delegation. Augustine at the end of the sixth century and Theodore near the end of the seventh was each given a task, and it was then very largely left to them and to others on the spot to accomplish it. The second point is that it all took rather a long time. There was no quick solution to the problem of overcoming generations of paganism. The third point is that the conversion of the English lasted. Two hundred years after Theodore, when pagan Danish invaders had already conquered all except one of the Angle and Saxon kingdoms, Alfred, the king of the West Saxons, was able to persuade his people that it was worth fighting, because their kingdom represented Christian civilisation, with its associated benefits of learning and literature and the rule of law. It was much the same message that Churchill was to proclaim to their descendants more than a thousand years later.

Conversion of the Germanic tribes

Just as Pope Gregory the Great sent Augustine to convert the Angles and Saxons, so his successors encouraged many other missionaries in the work of conversion of the Germanic tribes on the continent. One of the most famous of them, partly because of his achievements and partly because so many of his letters have survived, was a monk from Devon called Wynfrith, who in the early eighth century, when Christianity was well established in Britain, went as a missionary to the barbarian tribes of North-west Europe and established and organised the Christian church in large tracts of the area we now call Germany. He

operated very largely on his own initiative, and when he wrote to
other bishops he would send them the present of a towel as a
reminder of the example Jesus had set by washing his disciples'
feet. He maintained a correspondence with Rome, in which he
tried to check that what he was teaching was in line with the
teaching and practices of the catholic church, and in 722 Pope
Gregory II consecrated him as archbishop and gave him the
name Boniface ('He who does good'). During the last years of his
life, as Archbishop of Mainz, he retained his zeal for missionary
work, and he died a martyr at the age of 79 when cut down
by seafaring raiders while trying to bring the gospel to the Frisian
coast. Another important Anglo-Saxon missionary, Willibrord,
consecrated in 695 by Pope Sergius I as archbishop of the Frisians,
was also a monk, but in his case from Northumbria. They are two
of a substantial number of monks who devoted themselves at this
time to the task of evangelism.

Monasticism

The monastic movement developed on a vast scale during these
centuries and became an integral part of the economic as well
as the religious life of society. There is a sense in which one can
see the monasteries of the West as educational institutions
preparing Christians for a life of service in the world. It was right
that men should withdraw from the world into the cloister to pray
and worship God. But it was also seen as desirable for that
experience to fit them for returning to the world to undertake a
wide range of tasks, including colonisation, administration and
missionary work.

Kings and other great landholders found monasteries an
extraordinarily effective device for the development of previously
uncultivated land. Monks lived in disciplined communities
following the Rule of St Benedict, and they worked hard and
regularly. They were literate and could keep accurate accounts.
If land was transferred to them they could be relied on to draw
up a plan for clearing the trees and providing drainage. What is
more, the monastic community was more durable than a lay lord.
Individuals might die. The community survived and would always

have more monks working hard, battling with the land and playing their part in helping to create Christendom.

But they were also concerned with the religious life and such consideration of theology as happened in the West usually took place in monasteries. There was scope to develop and give expression to differing views on such matters as eucharistic theology. In the 840s, for example, Charlemagne's grandson, Charles the Bald of France, received two treatises from the monastery of Corbie on eucharistic theology. The abbot of Corbie had written one setting out the case for transubstantiation. That is, he accepted the idea that any material thing has not only its physical characteristics, or 'accidents', but also an underlying or fundamental reality, which is its 'substance', and he argued that at the moment of consecration in the eucharist the 'substance' of the bread changes into the 'substance' of the actual body of Christ crucified, though the 'accidents' remain the same. Similarly the wine changes into the blood of Christ while retaining the physical characteristics of wine. The other treatise was by another monk of Corbie, who argued that the sacrament was primarily a memorial of Christ's passion and that any divine presence was spiritual and in no way physical. Perhaps the most illuminating thing about this is the unspoken assumption that fellow-Christians, even monks in the same monastery, could hold such differing views and remain in fellowship with one another.

The cultural shift

Throughout these centuries a distinctive Western Christian culture was developing. As the boundaries of Christendom were pushed out a lord would establish a settlement and provide it with a church and a priest. The church would eventually become the parish church and the lord would expect to provide for it and appoint the priest. He was not consciously denying the authority of the local bishop. The right, or duty, of a local lord to run his own church and appoint its priest was much the same as the right, or duty, of a king to establish bishoprics. Similarly kings and other laymen founded monasteries and expected to have some say in how they were run. Monks in a monastery might need to elect, or choose, their next abbot, but it would often be made clear to them who should be chosen.

In time churches were built in almost every village and generation by generation Christian ideas were more and more embedded in people's thinking. Converts to Christianity were told in their own language about the need to renounce the devil, behave well, give alms to the poor and look for the coming of the Day of Judgement. They were baptised using the so-called Apostles' Creed, which developed long after the theologically more complex Nicene Creed to provide a simple statement of basic Christian beliefs and is not found in its final form until the mid-eighth century. They learnt the Ten Commandments, the Lord's Prayer and the Apostles' Creed in their own language.

Stories about martyrs and about holy men and women were passed on from one generation to the next and saints were created by popular decision (It was not till the second millennium that the papacy became involved in official canonisations). Churches were often painted with pictures expressing the ideas of Good and Evil, or Heaven and Hell, in symbolic form, and, since it was a simple and primitive society, the visual imagery, such as angels with wings and devils with horns, came over time to be interpreted literally. At the same time the crucifix, with Christ hanging in agony on the cross, rather than the traditional image of Christ reigning triumphant from the cross, became an important symbol of Western devotion.

Meanwhile Latin was used for church services and the only versions of the Bible available in the West were in Latin. Latin had been adopted for church services in Rome in place of Greek in the early third century because it was the language of ordinary people, and in the early fifth century St Jerome had produced a more accurate Latin version of the Bible than was already available. Paradoxically Latin survived in a barbarian world as the language of religion and scholarship. Thus literate priests came to be intermediaries between ordinary people and the sacred and Latin mysteries of their religion. The liturgy developed and was gradually standardised. Music became a regular part of worship, in accordance with St Augustine's aphorism, *quis cantat bis orat*

(Whoever sings prays twice). Learning, literature and law were all permeated with Christian thought.

The political world

The Franks who dominated Gaul were much involved in the fighting against the Germanic tribes across the Rhine and in the fighting against the Arabs in the South. Success against the Arab invasions of the early eighth century resulted in the creation of a powerful Frankish kingdom, and by the time Charlemagne was crowned as emperor in 800 AD he was ruling a wide range of different peoples. But the Carolingian Empire was short-lived. It was too large and cumbersome to be able to cope effectively with the threats facing Western Europe in the ninth and tenth centuries and within two generations it had been divided into three. One of Charlemagne's grandsons ruled the lands in the West which eventually became France. Another ruled the lands in the East which many centuries later became Germany. A third was emperor and ruled a middle kingdom reaching from the Netherlands to Rome. But even these kingdoms were too large.

Throughout the ninth and tenth centuries pagan Vikings, or Northmen, attacked from the North, sailing their boats up the rivers which flowed into the North Sea and the English Channel. The Saracens attacked in much the same way from the South, sailing up the rivers which flowed into the Mediterranean. The Magyars rode in on horseback from the East. It is a measure of the vulnerability of Western Europe that the monastery of Luxeuil in Burgundy was sacked in the early tenth century by all three. Some of these raids were on a very large scale, but many were by no more men than could get into a couple of boats, and the appropriate response to that was not the deployment of large armies. The only way for Western Europe to survive was to break up into self-sufficient political units small enough to defend themselves from raids. The former Roman province of Britain was already divided into the seven kingdoms of Wessex, Mercia, Northumbria, East Anglia, Essex, Kent and Sussex. The former Roman province of Gaul was in theory one West Frankish kingdom, but in practice counties such as Anjou, Maine, Blois and

Champagne operated as independent states, as much as did the Ile de France, the area around Paris ruled by the King of France. Trade dried up. Men tilled the fields, worshipped God in their local churches, and looked to their local lord to defend them from attack.

In the ninth century the Vikings, also known as Danes or Northmen, established themselves in the north and east of Britain in an area which came to be known as the Danelaw, and in the tenth century they established themselves in an area of Gaul which came to be known as Normandy. But they were converted to Christianity. The Saracens, however, could not be converted. But they were driven off. The last great threat was from the Magyars, or Hungarians, and in 955 the German king, the Saxon Otto I, with the help of the four great duchies of Franconia, Suabia, Saxony and Bavaria, finally defeated them at the battle of Lechfeld in Bavaria. After their defeat they were treated leniently, and the outcome was that by the end of the century there was an independent Christian Kingdom of Hungary on the eastern border of western Christendom. Otto's success was followed by a revival of the imperial ideal in the West, and in 962 he was crowned as Roman Emperor by Pope John XII and is remembered as Otto the Great. But this new western empire ruled by a German king and later known as the Holy Roman Empire, was very different from either the old Roman Empire in its heyday or the continuing Byzantine Empire in the East.

The Papacy

The authority of the pope as the representative of St Peter on earth had for centuries been widely accepted in the West. It was believed that he held the keys to Heaven on behalf of St Peter and could and would decide whether or not any individual should be allowed in. Any new archbishop had to make a written statement of faith which was acceptable to the pope and receive a *pallium*, a woollen mantle worn as a mark of honour, before he could exercise his metropolitan functions. But communications were poor and the opportunities for enforcing papal commands negligible, so it is a mistake to see these years as a time in which the western church was dominated by a vigorous and centralising papacy. It was not. The papacy maintained its extensive claims to Petrine authority, but that authority was latent rather than effective. The further Christians were from Rome and the less there was any direct contact, the more potent it seemed.

Back in Rome the position was very different. Rome had declined into a provincial Italian city and the papacy had reverted to being a local bishopric. As in other parts of Europe the bishop was usually appointed by a local ruler, but the instability of Roman politics made for trouble. In the early ninth century the Carolingian Empire had disintegrated, in 846 Rome was sacked by the Saracens and in the late ninth century effective government broke down both in the city and in the surrounding area. Pope John VIII was assassinated in 882, and in the following century most popes died violent deaths. Local families competed for control of the papacy, which remained important locally but was far from being a model of a good bishopric. For example, Sergius III, who seized the papacy by force in 904 and held it until his death in 911, had a teen-age mistress called Marozia. Their illegitimate son became Pope John XI in 931, and her grandson became Pope John XII in 955 at the age of eighteen. It was he who crowned Otto I as Emperor in 962, but he was deposed by the emperor the following year and was reputed by bishop Liutprand of Cremona to have died of sexual excess in 964 at the age of twenty-seven.

The reform movement

In the last centuries of the first millennium the Christian church had become an integral part of the society of Western Europe. It was not an additional extra added onto an essentially barbarian world to provide a moral and spiritual dimension to life in a hard, dangerous and difficult world. It was as much part of that world as agriculture and warfare, and its very success threw up problems. Could bishops really combine spiritual leadership with their function as local administrators, and even more, could they properly lead fighting men in battle? Should monasteries own such vast lands and wealth? When positions such as those of abbots, bishops and archbishops were so important and endowed with so many resources and so much power, both material and spiritual, then was it not natural that some conflict should arise over control of those positions? If the pope was the supreme spiritual leader of Western Christendom, or even, as he claimed, of all Christendom, should he not be setting a good moral example?

Reform of some sort was needed. Genuine idealism, combined with hard fighting and hard work in the fields, had achieved a vast amount in Western Europe. But it was time for some self-criticism. Many monasteries had become so rich and self-indulgent that there were now new foundations conscientiously seeking to be more holy. No one questioned the right of lay rulers to appoint to high ecclesiastical office, but if they appointed a close relation whose life was scandalous, or who was plainly incompetent, then it would be condemned as nepotism. If money changed hands when an ecclesiastical appointment was made, especially if it was a bad appointment, that was likely to be seen as the sin of 'simony', which takes its name from the incident in *The Acts of the Apostles* when Simon Magus came to Peter and tried to buy the gift of the Holy Spirit with money (*Acts 8.18-24*). Despite the papal instruction issued in 385 AD that bishops, priests and deacons should avoid sexual intercourse, clerical marriage was widespread and was seen as a serious problem when senior churchmen made arrangements for their children to inherit church lands or appointments. Above all the papacy itself was falling short of the high ideals many people had for it. If the church in the West was to be reformed and tackle the problems of nepotism, simony and clerical marriage, the starting point was going to have to be the reform of the papacy itself, and the initiative would have to come either from the German king in his capacity as Roman Emperor, or from the new reformed monasteries, or both.

The Golden Age

The centuries after the destruction of the Roman Empire in the West are sometimes described as the Dark Ages – and certainly they are dark in the sense that historical source material is scarcer than for the preceding and following centuries, and thus historical scholarship has not been able to illuminate them as much as it has other periods. But in another sense they were a Golden Age. Christianity spread throughout the tribes of Western Europe. Bishoprics were established universally and churches were built for every community. Monasteries maintained learning for men and women alike. Every member of society was a member of the church. There was fruitful co-operation between all elements in society as they faced external enemies and worked together for good. Peasants relied on fighting men for their protection and fighting men relied on peasants for their food and equipment. Bishops provided an ideology worth fighting and even dying for, and they also provided the administrative support. By the beginning of the second millennium local parish priests were spreading the ideals of Christianity throughout society, tilling the fields alongside their parishioners and providing them with moral guidance. Kings and barons, knights and peasants, bishops and priests, abbots and monks were co-operating in the development of vigorous and flourishing Christian communities. They were divided from their fellow Christians in the East, but they were self-reliant and increasingly self-confident.

Section 4
The High Middle Ages
(1000 AD to the 1330s)

Chapter 11

Reform and Conflict

Monastic Reform

By the end of the first millennium Western Europe was a Christian society. It was divided into kingdoms and into bishoprics, and anointed kings appointed the bishops, who co-operated with them in government. It was divided into parishes, and local lords ensured that each village had a church; they appointed the priest and very often they collected the tithes, the local tax due to the church. Both kings and lords founded monasteries, partly as acts of piety and partly because monasteries, holding land on favourable terms, were an economically efficient way of exploiting the land. The church and lay society were closely integrated, but precisely that integration, which had achieved so much, came to be a cause for concern.

A reform movement developed in a number of monasteries. Cluny in Burgundy took the lead. It had been founded in 910 AD by Duke William I of Aquitaine with an unusual measure of independence from any lay authority, and it was the most important single monastery involved in this movement. Its first concern was the development of the liturgy, the *opus Dei*, and as its fame spread other monastic houses, conscious of falling short of perfection, called Cluny in to help them with the process of reform. During the eleventh century Cluny devised a way of establishing a permanent link with these reformed houses: their abbots still ruled their own houses but were now subordinate to the abbot of Cluny. The next step was for Cluny to found a number of new houses, and it did this on a large scale. Each of the new houses was ruled by a prior on behalf of the abbot of Cluny, so both in theory and practice these Cluniac priories were extensions of the great mother house.

In all of these houses reform centred on the liturgy and included the idea that an offering of worship to the Lord should not be made by men whose hands were sullied by contact with money or whose bodies were sullied by contact with women. What began as a monastic ideal was before long being recommended to the rest of the Western church as well, though in the Orthodox church in the East there was still a general expectation that parish clergy should be married. The reformers went on to attack simony, the sin of treating spiritual things as commodities to be bought and sold, and the definition of simony was eventually extended to include all lay involvement in ecclesiastical appointments. Their attack at the same time on clerical marriage or co-habitation was both because they feared that spiritual things would be contaminated by the involvement of priests in sexual activity and also because of the danger that ecclesiastical offices might come to be inherited. This reform movement spread from the monasteries through the Western church and eventually influenced the papacy.

The Papacy

At the end of the first millennium the papacy was clearly the most important ecclesiastical institution in Western Europe, but during the tenth century it had become a prize in the politics of the noble families of Rome and central Italy, such as the Crescentii and the family of the counts of Tusculum. German kings who became Roman emperors in the West saw it as their duty to make the papacy more respectable, so they intervened and made their own appointments. But the involvement in Italy of the emperors Otto I (936-73), Otto II (973-83) and Otto III (983-1002) was inevitably intermittent, and in the first half of the eleventh century the papacy was very largely in the hands of the counts of Tusculum. By the mid-1040s three different men were claiming to be pope. One was the last Tusculan pope, one was his Crescentian rival and one was a reformer who had, despite his reforming principles, paid a large sum of money to obtain the papacy. The Emperor Henry III (1039-56), a descendant of Otto I, was in sympathy with the reforming movement and at the Synod of Sutri in 1046 he deposed them all and went on to appoint a succession of worthy German bishops. The most significant of these reforming popes was Leo IX (1048-54), who spent only six months of his five-year pontificate in Rome. He crossed the Alps to France and Germany five times, held synods, settled disputes and issued decrees against simony and clerical marriage and against violence and moral laxity generally. By the end of his pontificate he had made it clear that the central element in papal policy in the coming years was going to be the assertion of the ideal of papal authority throughout the church.

At this stage there was no attack on lay authority, but the way things were changing is indicated by the critical view being taken in the eleventh century of the document known as *The Donation of Constantine*, a papal forgery of the mid-eighth century representing the Emperor Constantine as conferring authority on the pope. The view was developing at the papal court that God had given all authority to the successor of St Peter, who in turn might choose to confer part of that authority on an emperor. The *Donation* was at fault in seeming to suggest that papal authority in the West derived from the supreme authority of the emperor. In fact, it was suggested, the supreme authority of the pope throughout Christendom owed its origin not to any imperial gift but rather to the declaration by Christ to St Peter of the authority he was giving to him (and, by inference, to his successors) to lead the church and decide whom to bind and whom to loose (*Matthew 16.18 and 19*).

The clash with the East in 1054

Meanwhile Pope Leo IX had to face the immediate problem that a group of Normans (Northmen or Vikings who after a generation or two in Normandy had been transformed into mounted Norman knights and had invaded South Italy early in the century) were threatening his interests. He launched a military campaign against them and in 1053 was defeated by them and imprisoned. From captivity he wrote both to the Byzantine Emperor Michael III and to the Patriarch Michael Cerularius of Constantinople, and sent the letters with three legates, or papal representatives. To the emperor he wrote a letter which, while conciliatory in tone, assumed a position of strength rather than weakness, complained about the patriarch and asked for help. To the patriarch he wrote as if to a disobedient subordinate, asserting the supremacy of Rome, criticising him for a range of different offences, real or imagined, and requiring repentance. The language was strong, but it expressed Rome's position clearly. Obedience to Rome's orders and conformity to Rome's practices was demanded as the way to the unity of the church.

The visit of the legates to Constantinople was a disaster and ended with the legates placing on the altar of the church of the *Hagia Sophia* a sealed papal document (known as a 'bull' because the Latin for 'seal' is *bulla*) excommunicating the patriarch and listing a range of offences, one of which was the omission of the *filioque* clause from the Nicene Creed. The reality, of course, was not that the clause had been omitted in the East but rather that it had been introduced in the West. The departure of the legates was followed by a synod at Constantinople which condemned the visitors from the West who had behaved so offensively.

These events are often seen as marking the start of the schism between the eastern and western churches, but in reality it was no more than a dramatic episode in a problem which went back for centuries and was still unresolved. There had been a serious rift exactly three hundred years earlier in 754. That was the year in which iconoclasm was proclaimed in the East as orthodox, and was also the year in which Pope Stephen II allied with King Pepin of the Franks, relying on him for support against the Lombards rather than on the iconoclast Emperor Constantine V. In April 1054, before his legates had excommunicated the patriarch, Pope Leo IX died, so technically their action was invalid. The opportunity for reconciliation was still there if and when the main protagonists were prepared to treat each other with sympathy and understanding.

The Orthodox East and the Catholic West

There were three ways in which Christendom might possibly have been re-united. One was the route of political negotiation, which had just failed so badly. This was likely to involve papal support for the Byzantine emperor in return for the subordination of the eastern church to Rome, and that would be tried again two hundred and twenty years later. An alternative was military conquest, which Justinian had attempted in the sixth century. But Byzantium was no longer powerful enough for that, and the West was not yet powerful enough. The third possibility was the way of understanding and reconciliation. For that to work both sides needed to be prepared to see some faults in themselves and some good in their opponents.

Some of the very best churchmen on both sides were prepared to approach things that way. Towards the end of the century the wise and scholarly Greek Archbishop Theophylact of Ochrida in Bulgaria was asked his views on the errors of the Latins, whose customs, and even beliefs, were in so many ways different from those of the Greeks. Priests in the West were expected to be celibate and shaved their beards. They used different ceremonials at weddings and baptisms, and they fasted at different times. They bent the knee to the altar, while the Greeks bowed. Theophylact's view was that East and West should accept such differences. With goodwill and mutual tolerance there should not be a problem. But some differences had symbolic importance. The West used unleavened bread in the eucharist, while the East used leavened bread and thought it important to do so, because the leaven was a symbol of the living Christ. Even that, thought Theophylact, was not an issue which should divide fellow-Christians. More important was the Western inclusion in the Nicene Creed of the *filioque* clause, suggesting that the Holy Spirit proceeded from the Son as well as from the Father. Theophylact had no doubt that the West was wrong, but he ascribed the problem to the poverty of the Latin language, which could not convey the theological subtleties which could be expressed in Greek. Just as Greek had a range of words to convey different aspects of the meaning of 'love', so they had a range of verbs with different shades of meaning which were all misleadingly translated into Latin by the one verb *procedere*, 'to proceed.' He was even prepared to accept that the West could have its own reasons for adding the *filioque* clause. So long as they recognised that the creed approved by the ecumenical councils of the church did not include the *filioque* clause, and so long as they did not seek aggressively to require the use of that clause in the East, Theophylact believed that one should not be too critical.

That last point, the question of how far Rome might impose its views on the rest of the church, was crucial. The East had long acknowledged the primacy of Rome, partly because it was the see of St Peter (though Antioch was as well) and partly because it had once been the capital of the empire (though Constantinople was now). But primacy was never seen in the East as implying supremacy. The pope might be *primus inter pares*, the first among equals, but he could not dictate to the others. The four eastern patriarchs could not possibly let him overrule them or the decisions of an ecumenical council.

Empire and Papacy

Meanwhile the exalted papal claims which were the crucial issue in the schism between the eastern and western churches also produced a clash between emperor and pope in the West. The decade after the death of Leo IX in 1054 saw some significant changes. The Emperor Henry III, who had deposed and appointed popes in order to create a reformed papacy, died in 1056 leaving a child of nine years old to succeed him as the Emperor Henry IV, and the period of Henry IV's minority saw a serious weakening of the German monarchy. By the time he started to rule for himself in 1065 at the age of eighteen, a significant body of opposition among the German princes was determined to assert its own power at the expense of the emperor.

At the same time the power and authority of the papacy increased. Nicholas II, in his brief pontificate from 1059 until 1061, produced an electoral decree which would transform the selection of popes. A substantial number of bishops, priests and deacons in Rome who helped with papal affairs were known as 'cardinals' (from the Latin *cardines*, 'hinges'). Just as hinges enabled a door to work, so cardinals, it was suggested, enabled the church to work. In future the cardinal-bishops were to choose papal candidates and the whole body of cardinals was to select the pope from among them. Next Nicholas met the Norman leaders in South Italy and reached an agreement with them. He invested them with their conquests; they acknowledged his ecclesiastical jurisdiction and undertook to protect the new system of papal elections. Both that new system and the acknowledgement of Norman territorial authority in Italy were infringements of the emperor's prerogatives. But the western emperor was a small child unable yet to assert himself, and the papacy had acquired a valuable new ally as well as new moral authority. In any future clash between empire and papacy the balance of power had shifted significantly.

Hildebrand

In 1073 a monk called Hildebrand, who had played a large part in developing and setting out the new papal position, became Pope Gregory VII and was pope for the next twelve years. He informed the emperor of his election instead of, as was customary, asking for imperial assent. In 1074 he ordered the deposition of all priests guilty of simony and forbade married priests to celebrate the eucharist. Early in 1075 he issued a decree forbidding the investiture of bishops by laymen and at some time he drew up a private document, commonly referred to as the *Dictatus Papae*, which he kept on his desk as a guide to action. It included the following principles: the Roman church has never erred and never will err to the end of time; a duly ordained pope is undoubtedly made a saint by the merits of St Peter; the pope alone can depose and restore bishops; he can depose emperors; he can absolve subjects from their allegiance. Gregory claimed that all he was doing was gathering together the writings, or authorities, of the past. In reality his programme was revolutionary, and later that year he clashed with the emperor over the appointment of the archbishop of Milan.

Conflict

Early in 1076 Henry IV, now aged twenty-eight, summoned a synod at which the German and Italian bishops withdrew their allegiance from 'Hildebrand, no longer pope, but false monk' and he called on Gregory VII to give up the papacy. The pope responded by excommunicating the emperor and suspending him from government. Henry's opponents in Germany took advantage of this to demand that the emperor should free himself from excommunication or lose his crown. In an extraordinary and brilliant manoeuvre Henry in January of 1077 came to meet the pope at the castle of Canossa in North Italy and waited outside as a penitent, barefoot in the snow, until Gregory VII absolved him. Under the circumstances the pope could scarcely avoid doing so. But the conflict was not yet resolved and by the end of 1080 the pope was supporting an anti-king and the king was supporting an anti-pope.

From now on Gregory's position disintegrated. He was a man with a talent for making enemies. He had denounced Philip I of France as a tyrant. In 1080 he excommunicated the Norman leader in South Italy, Robert Guiscard, but when he needed help in 1081, he removed the excommunication. He excommunicated the Byzantine emperors Nicephorus III and Alexius I. He even clashed with William the Conqueror, the Norman duke who had taken a papal banner to proclaim the cause of reform when he sailed to conquer England. Gregory demanded that William swear fealty to him (In a feudal society fealty was the promise of faithfulness which a man would swear to his lord on becoming his vassal). William refused, and there was nothing Gregory could do about it.

It was not only lay rulers whom Gregory offended. Archbishop Liemar of Bremen said of him that 'this dangerous man wants to order the bishops about as though they are bailiffs', and by 1083 thirteen cardinals had abandoned him for the anti-pope. Then in March 1084 Henry IV captured Rome and was crowned emperor by his anti-pope.

Conflicting theories of authority

Gregory had taken over a reformed papacy after some years in which he had been closely involved in helping to devise the reform programme. He genuinely abhorred the contamination of spiritual things with either money or women, and his decrees against simony and clerical marriage were the natural outcome of that abhorrence. But he extended the definition of simony to the point at which it included the traditional appointment of bishops by lay rulers, and he either adopted or came close to the heretical position of believing that the sacraments were invalidated if administered by men guilty of co-habitation with a woman. That was an issue which had been settled by Bishop Stephen of Rome in the third century when, contrary to the position adopted by the Donatists, he asserted that the validity of the sacraments was independent of any merit or virtue of the minister.

Gregory VII's conflict with the emperor is rather peculiarly known as the Investiture Contest after the compromise which ended it. But that name is misleading, since the real issue was the question of who was entitled to appoint bishops rather than who was to invest them with their spiritual functions by the grant of a ring and pastoral staff. Gregory VII's view was that Christendom was one and indivisible and that all authority derived from God. But, he believed, there were two different sorts of authority: spiritual and temporal. The spiritual function was higher, was exercised directly by the papacy and extended over all ecclesiastical and moral matters. Temporal authority was wielded by a range of rulers under 'the care and authority of the apostolic see', and in the last resort the pope had the authority to depose bad rulers.

The contrary view, held by emperors and kings alike, was partly an assertion that they ruled by divine authority and partly an appeal to custom. The kings of western Europe had always appointed bishops in their own lands. It was one of their duties as Christian kings. Canon Law demanded the free election of bishops 'by clergy and people.' But *electus* is simply the Latin word for 'chosen' and Canon Law did not indicate how the choice was to be made. For many years the ideal had been the royal appointment of bishops who were acceptable to both lay and ecclesiastical authorities.

Difficulties arose when kings were more concerned with the value of bishops as administrators than with their spiritual functions, and it was even worse when they kept a bishopric vacant for some years in order to collect the revenues, as William II and Henry I both did in England. The system could and did work well in the right hands, but when it went wrong it helped to produce a bitter clash between papal authority an the one hand and imperial and royal authority on the other.

Lay appointments and patronage

Everyone agreed that Church and State should live in harmony and that lay and ecclesiastical authorities should operate separately, fulfilling their separate responsibilities in such a way as to help each other. The problem which divided western Christendom was first of all over what should happen when something went wrong or if there was a disagreement about what was right. Secondly, and more importantly, it was over who, in the case of a dispute, was entitled to make the final decision. Gregory VII was entirely clear that the final decision should rest with the pope, and he demanded two things. First, he insisted that laymen, including the emperor and kings, should no longer make appointments to bishoprics and abbacies. Secondly, he required that layman should not treat bishoprics, monasteries or parish churches as property which they owned and whose revenues they were entitled to collect and use as they saw fit.

The first of these points was unacceptable to the emperor and to other lay rulers, such as the kings of France and England. The government of their kingdoms depended on having a literate civil service, and the only literate civil servants at their disposal were the clergy. It was essential to be able to appoint the bishops in their kingdoms and equally essential to be able to pay them with the revenues of their dioceses. What is more, they often held very considerable lands, and just as lay barons and knights typically held their land in return for the regular provision of a given number of knights' service each year, so did bishops and abbots. In the middle of the twelfth century the archbishop of Canterbury held his lands from the king in return for the service of sixty knights. So did the bishop of Winchester and the abbot of Peterborough. The bishop of Norwich and the abbot of Glastonbury each held theirs for forty. The second point is similar and affected a large number of the ruling class. The proprietorship of churches and monasteries arose from their own or their ancestors' generosity. It had been a source of income in the past and still was. In practice the lay power, barons and knights as much as the emperor and the kings, could not and would not give in on the issues of lay appointments and lay patronage. Gregory VII could not and would not give in on the issue of the supremacy of the papacy. He left his successors with the difficult task of moving away from the assertion of papal supremacy over all lay authorities to the more limited assertion of papal supremacy in the church.

Compromise

After Gregory VII's death in 1085 the search for a compromise began and Pope Urban II, a French nobleman, Odo of Lagery, who was also a monk of Cluny, managed during his pontificate from 1088 until 1099 to effect a significant change in the climate in which the controversy was conducted. The conflict was not resolved, and the emperor continued to appoint and support a succession of anti-popes. But Urban established friendly relations with other rulers, such as the kings of France and England, and paved the way for a resolution of the conflict by shifting the emphasis of the papal argument away from the issue of power and authority, which had so obsessed Gregory VII, to the very particular issue of lay investiture.

His successor, Paschal II, another monk who was pope from 1099 until 1118, suggested the solution that bishops should renounce their fiefs and all temporal responsibilities and thereafter exercise purely spiritual functions. He had moved to the opposite extreme from Gregory VII. Instead of being concerned with the issue of power, he was concerned only with the principle. But his solution was rejected both by the lay powers, who needed bishops and other churchmen for the government and administration of their countries, and also by his own supporters. All the same it was a conciliatory move which brought a solution closer and in 1107 a compromise was reached with the kings of France and England. In practice the king was left free to choose any new bishop, who would then do homage to the king for his temporal possessions and swear fealty before being invested with his spiritual authority by other bishops.

Compromise with the empire was not yet possible because the rift had gone too deep, but negotiations began with the accession of a new emperor, Henry V, the son of Henry IV and grandson of Henry III. In 1122 Pope Callistus II and Henry V at last brought the long quarrel to an end with the Concordat of Worms on much the same terms as the agreements of 1107. The empire had in the end lost very little in practical terms, but it had given up the symbol of lay investiture, so in that sense it had lost what came to be known as the Investiture Contest. The papacy had gained very little other than a symbol. But symbols can be important, and this one could be seen as proclaiming the political independence of the papacy from imperial authority.

Reconciliation with the East

Urban II looked for reconciliation with the East as well. In 1089 he sent an embassy to the Emperor Alexius Comnenus with a letter lifting the sentence of excommunication imposed on him at his accession in 1081 by Gregory VII and avoiding any reference to the papacy's claim to supremacy in the church. Relations improved, and a few years later Alexius felt able to turn to the West for help. A new wave of invaders, the Seljuk Turks, had overrun the Arab Caliphates of Baghdad and Damascus but then accepted Islam. They had gone on to defeat the Byzantine army and advance into Asia Minor. The threat was imminent, so in 1095 the Eastern emperor sent envoys to the West in a bid to recruit manpower for his army.

Urban II was anxious to help and in November of the same year he preached a sermon at Clermont calling on western Christendom to go to the aid of the East. The response was overwhelming. All over western Europe people responded to the call and during 1096 a number of armies set out for the East. The emperor had wanted fighting men to serve under his orders against the Turks. What arrived were large armies which saw all Muslims as enemies, were looking for land and booty, and were moved by zeal to recover Jerusalem and the Holy Land for Christ. The emperor's daughter, Anna Comnena, described how 'all the barbarian tribes as far as the Pillars of Hercules (i.e. Gibraltar) were on the move.' She and her fellow-Christians in the East had good reason to fear these 'crusaders' and their aggression.

In 1098, while warfare raged in the East, the pope held a council at Bari on the east coast of southern Italy, in territory which had formerly been part of the Byzantine Empire but was now under the control of the Normans, and tried to reach an understanding with the Greeks. One of the biggest problems was the *filioque* clause. Anselm, archbishop of Canterbury, accompanied the pope. He was in exile after a quarrel with King William Rufus about the poor training and equipment of the knights he had provided for a Welsh war the previous year. But he was better at theology than he was at training and equipping knights, and he addressed the assembly at Bari. He assured the Greeks of the West's veneration for the original form of the creed and explained how the Western view of the Trinity led to the idea of the procession of the Holy Spirit from the Son as well as from the Father. He in no way suggested that the Greeks were wrong and he avoided any mention of papal supremacy. The Greeks went away satisfied. If men like Anselm of Canterbury and Theophylact of Bulgaria could deal with these matters, prospects for continued communion between East and West and for developing co-operation would be good.

Crusade and division

Meanwhile the crusaders advanced into Syria and besieged and took first Antioch and then Jerusalem. A literate Western knight wrote an account of the deeds of the Franks and others who went on the journey to Jerusalem: the *Gesta Francorum et aliorum Hierosolimitanorum*. He describes the taking of Jerusalem, where 'there was such a massacre that our men were wading up to their ankles in enemy blood...After this our men rushed round the whole city, seizing gold and silver, horses and mules and houses full of all sorts of goods, and they all came weeping from excess of gladness to worship at the Sepulchre of our Saviour Jesus, and there they fulfilled their vows to him.' There is no irony in that. It is the integrated view of a Frankish knight for whom killing, looting and religious fervour were all part of a holy war.

None of the captured land was handed over to the Byzantine emperor. Instead four crusader states were set up: the Kingdom of Jerusalem, the Principality of Antioch and the Counties of Edessa and Tripoli. In the next two years Latin patriarchs were established in Jerusalem and Antioch, and that, more than anything else, ensured the continuing division between the Latin Catholic West and the Greek Orthodox East. Jerusalem was won, Christendom was divided, and the Muslims were provoked into responding with their own *jihad*, or holy war.

Chapter 12

A Medieval Renaissance

The re-birth of the West

The energy which flowed from Western Europe into the first crusade at the end of the eleventh century found expression in a range of different ways. The economy of Western Europe had been growing for centuries in an entirely different way from that which had characterised the Roman Empire. It was less urban, more agricultural, less dependant on trade, more geared to self-sufficiency. By the twelfth century things had changed. The era of incessant raids by Vikings, Saracens and Magyars was over. Trade was developing. Water and wind power had been developed. Towns were growing. New ideas could spread more easily. Intellectual life developed. Artistic tastes changed. There were new developments in building techniques and in military technology. The West had acquired the strength and self-confidence to challenge not only the Muslim World but the Greeks as well.

The Cluniacs

Part of the energy in the barbarian, Christian society of the West had gone into monasteries, and monks had played a remarkably large part in the economic development of the West. That in turn produced a further expansion of monasticism. For more than five hundred years, from the death of St Benedict in 550 AD until the end of the eleventh century, the Benedictines had a virtual

155

monopoly of organised, or institutional, religious life. But success carries within it the seeds of its own failure. Each Benedictine monastery was a separate institution, often holding its land in return for rent payable to a lay patron. They were linked to each other only by their attachment to the Rule of St Benedict. Some of the greatest monasteries were now so well-endowed and rich that life for a monk could be one of ease, with good food and wine, rich clothing and servants to care for their needs, while they neglected both the liturgy and the hard work in the fields.

But just as success can breed laxity and decay, so decay can become fertile ground for reform, and the tenth century saw a conscious attempt to revive or reform Benedictine monasticism. The foundation of Cluny in 910 by Duke William I of Aquitaine, with its virtual freedom from lay control and its reform of the liturgy led to the development of what was in effect a Cluniac Order, with daughter–houses headed by priors subordinate to the abbot of Cluny. The next step was to seek independence from lay control for all of them, and that was very largely achieved by placing Cluny and all of its daughter-houses in a position of direct subordination to the papacy. This was good for the prestige of the reformed papacy, it gave Cluny a vested interest in papal supremacy, and the Cluniac houses flourished in the eleventh century. But the very success of Cluny, with its magnificent liturgy and a vast and exotically decorated church in the Romanesque style, produced in some men a reaction and a yearning for greater simplicity.

The Cistercians

Early in the twelfth century there were several experiments at a simpler monastic life. The most successful was a foundation in Burgundy called Cîteaux, where the monks tried to get back to the purity of *The Rule of St Benedict* and live a simple life with the day rigidly divided into the *opus Dei* (the liturgy), the *opus manum* (manual work) and *lectio divina* (spiritual reading). So popular did Cîteaux become under its third abbot, an Englishman called Stephen Harding, that in 1112 it founded a daughter-house and shortly afterwards three more. In effect it had created a new monastic order. Each daughter house went on to found its own daughter houses, preferably in a *loco horroris et vastae solitudinis*, 'a place of horror and vast solitude', away from secular life. A system of inspection was put in place, with mother houses inspecting their daughters and the daughter-houses in turn inspecting the mother house to ensure that the purity of the Rule was maintained. It was one of the great success stories of the twelfth century. A dominant figure in European religious and political life in the first half of the century was St Bernard, a monk of Cîteaux who was sent by Stephen Harding to be the founder and first abbot of Clairvaux, the fourth and most famous of the four daughter-houses of Cîteaux. In the middle of the century Pope Eugenius III (1145-53) was a Cistercian, and by the end of the century there were more than five hundred Cistercian monasteries, many of them with hundreds of choir monks and hundreds more lay brethren. Again, success attracted endowments and large numbers of new recruits, and that in turn led eventually to decline and the need for reform.

The Augustinian Canons

A quite different development, but also in its own way a reaction against the grandeur and splendour of houses such as Cluny, was the establishment of the Augustinian Canons. While the Cistercians were in a sense a conservative or even reactionary movement, trying to get back to the purity of *The Rule of St Benedict*, the Augustinians deliberately turned away from traditional monasticism. Some six hundred years earlier St Augustine had set out some advice about how to live a religious life in a community, based on the experience of his own household in Hippo. The Augustinians now adopted not only his name but also his advice, which was so general that it allowed flexibility for solving a range of different problems in a range of different ways.

Most Augustinian Canons lived in a community under a superior and held such goods as they had in common. But they usually had far less property than a Benedictine or a Cistercian monastery and ideally they used it not so much for the perpetuation of their own community as for running hospitals and schools, retirement homes and hospices, and homes to care for lepers or for the blind. Groups of Augustinians would repair a dilapidated church; they would provide comfort and reconciliation for penitent sinners; and they also preached to local communities, which in turn led them to emphasise the importance of learning.

Monasteries, of course, were grander, and men who retreated into the 'paradise of the cloister' to care for their own souls might sometimes emerge to do great works as bishops or even as pope. Augustinian Canons were seldom grand and they were more accessible. If there was no longer a need for a particular service provided by an Augustinian community, that community could fade away and its resources be diverted to other purposes, whereas some great monastic houses eventually found themselves in the embarrassing position of accommodating only a few dozen monks in buildings designed for several hundred.

Other religious orders

Other religious orders came into existence to meet particular needs. For example, there continued to be a relatively small number of men who felt the urge to live a religious life in solitude. The Carthusian Order, founded by St Hugh of Chartreuse, provided a good practical solution, with a monastic house in which each monk had his own cell and the monks came together in church to say the liturgy but did everything else in isolation and with strict discipline.

The two great religio-military orders, the Knights of St John of the Hospital, or the Hospitallers, and the Knights of the Temple, known as the Templars, both came into existence to meet needs thrown up by crusading. They were founded to look after pilgrims travelling to the Holy Land. But because of the circumstances of the time both soon became substantial orders of fighting men who were not only knights but also celibate monks. Both orders were supported by massive pious endowments and gifts from the West and they were in a sense the ultimate expression of that marriage of Christianity and Barbarism which can be seen as the distinguishing characteristic of the church in the West. For centuries they gave vigorous expression to their religio-military fervour in the colonised lands of *Outremer*, the crusader lands beyond the sea, and their example was followed in the fourteenth century by the Knights of the Teutonic Order, who colonised the lands along the south-eastern shore of the Baltic.

From Romanesque to Gothic

Throughout Western Europe surplus resources went into the building of churches. Just as nineteenth century Europeans built railway stations in a grand, or triumphalist, style and twentieth century Europeans celebrated banking and insurance with their buildings, so in the Middle Ages men built churches and cathedrals. For centuries West Europeans had built churches using round arches resting on substantial pillars. That was the way Romans had built, and the barbarians copied them, at first clumsily but after some centuries confidently, in a style which is understandably called Romanesque. The buildings were usually highly decorated and the stonework carved with a mixture of Biblical characters and grotesque mythological figures. The grandest churches were for the great monasteries. A great new church was completed for Monte Cassino in 1071 and the largest church ever yet built was begun at Cluny in 1088.

But in the twelfth century masons began to use new techniques and those who commissioned them sought to incorporate new ideas. Thus Durham cathedral, which is often seen as the culminating glory of Romanesque architecture, has its massive roof built with the new technique of stone vaulting, which produces what look like pointed arches. Internally, but hidden from view, it even has flying buttresses to take and transfer some of the weight of stone. Stone vaulting, the pointed arch and flying buttresses are characteristic of a new style of church building which we now call Gothic. That is, no longer were the barbarians imitating the style of the Romans. Instead they were building in their own style and with their own techniques, and they gloried in them. The canons of Chartres had a new cathedral built in the early twelfth century in this new Gothic style, with arches pointing up to heaven, windows letting in the divine light and with one of the towers built in accordance with geometric principles to reflect the creative design of the Almighty, and it was rebuilt on an even grander scale when most of it burnt down in 1196.

Significantly Chartres was not a monastic building. It was a large cathedral church built by public subscription and for public worship in one of the towns which were now developing all over Western Europe. During the twelfth century one town after another in the North of France built a cathedral in the new Gothic style. In the thirteenth century towns in the South, in the Empire, in England and in Spain followed suit.

St Anselm

Such intellectual life as there was in Western Europe in the eleventh century was still in the monasteries, and the flowering of monastic philosophy and theology was the work of St Anselm, who believed that faith should lead to understanding. He had gone from Aosta in Italy to the monastery of Bec in Normandy because its prior, Lanfranc, was a great teacher who had created a flourishing school there. Later Anselm, like Lanfranc, became archbishop of Canterbury. One of his greatest intellectual achievements was the so-called ontological argument for the existence of God, which still seemed impressive to the non-Christian philosopher Bertrand Russell in the twentieth century. Anselm took as his starting point the opening words of Psalm 14: 'The foolish man has said in his heart, there is no God.' In the form of a meditation he asked what, in this context, was meant by the concept of God, and he decided that it must be *aliquid quo maius nihil cogitari potest*, or 'that than which nothing greater can be thought.' This led eventually to the proposition that a God which existed *in re*, 'in reality', as well as *in intellectu*, 'in the mind', must be greater than a God which existed only *in intellectu*, and from that to the conclusion that God must therefore exist.

He also produced a novel justification for the doctrine of the Incarnation in a meditation known as the *Cur Deus Homo*, or 'Why a God-Man?' At the time the conventional explanation of the Incarnation, characteristic of feudal society, was along the lines that sinful Man had thrown off his allegiance to God and voluntarily subjected himself to the Devil. God could not free Man from subjection to the Devil without a breach of Justice. But He found a way out by taking human form, which led the Devil to crucify Him and thus forfeit his right to Justice. So God could now accept the allegiance of those who were willing to be faithful to Him. Anselm did not think that a very satisfactory explanation and produced an alternative which began with the proposition that Man was created by God for eternal blessedness. By his sinfulness Man seemed to have frustrated God's purpose. But it is impossible for the will of God to be frustrated, so there had to be some means of redemption. What was needed was an offering which outweighed Man's disobedience. Such an offering ought to be made by Man, but only God could make it; it had to be made by someone who was both God and Man. Therefore the Incarnation was necessary. It was not just something which a loving God did to help human beings. It was needed in order to fulfill the purpose of Creation.

Peter Abelard

In the twelfth century intellectual life shifted increasingly from the monasteries to schools, later known as universities, which grew up attached to cathedrals in the developing towns, such as the cathedral of Our Lady, or *Notre Dame*, in Paris. There schoolmen worked at discovering, translating and writing down the works of great thinkers of the past. Little was original, but they were laying the foundations of future scholarship. One of the early schoolmen, Bernard of Chartres, is reported as saying that modern men were like dwarfs by comparison with the giants of the past; but if a dwarf could keep his seat on a giant's shoulders, he could see further than the giant.

While the schoolmen worked at rediscovering the past, young men with a zeal for learning could travel from place to place and learn from masters, who were no longer necessarily bishops or monks, and without needing to join a monastic community. One of these wandering scholars was Peter Abelard, who possessed the most original mind of all the twelfth century schoolmen, and studied, argued and made his reputation at the school attached to the cathedral church of Notre Dame in Paris. He turned round Anselm's concept of faith seeking understanding and thought in terms of understanding leading on to faith. He saw doubt as a virtue. Doubting would lead to enquiry. Enquiry would lead to truth. He encouraged his pupils to think by setting out for them a series of conflicting authorities in his great teaching manual, *Sic et Non*, (Yes and No), and challenging his pupils to resolve them.

Abelard's fame as a teacher resulted in one of the canons of Notre Dame, Fulbert, employing him to teach his niece, Heloise, of whom Abelard said that she was 'a lady of no mean appearance while in literary excellence she was the first' (*Historia Calamitatum*, translated by J.T.Muckle). Abelard and Heloise fell in love, spent their lesson time in making love, had a baby and got married secretly, because, since Abelard was a canon of Sens cathedral, it would be damaging to his career for the marriage to be public. But thugs employed by Fulbert attacked and castrated Abelard and the marriage was dissolved in the only way then possible by both of them going into religious houses, he to continue writing and teaching, she eventually to become a distinguished abbess.

It was Abelard who gave the medieval world the idea of a God who loves rather than judges mankind and who, in the Incarnation, entered into sympathetic understanding of mankind and, by paying the price for the sins of mankind on the cross, offered salvation to all. His Christ is suffering on the cross in agony rather than ruling in majesty, and Abelard's view of God and his insight into divine love probably owe a lot to Heloise, to his love for her and to her love for him. He continued writing with brilliant and original insight on such topics as the doctrine of the Trinity, no doubt straying in and out of heresy in the process. But it was because Abelard was seen as scandalous in view of his past personal life that that great Cistercian puritan, St Bernard of Clairvaux, decided that his writings on the Trinity should be publicly recognised as heretical, and at the Council of Sens in 1140 they were condemned and burnt.

Heresy and unofficial preaching

Heresy was becoming an increasing concern of church authorities. The rise of towns produced concentrations of people among whom new ideas could spread rapidly. That led to a rise of popular religion and the spread of heresy. It had been difficult to be a heretic in western Europe for some centuries. The requirements of belief had been few and were set out simply in the Apostles' Creed. For most people religion had concentrated more on behaviour than belief, and few openly questioned what appeared to be the fundamental beliefs of the Christian Faith. Nor did they usually challenge the authority of the church in either spiritual or moral matters.

But some preachers in the first half of the twelfth century did challenge the church on the grounds that it fell short of the high ideals it proclaimed. Individual clergy could be seen to be corrupt. A parish priest living with his concubine in greater comfort than his neighbours, and on the fruits of the tithes they paid, could cause resentment. So could a great bishop, living in splendour with his wife in the cathedral close, and with his sons and other relations benefiting from the patronage at his disposal or at the disposal of his friends. A great monastery, with its vast corporate wealth, could appear as an offence to the ideal of monastic poverty. In a way these criticisms were an extension of the monastic reform movement's ideals of the previous century, and similar criticisms could be heard from reforming popes or the abbots of Cistercian monasteries. But they came to be seen as heresy at the point at which the critic suggested that the whole church was corrupt from top to bottom and incapable of being reformed.

The Albigensians

Another quite different kind of heresy was the Dualist view that all matter was of its nature evil, while the things of the spirit were good. The Cathars (the name comes from the Greek word for 'the pure') believed that God, who was spirit, had created the things of the spirit, while the Devil had created the material world and all things material. They came to be firmly established in the South of France, where members of the nobility and even bishops joined them. For a while they dominated the religious life of the area and were widely known as Albigensians because one of their main centres was the town of Albi.

As seen by their enemies they can be divided into two extreme and very different groups. On the one hand there were those who sought perfection, abstained from sexual intercourse and from all food which was the product of sexual intercourse, and rejected the whole material world as evil. On the other hand there were those who took the view that, since all matter was evil, they might as well indulge themselves in whatever ways they chose until the time eventually came for them to leave their corrupt earthly bodies and enter into a new spiritual life. Both perceptions are some way from the truth, but they provided sufficient justification for launching a crusade against them, which is what Pope Innocent III did in 1207. A substantial army moved from the North into the South of France. 'Kill and let God recognise his own', the papal legate was reputed to have said at the siege of Béziers. The crusaders did, and the Cathar heresy never recovered from the wholesale slaughter of its adherents.

Waldensians, Franciscans and Dominicans

Meanwhile there was an increasing number of poor preachers who sought to live a life of poverty, emulating Christ and his disciples, and preaching the gospel. Far from attacking the church, they saw themselves as its loyal servants. But it could be difficult for those in authority to draw a line between poor preachers regarded as missionaries, engaged in the admirable task of the internal conversion of society, and others who were seen as heretics. The growth of towns made it easier for people to come together and talk about their religious faith, and a group known as the Waldensians after their leader, a French merchant called Peter Waldo, was suspect because they gathered together to read the scriptures and expound them to each other. For the first time the western church was faced with the problem of educated laymen unwilling to defer to the official church. So the official church made the mistake of persecuting them and turning them into what was perceived as an heretical sect.

On the other hand Pope Innocent III, to his credit, recognised the merits and the value of St Francis of Assisi and his followers, who walked from place to place with a staff and begging bowl, living off charity, preaching devotion to their crucified and resurrected Lord and love for all creation, and very often caring for the sick and homeless. The Franciscan movement exploded across Europe and was already turned into a religious order in the lifetime of St Francis. That produced problems. The friars would come to a town or a village preaching, hearing confessions and offering spiritual guidance. But these activities encroached on the territory of local clergy, and they were not always welcome. Local clergy protested and there was often conflict rather than co-operation. The friars eventually offended the papacy as well, when their attachment to the rule of poverty led to a general condemnation of the ownership of property. Pope John XXII denounced the Franciscan doctrine of poverty as heresy in 1323, and the leaders of the Franciscans then denounced the pope as a heretic.

Innocent III also recognised the value of a group of preachers who had been gathered together by a Spanish canon called Dominic to preach against the Cathar, or Albigensian, heresy. They also were formed into a religious order, and the papacy made considerable use of the Dominicans in commissions of inquisition into heresy, which at first were probably not as threatening as they later became. The two orders of friars, the Franciscans and the Dominicans, were both important elements in the religious life of the later Middle Ages. They suffered the consequences of popularity and success in much the same way as had the successful monastic orders, and they also suffered criticism when they fell short of the standards of their early predecessors. It was impossible to maintain on a large scale what was so impressive on a small scale in the lives and the work of St Francis, St Dominic and their small bands of followers.

Gratian and Aquinas

By the end of the thirteenth century it was possible to be a lot clearer than ever before about what was heresy and about what behaviour was or was not acceptable to the church authorities.

Some of the cathedral schools of the twelfth century had developed into what we call universities, and scholars had made an attempt to find an all-embracing theological system as well as an all-embracing system of canon law. Theology was seen as the study of God and His relationship to Creation. Canon law was, and is, a legal system for regulating morals and religious practices and structures. To begin with there was no clear distinction between them. It was only as both things were codified that a distinction emerged between what the church expected Christians to believe and how it expected them to behave.

By about 1140 a monk called Gratian working in Bologna drew up a collection of canon law cases intended as a guide to decision-making on all matters moral and spiritual. When Pope Gregory IX in 1234 issued the first set of papal decretals, or edicts, as a supplement to it, the church had a collection of answers to all, or more or less all, problems of human behaviour. A Dominican friar, Thomas Aquinas, tried to do much the same for theology at the University of Paris. By his time much of Aristotle had been re-discovered, translated and subjected to careful thought and criticism by Arab, Christian and Jewish scholars. So Aquinas set out to reconcile Aristotle with Christianity and unite Reason with Faith. By his death in 1274 he had developed a complete, coherent and remarkably durable theological system.

Between them Gratian and Aquinas had created the ideological framework for the church as a totalitarian society – that is, a society in which those in authority would expect to care for and control every aspect of human thought and behaviour. What was missing was the power to enforce the ideology.

Marriage

One area in which the church did intervene and gradually developed and asserted a common view was that of marriage and divorce. For centuries marriage had been a far more informal matter than it became later. Among the ruling class it had always been important as a way of symbolising alliances and transfers of land. Among ordinary people it was the consequence of mutual attraction, or of a family wish to consolidate land-holdings, or both. The circumstances and practicalities of life tended to make for durable unions until the wife died in childbirth or the husband in battle or from illness. But customs and attitudes varied from place to place, and the woman's position could be insecure. Moreover, since the time of St Augustine the church had taken the view that sexual intercourse was the means by which sin was transmitted from one generation to the next. But in the twelfth century it was coming to the view that marriage, though it should be illegal for clergy, was a holy sacrament for the laity, entered into by mutual consent, preferably in public and preferably in church, and made binding by consummation. Under canon law a valid marriage could not be ended, but an invalid marriage could be annulled, and marriage to anyone to whom one was related within seven degrees of kindred was deemed to be invalid. In practice annulment was widely available to members of the ruling class, but not to the rest of society. At this stage the church's intervention can be seen as a humane attempt to protect the interests of women and require them to be treated with more respect than was customary. But there was some way to go before churchmen would recognise that ideally marriage involves that love which in other circumstances plays so important a part in Christian thinking.

Unity, division and personal piety

The church lacked the power to intervene effectively and in detail in most areas of human behaviour. In a very loose sense western Christendom could be seen in the early centuries of the new millennium as a united Christian society. The church was an integral part of society, the authority of the papacy was increasingly recognised, an elite of monks and priests offered the liturgy to God, ordinary people gave assent to basic Christian beliefs expressed in the relatively simple Apostle's Creed, the Ten Commandments and the Lord's Prayer, and they were expected to live their lives in accordance with the customs of their own tribe or nation. But western Christendom was not united. It was divided into emerging nation states and was subdivided into small political units for the purpose of defence in a dangerous world. Within those units the apparatus for detailed control of thought and behaviour simply did not exist.

All the same, over the coming centuries there was a spread of personal piety among ordinary people. That was particularly so in centres of population, where it was often encouraged and guided by priests and friars. St Francis had spread the idea of venerating the infant Jesus and his mother by the innovation at Christmastime of a crib illustrating the Nativity story. Devotion to the Blessed Virgin Mary was accompanied by a higher view of women and of men's obligations to them. There was a gradual shift from awed awareness of Christ the King, reigning in majesty on the cross, to devotion to the crucified Christ hanging on the cross in agony and bearing the sins of mankind. And at some stage people adopted the practice of kneeling to pray with the palms of their hands placed together in front of them in imitation of a member of the feudal aristocracy swearing fealty to his lord. This practice illustrates the continuing relationship between Barbarism and Christianity in a world in which warfare and conflict were still important aspects of Western life, especially among the ruling class. But meanwhile Christian ideas and values were having a civilising effect on many ordinary people and both spiritual and moral awareness were more widespread than they had been three hundred years earlier.

Chapter 13

The Papal Monarchy

Papal aspirations and practice

'Render unto Caesar the things that are Caesar's', said Jesus, 'and unto God the things that are God's' (*Luke 20.35*). So in the fourth and fifth centuries the emperor ruled the empire and the patriarchs presided over the church. But after the fifth century there was no longer an emperor in the West exercising imperial authority. The pope established his authority in what had been the capital of the empire, while beyond Rome it was barbarian kings who usurped the place of Caesar. Both the spiritual and the temporal claims of the papacy developed and in the late eighth century the papacy produced the forged *Donation of Constantine* to assert its right to the spiritual overlordship of all Christendom and the temporal overlordship of the West. In the eleventh century the monk Hildebrand, coming to Rome from Cluny with high expectations of the papacy, was disappointed with what he found. Others, particularly monks coming from reformed monasteries, felt the same. They set out to clarify their aspirations and close the gap between the aspirations and the reality. Towards the end of the century Hildebrand, now Pope Gregory VII (1073-85), asserted that all legitimate power on earth derived from the pope. He pointed out that the disciples had said to Jesus at the Last Supper, 'Look Lord, here are two swords,' and he had replied, 'It is enough' (*Luke 22.38*). On the strength of that Gregory asserted that the two swords were those of spiritual and temporal power. He expected to wield the former directly, and he expected lay rulers, emperors and kings, to wield the latter on his behalf. But there was a vast gap between his aspirations and the reality of how power was wielded beyond Rome.

At the end of the century Pope Urban II (1088-99) gave the papacy the beginnings of an effective administrative structure. He was a French nobleman, Odo of Lagery, who was also a monk of Cluny, and he imported ideas both from the French court and from Cluny. He established a writing-office, with another monk from Cluny, John of Gaeta, later Pope Gelasius II (1118-19), at its head as *cancellarius*, or chancellor, and he appointed yet another Cluniac monk called Peter to be the first papal chamberlain, or *camerarius*, responsible for the papal finances. He improved relations with lay rulers in the West by moving away from the Hildebrandine insistence on the temporal authority of the papacy, he sought reconciliation with the East, and he established the papacy's moral leadership of the West by his proclamation of the First Crusade. Urban II's aspirations were not as high as those of Gregory VII, but he took the practical steps which laid the foundations of the papal monarchy. His successors built on those foundations.

Accumulating power

During the twelfth century papal administration developed significantly and the papal curia became a court comparable with that of any lay monarchy. Innocent II (1130-43) found a relatively inexpensive way of staffing the papal administration. He would recommend a particular clerk for a benefice and then employ him at the curia, while the clerk received the revenues of his neglected benefice. By the middle of the century this practice of so-called 'papal provisions' had become widespread. The first and only English pope, Nicholas Breakspear, Adrian IV (1154-59), issued orders rather than recommendations and claimed the right to dispose of the benefice of any clerk who died while at the papal curia. Then Alexander III, when engaged in his expensive conflict with Frederick Barbarossa, tried to solve the problem of inadequate funds to pay his officials by granting 'expectancies' to benefices which were not yet vacant.

The system of canon law was developing at the same time, and in the middle of the century, when a Cistercian monk from Clairvaux was Pope Eugenius III (1145-53), his former abbot and teacher, Bernard, complained to him that the papal court was concerning itself with legal rather than religious matters and, what is more, it was 'Justinian's law, not the Lord's.' The legal system and the administrative system, continued to grow and both generated increasing costs. Meanwhile the papacy dissipated its resources in conflict with the empire, and one of the sad effects of that conflict was that by the time of Alexander III's death in 1181 there was no money to pay the officials of the papal court. Bribery and corruption flourished because unpaid papal officials had to rely on charging fees for their services.

Accumulating problems

Meanwhile problems were accumulating. The ending of the Investiture Contest in 1122 could be seen as a success for the reformed and reinvigorated papacy. For forty out of the previous sixty years there had been two popes in Western Europe, one appointed by the emperor and one appointed, or at least accepted, by the college of cardinals, and that had been one of the reasons why it was so difficult to bring the Investiture Contest to a satisfactory conclusion. Now it seemed that there would be just one generally accepted pope. But not for long. Pope Nicholas II's election decree of 1059 had failed to specify how the cardinals should choose a pope, and disputes continued. In 1130 the older and more experienced cardinals, the *senior et sanior pars*, elected one of their number as Pope Anacletus II. The rest of the College of Cardinals elected an alternative, Pope Innocent II. Europe was divided and for some time it was not clear who would emerge as the victor. Among those campaigning on behalf of the eventual victor, Innocent II, was Bernard, Abbot of Clairvaux, and four months after the death of Anacletus II in 1138 the schism was ended, with Innocent II generally accepted.

Bernard later involved Innocent II in his vendetta against Peter Abelard and in 1141 the pope condemned Abelard's teaching. In 1144 Edessa fell to the great Muslim leader, Imad-ad-Din Zengi. Support for the Frankish, or Latin, colonies of *Outremer*, the lands 'beyond the sea', had been a consistent element in papal policy ever since the capture of Jerusalem in 1099, and now Bernard of Clairvaux emerged from his monastery again to preach the Second Crusade. He persuaded the king of France and the German emperor to go crusading. They both led armies into Asia Minor and both suffered disasters. The crusade achieved nothing of value, and it damaged even further relations with the Byzantine Empire, which needed peace rather than war on its Turkish frontier.

Before long the papacy was again involved in a clash with the Western Empire. This time the quarrel was not over any fundamental principle, as the quarrel between Gregory VII and Henry IV had been. It was territorial. Pope Alexander III, in his relatively long pontificate from 1159 until 1181, sought to free the papacy from lay interference by controlling the lands of central Italy. This was a political misjudgement. Over a period of twenty years the Emperor Frederick Barbarossa set up a series of anti-popes and generally retained the loyalty of the German church. Alexander III poured energy and resources into a conflict which in the long run damaged both empire and papacy.

Then in 1187 Jerusalem fell to another great Muslim leader, Saladin, and the Third Crusade was launched. This time the Emperor Frederick Barbarossa, King Philip II of France and King Richard I of England all set out with their armies for the east. The emperor died *en route*. The king of France, having made the gesture of going to the Holy Land, returned home to look after his own interests. The king of England failed to take Jerusalem. All that remained of the Frankish lands in the East by the end of 1192 was a coastal strip reaching from Acre about a hundred miles south to Ascalon, and the island of Cyprus, which Richard of England had captured from a Greek ruler *en route* to the East.

Innocent III

Innocent III, who became pope in 1198 at the early age of thirty-seven, inherited both the power and the problems. During the twelfth century the papacy had shaken itself free from secular control, and had developed an administrative system, a code of canon law, legal apparatus to go with it, and even its own lands and feudal authority. The pope was literally a monarch as well as the successor of St Peter. He could scarcely be seen as *servus servorum Dei*, 'the servant of the servants of God', for he was a monarch at the head of a temporal state, reigning in the papal curia, or court, anxious like other monarchs to defend his lands, maintain his privileges, exercise his customary rights, push out the bounds of his jurisdiction and of his feudal overlordship, and insistent on the obedience of his servants. Everywhere his lordship overlapped and conflicted with that of temporal lords. Innocent III, unlike Gregory VII, did not rest a claim to temporal authority on any theory of papal sovereignty, but for a man whose theoretical claims were limited, the extent of his intervention in temporal matters was remarkable. It was largely the result of the powerful position the papacy had attained. Having achieved temporal power through its activities in the twelfth century, it was now scarcely possible to refrain from the exercise of that power.

During Innocent III's pontificate Aragon, Portugal, Hungary and England all became at least nominally fiefs of the papacy; he established a firm base of papal territory across the middle of Italy, and he intervened in the internal politics of the Holy Roman Empire and the Kingdom of Sicily to try to ensure the future independence of the papacy from lay interference. He also found a way of helping to pay for the expenses of the papacy by taxing the clergy throughout Europe. But there was no way in which he could exercise effective control even in those countries which recognised his overlordship. Lack of adequate resources caused him to hand over the papal lands in central Italy as a fief to a lay ruler, and his involvement in the affairs of the empire and Sicily had disastrous long-term consequences.

The Fourth Crusade

From the start of his pontificate Innocent III was understandably anxious to recover Jerusalem, and eventually a plan was made to do so with a new and different strategy, avoiding the perils of Asia Minor. With the assistance of Venetian sea power Frankish forces would invade Egypt and, after establishing a secure base there, would take the Holy Land from the south. But the crusade, which set sail in 1202, was diverted to Constantinople and in 1204 the Westerners took the imperial city by assault. The soldiers were given three days to sack it. Men, women and children, clergy, monks and nuns were assaulted. The booty was on a scale larger than anyone had known before. Libraries with their manuscripts from the ancient world went up in flames. Churches were desecrated. Soldiers paid mock homage to a French prostitute sitting on the throne of the patriarch in the church of the *Hagia Sophia*.

Count Baldwin of Flanders was installed as emperor and a Venetian was installed as patriarch. The pope was shocked by the means used to establish a Latin empire in the east and a Latin patriarch in Constantinople, but he could not resist the temptation to accept the outcome. Technically the schism between East and West was ended. In reality it was made worse, with consequences which persist to the present day. The leaders of the Greeks retreated to those parts of the empire which had not been overrun and bided their time. As early as 1208 a new Byzantine emperor was established in Asia Minor with his capital at Nicaea, and an Orthodox patriarch was appointed at Nicaea as well. Meanwhile the crusaders gave up any idea of going on to Jerusalem and devoted their energy to colonising Byzantium. But the western political system was never firmly established and the Latin Church was bitterly resented by the Greeks.

The Fourth Crusade was regarded in the west as a success, but in the long run it damaged the crusading ideal. The same is true of the Albigensian Crusade which Innocent III launched against the Cathar heretics in the South of France. As with the Fourth Crusade his aims were obscured by the aims of his allies. In the

Fourth Crusade an attack on the infidel was diverted into an assault on fellow-Christians in Byzantium. In the Albigensian Crusade a heretic hunt turned into a war of conquest. In both cases the pope made the best of a bad job.

The *plenitudo potestatis*

Innocent III's pontificate raises in an acute form the question of how far the pope should have been contented to be a spiritual leader of the Christian Church and how far he should have aimed to be a papal monarch, relying on taxation, alliances, diplomacy and warfare to achieve his aims. Innocent III tried to do both, but in the long run the two functions were incompatible. His position as a spiritual leader could not allow him to become an effective ruler using all the means at the disposal of an emperor or a king. Meanwhile the attempt to be a powerful ruler damaged his spiritual leadership. His claims in that area were high. To be the Vicar of St Peter was no longer enough. 'We are the successor of the Prince of the Apostles', wrote Innocent III, 'but we are not his vicar, nor the vicar of any man or apostle, but the vicar of Jesus Christ himself.' He believed in the *plenitudo potestatis*, the 'fullness of power', of the papacy in the affairs of the church, and he stated the position explicitly: 'So extensive is the authority of the apostolic see that nothing can reasonably be determined in all the affairs of the church except by its authority.' He confined his claims to the church, but even within the western church the papacy lacked adequate resources to give effect to its claims. Its claims were always, even at the height of its authority, far greater than its effective power.

The western councils

In 1215, the year before he died, Innocent III summoned a council which can be seen as marking the high point of the medieval papacy. It was the fourth of a series of seven councils summoned by popes in the two centuries after the ending of the Investiture Contest. In the fourth to the eighth centuries there had been seven ecumenical councils in the East. All had been called by the emperor and representation from the West had usually been thin.

Now there were seven councils in the West. The first four were held at the papal palace of the Lateran in Rome. They were all summoned by the pope, the pope presided over them, each was important in the development of both doctrine and church government, and the pope promulgated their decisions in his own name. The First Lateran Council in 1123 celebrated the ending of the Investiture Contest and the supremacy of the pope in the western church. The Second Lateran Council in 1139 celebrated the ending of the eight year schism in which there were two contending popes. The Third Lateran Council of 1179 similarly celebrated the ending of the twenty-year schism, again with two contending popes, which had arisen from the clash between Frederick Barbarossa and Alexander III.

The Fourth Lateran Council of 1215 was more splendid than any previous western council. More than 400 bishops and more than 800 abbots gathered in Rome. The Orthodox Church had been subjected to Rome in 1204 as a consequence of the Fourth Crusade, so the council set out regulations for the conduct of its affairs. It made an attempt to deal with the disorder produced in the south of France by the Albigensian Crusade. It tried to make new arrangements for the reconquest of Jerusalem. It produced plans for reforming the clergy and disciplining the laity, and it introduced legislation against Jews, who were required to wear distinctive dress and had their books burned. It was the last and greatest of the councils of the undivided western church held in Rome, and it represented a peak of papal power and authority. The trouble with peaks is that they go downhill on the other side.

The last three of this group of seven councils were all held in France – at Lyon in 1245 and 1274 and at Vienne in 1311-12. The first four of the seven western councils had done a lot to establish the leadership of the papacy in the religious life of Western Europe. But by the middle of the thirteenth century the papacy was no longer leading the reform movement. It was itself under attack both over the practice of 'papal provisions' and over what was seen as extortionate taxation of the clergy. The later councils generated more problems for the papacy than they solved, so the popes ceased to call councils. In the long run the fact that the seven western councils had been called at all acted as a reminder that traditionally decisions on belief and practice were made by the bishops of Christendom meeting together in council rather than by the authority of the pope acting alone.

Church and State

During most of the twelfth century and in most of Europe church and state co-operated. From a king's point of view the appointment of talented clergymen to posts in the royal administration was a sensible way of paying for his government out of the resources of the church. From the church's point of view it was an effective way of maintaining ecclesiastical influence in secular affairs. In England, for example, Henry II appointed a particularly able clerk, Thomas Becket, the archdeacon of Canterbury, to be the head of his writing-office, or chancellor, and precisely because he was so effective Henry later made him Archbishop of Canterbury. But once Becket was archbishop he saw it as his duty to uphold the rights and privileges of Canterbury. That produced conflict with the king, and the outcome was that four of Henry's knights killed Becket in his own cathedral. The king did penance and agreed to abolish all the customs introduced in his own time to the detriment of the church. In the short run he lost little of practical importance, for he reckoned, as he always had, that such customs were 'few or none.' But the symbolic value to the church of the martyrdom of Thomas Becket was immense, and the papacy also benefited from a moral victory of church over state.

A generation later Innocent III clashed with King John of England over the appointment of another Archbishop of Canterbury and as a consequence England was placed under an interdict and the king was excommunicated. For four years there was no eucharist celebrated in English churches and there were no Christian marriages or Christian burials. But throughout those four years John was powerful enough to disobey the pope and otherwise life in the country carried on as normal. Eventually other pressures, political and military, led him to the conclusion that it was worth making an ally of the pope and he went so far as to hand England to Innocent III and accept it back as the pope's vassal.

Both the interdict and the later feudal relationship illustrate the strength and the weakness of the papacy. The papacy was weak enough and far enough away for John to defy it throughout the interdict, but it was strong enough that it never occurred to him to disregard it and operate the *ecclesia Anglicana* separately, as Henry VIII did three hundred years later. When John accepted the pope as his overlord, that was partly an empty gesture in that the pope was so far away that it made no real difference to John's sovereignty. On the other hand, it was worth doing because the prestige of the papacy was so great that it was more difficult, for example, for Philip II of France to attack John, or for John's own barons to fight against him, if he was a loyal vassal of the pope.

The papacy had done little to support Thomas Becket because Pope Alexander III was more concerned with his own clash with the Hohenstaufen Emperor Frederick Barbarossa over control of lands in Italy, and that conflict, though ostensibly settled in 1179, in practice continued for nearly another century. After years of political manoeuvring the papacy found itself facing just the position it dreaded most, with a Hohenstaufen emperor, Frederick II, ruling both the Holy Roman Empire and the Kingdom of Sicily. Successive popes in the thirteenth century squandered their resources in a long drawn out attempt to destroy the 'viper brood' of the Hohenstaufen. They succeeded and destroyed forever the possibility of a Holy Roman Emperor exercising effective power throughout Germany in the way in which the kings of France and England could rule their increasingly powerful nation states. But in the process the conflict seriously damaged the prestige and moral authority of the papacy.

The East

Apparent success against the western emperor was followed by problems in the East. In 1261 the Greeks recaptured Constantinople and Michael VIII Palaeologus, the first emperor of the dynasty which was to rule the Byzantine Empire for nearly two hundred more years, entered the city. The church was restored to the orthodox faith and the orthodox patriarch returned to the city. But the Byzantine Empire was still under threat, both from the West and from a new wave of Turkish invaders, the Ottomans, in the East. One possible option was to buy western support against the Turks by submitting the eastern church to Rome, while the pope recognised the imperial authority of the Byzantine emperor. This had the possible double advantage for a Greek emperor that it could give him security from western attack as well as western support against the Turks. It had even more advantages for the pope. He would get a united church under his own authority, freedom from a western emperor inclined to interfere in Italy, and the possibility of a united Christendom which could go on to launch a successful crusade against Islam and recover Jerusalem for ever.

Essentially that was the deal agreed in 1274 at Lyons. The problem with it was that it was agreed between a Byzantine emperor and a pope. Neither could be sure of being able to deliver his own part of the bargain. The pope could not guarantee to deploy the forces of Western Christendom. The emperor could not get the clergy and people of Byzantium to accept what he had negotiated on their behalf. The Greek emperor had to face the ever-growing threat from the Turks without western support. The pope, far from uniting Christendom, was going to find it increasingly difficult to keep even the western church united. The agreement reached in 1274 at the Council of Lyons was short-lived, as was a similar agreement at Florence in 1439. In 1281, even though Michael Palaeologus did what he could to keep his side of the bargain, the newly elected Pope Martin IV denounced him as a schismatic and declared him deposed – though to no effect. The Byzantine Empire, the continuation of the old Roman Empire in the East, carried on.

The western colonies in the east did not. Successive crusading expeditions failed and in 1291 the last Christian stronghold in Syria, Acre, was lost. There was serious disillusionment. The popes had launched crusades against the Greeks, the Albigensians and the Holy Roman Emperor, but they had neglected Jerusalem.

God seemed unable to look after the crusaders. The idea of crusading was not yet abandoned. It was still to be deployed against the Baltic peoples and the Bohemians. But public opinion was no longer enthusiastic.

Boniface VIII and Philip IV

In the early fourteenth century the papacy, which had very largely destroyed the power of the Holy Roman Emperor, found that instead of achieving clear papal supremacy in the West, it was now involved in clashes with the developing nation states. The pope expected to raise revenue by taxing the clergy, but the kings of France and England wanted to tax their own clergy for themselves. A quarrel which began over the question of who was entitled to approve taxes turned into an ideological issue, and in 1302 Pope Boniface VIII issued the bull *Unam sanctam*, which included the statement 'that it is altogether necessary for the salvation of all men that they should be subject to the authority of the Holy See.' Boniface VIII was reviving the Hildebrandine view that all authority, both ecclesiastical and secular, was ultimately the prerogative of the pope. He exercised ecclesiastical authority directly. He exercised secular authority by delegation. But the theory bore no relation to reality.

The French king had usually supported the papacy in the thirteenth century, but in 1303 French troops invaded the papal palace at Anagni, captured the pope and sacked the papal treasury. Boniface VIII died within a month and two years later a French archbishop was elected as Pope Clement V. He was crowned at Lyons and never left France.

This intervention by King Philip IV of France in the affairs of the papacy had its origins in an attempt to improve the royal finances. But looting the papal treasury did not resolve his financial problems and he saw a further opportunity to improve his financial position by taking over the very considerable wealth of the Order of Knights Templar, who were now no longer actively engaged in crusading. One night in 1307 all the members of the order in France were arrested and soon afterwards they were accused of all sorts of evil, including Devil-worship. Many were tortured. Some were burnt to death. The king confiscated their property.

Then in 1309 Clement V established the papal court at Avignon. He eventually created enough new cardinals to give the French a permanent majority on the College of Cardinals, and in 1311, at the Council of Vienne, he gave in to Philip IV's demand that he should dissolve the Order of Knights Templar. Three hundred years earlier the papacy had been a small Italian bishopric very largely in the hands of the counts of Tusculum. Now it was altogether grander and more powerful, but it had been transported to France and appeared to be very largely under the control of the king of France.

From success to failure

At the end of the eleventh century the reformers had been particularly concerned to root out the sin of simony and avoid the contamination of things spiritual with money. But as the papacy pursued its temporal ambitions the need for money had led to corruption at the curia and to public scandal. Already by the end of the twelfth century satires such as the *Gospel according to the Mark of Silver* were circulating and it was being pointed out that the letters ROMA, which spelt 'Rome' in Latin, were also the initial letters of the words *Radix omnium malorum avaricia*: 'The love of money is the root of all evil.'

During the next three centuries respect for the papacy was eroded by its use of spiritual authority to make money. At the end of the eleventh century Pope Urban II had offered the complete remission of sins to those who went on the first crusade. In the twelfth century it was argued that, if St Peter had the power to bind and loose, then it was reasonable to use that power in the service of the church. So Innocent III offered what came to be known as 'indulgences' to people who helped the papacy with money and advice, and by the end of the thirteenth century people were buying indulgences from their confessors on their deathbeds. In 1300 Pope Boniface VIII celebrated the end of the century by granting a plenary, or full, indulgence to anyone who came on a pilgrimage to Rome. In 1343 Pope Clement V decided to do the same every fifty years. In 1389 the interval was reduced to a third of a century and in 1470 to a quarter of a century. Pilgrims coming to Rome were a valuable source of income to the papacy, which had succumbed to the temptation to make money out of absolving sins. It had created a scandal with explosive potential for trouble.

In the eleventh century the reformed papacy had seized the leadership of Western Europe. It had instigated the crusades; but then Jerusalem was lost and crusading zeal expired. In the early thirteenth century it had united the eastern and western churches by force; but in the process it made genuine reconciliation impossible. It had sought to ensure clerical reform; but was now itself the object of criticism for its wealth and its misuse of power. It had encouraged the development of a universal system of canon law and tried to enforce conformity of behaviour. It had encouraged the development of an all-embracing system of theology and tried to enforce conformity of belief. But both things had generated resentment. A succession of outstanding lawyer popes had developed a powerful, centralised machinery of government. Often with admirable motives they had tried to create heaven on earth by regulation. From a practical point of view their achievement was massive. What they did not do was provide a vision of a Christian society moved by the ideals for which Jesus lived and died and which permeate the gospels and the letters of St Paul.

Section 5
The Era of Reform
(the 1330s to the 1660s)

Chapter 14

The End of the Middle Ages

The Babylonish Captivity

After the French capture of Pope Boniface VIII in 1303, the election of a French archbishop as Pope Clement V in 1305 and the settlement of the papal court at Avignon in 1309, a largely French College of Cardinals elected a succession of French popes for nearly another seventy years and the papacy underwent what Petrarch called 'the Babylonish Captivity.'

At first it looked as if the king of France was going to control the papacy in a way the emperor had never managed. But in the long run the papacy was a powerful enough institution to avoid permanent dependence on the king of France, and at Avignon it developed the largest and most efficient administrative and legal system in Western Europe. Clement V found a new way of raising money to make up for the loss of some of the papacy's Italian revenues by introducing a tax known as 'annates', which was the payment to the pope of the first year's revenue from any benefice conferred by him. This brought in substantial income, and meanwhile, as a result of the practice of 'papal provisions', many influential officials of the papal court in the fourteenth century were able to live in luxury on the revenues from a collection of archdeaconries and canonries which they never visited, just as influential businessmen in the twentieth century could live in luxury on the proceeds of non-executive directorships of companies.

The next step was for the theory of complete papal power to be applied to all ecclesiastical appointments. Four hundred years earlier the papacy had been asserting the principle that the local clergy and the people generally should be involved in the election of bishops, rather than just the lay ruler. Then in 1179 the Third Lateran Council had vested all episcopal elections in cathedral chapters. Now, at Avignon in 1335, the pope declared that all ecclesiastical appointments, from patriarchates and archbishoprics to parish clergy, were at his own disposal. It greatly increased his income from annates.

The national churches

Meanwhile England and Germany felt that papal taxation was taking money away from them for the benefit of France, and once the English were engaged in the fighting with the French which began in 1337 and has come to be known as the Hundred Years' War, they were determined to avoid that. Back in the thirteenth century King Henry III of England had summoned 'convocations' representing the two ecclesiastical provinces of Canterbury and York to grant financial subsidies to the crown, and now in 1351 King Edward III had Parliament pass the Statute of Provisors, which asserted that any senior ecclesiastic intruded into an appointment in England by papal 'provision' was to be expelled and replaced by someone chosen by the king.

His action was not unusual in a fourteenth century context. By now not only powerful kings outside the empire but even relatively minor rulers such as the dukes of Austria and Bavaria claimed authority over the church within their own lands. What was developing was the idea of a separate church in every kingdom, principality, duchy or even republic. The ideal of a united Christian *oikumene* presided over by the Roman Emperor had never established itself among the barbarian tribes of the West, and the Holy Roman Empire never for a moment looked like establishing its authority throughout Western Europe. Instead Europe was divided into innumerable kingdoms, principalities, duchies and even republics. In each of them the ruler expected to be master in his own house

Strangely enough the practical effect of the widespread extension of 'papal provisions' was to shift control of appointments back to the lay rulers. In the eleventh century lay rulers had usually appointed bishops. In the thirteenth the right of appointment had shifted to cathedral chapters. Now the pope had taken all appointments into his own hands. But in practice he could only exercise his authority with the agreement of the lay rulers, and it was to them that he therefore delegated the making of episcopal appointments. By the middle of the fourteenth century things were more or less back where they had been in the eleventh.

By now the idea of a universal church headed by the pope as the successor of St Peter was no longer as widely accepted as it had been in the twelfth and thirteenth centuries. If the pope wanted secular rulers to operate on his behalf he had to learn to work with them. In practice they would usually accept papal claims in relation to both the appointment of bishops and the collection of taxes so long as the pope had only theoretical authority while they themselves chose whom to appoint as bishops and could keep most of the taxes. Very widely that was the position by the end of the Avignon Papacy. The rulers of Europe got what they wanted. The pope had salvaged the ideal of supreme papal power.

The Great Schism

The Black Death, which recurred every few years from the mid-fourteenth century onwards, and the simultaneous ravages of the Hundred Years' War produced an increasingly dangerous and unsettled situation in France. As a result of this, and also because of a threat to the papal states in the turmoil of Renaissance Italy, the Avignon popes began to think of returning to Rome, and early in 1377, at the urging of the Italian mystic, Catherine of Siena, Gregory XI arrived there. When he died a year later the College of Cardinals elected an Italian as pope. Then in August they decided they had made a mistake and elected a Frenchman instead. Europe divided along political lines. The half which was pro-French supported one. The half which was anti-French supported the other. Half of the cardinals returned to Avignon; the other half remained in Rome.

The immediate practical effect was that the Western church as a whole now had to bear the expense of two papal administrations. But the schism also had a damaging effect on the view ordinary Christians took of the official church and in particular of the papacy. Two hundred years earlier the Third Lateran Council of 1179 had revised and clarified the arrangements for papal elections. It had required that for an election to be valid each cardinal should have an equal vote and that there must be a two-thirds majority. Ever since then there had only been one pope at a time. But now that had changed. Schism had reached the very head of the church and dragged on into the next century – and schism, like heresy, was known to be a sin.

Popular piety

While the Black Death and widespread fighting ravaged Europe, and while the papacy underwent the Babylonish Captivity and the Great Schism, popular religious movements grew. In Germany the Flagellants went around beating themselves to do penance for the sins of the world, and in particular for the corruption and excessive wealth of the church. Groups of women known as *beguines* lived in piety doing good works in the Rhineland. The Brethren of the Common Life in the Netherlands were moved by religious devotion and reforming zeal, and it was also in the Netherlands that Thomas à Kempis produced *The Imitation of Christ*, which came to be one of the most widely read and influential books of all time.

Thomas à Kempis and mystics such as Catherine of Siena and Juliana of Norwich adopted an approach to God which was quite new in the West. The characteristic way of looking at God in Western Christendom was to see him as the Creator of all things, the source of life and love, just and merciful, infinitely powerful and knowing all things. This is broadly the Old Testament view of

God. It is open to the charge that it makes God in Man's image, but the Christian response to that had always been that Man is made in the image of God, though even at his best Man is but a pale reflection of the Divine. The alternative view, which until the fourteenth century was more characteristic of Eastern Christendom than of the West, is that God is qualitatively different from Man and cannot be described in terms of human characteristics, however perfect those characteristics are in divine form. He is holy, or separate, utterly beyond the comprehension of the human intellect, and therefore indescribable. But he has given us a revelation of himself in Jesus Christ, so he is not entirely unknowable. If he is to be known, it can only be through Love. The way to union with God is through prayer and contemplation, not through reason.

Meanwhile among ordinary people devotion to the Virgin Mary had developed widely, and it had become common practice from the twelfth century onwards for church bells to be rung three times a day so that people could recite the *Ave Maria:* 'Hail Mary, full of Grace, the Lord is with thee. Blessed art thou among women and blessed is the fruit of thy womb, Jesus. Holy Mary, Mother of God, pray for us sinners now and in the hour of our death.' The distinction between worship and reverence, which had mattered so much in the iconoclast controversy, was relevant here too – though most ordinary pious folk, as they said the *Ave Maria*, would never have paused to consider whether their devotion to Mary was worship, and therefore heretical, or reverence, and therefore orthodox. The faithful often wanted to live good lives and yearned for some direct experience of Jesus or the Virgin Mary, or even for some direct contact with a local saint or martyr. There was a world of difference between that and the official view of the church that the only way to salvation was through the sacraments administered by priests mediating between ordinary people and God.

Wyclif and Huss

There was at that time little or no demand for reform of doctrine. The widespread assumption was that the church knew what was right and it was human sinfulness and frailty which had led to inefficiency and corruption. But the corruption of the church in the fourteenth century acted as a stimulus to an English clergyman and theologian called John Wyclif who lived from 1330 until 1384. His zeal for righteousness led to a range of new and disturbing ideas. Like the Donatists a thousand years earlier, and possibly Pope Gregory VII three hundred years earlier, he took the view that sinfulness could so corrupt a man as to invalidate the sacraments administered by him. He believed that the church should abandon its material possessions. He taught that the bread and wine of the eucharist did not change even after Christ became present in them. He encouraged the translation of the Bible to make it accessible to ordinary people and he set up a network of poor preachers to go round the country spreading these ideas. John Huss, a religious reformer in Bohemia, came into contact with Wyclif's ideas after Anne of Bohemia married Richard II of England, and he adopted them wholesale. The mixture of Wyclif's ideas with the Czech nationalism of Bohemia was an explosive combination. It produced a reforming movement which swept Bohemia and whose success was a warning to the rest of the church of what awaited it if it failed to put its house in order.

The Conciliar Movement

In the four Lateran Councils from 1123 until 1215 the papacy had taken the lead in promoting reforming projects affecting both clergy and laity. But the first Council of Lyon of 1245 was called mainly to mobilise support against the emperor and in the Second Council of Lyon of 1274 and the Council of Vienne of 1311-12 the papacy had to face a mounting barrage of criticism of itself. As a result no pope called another council throughout the following century. When a council was eventually called, in 1408, it was on the authority of the College of Cardinals and despite the opposition of two conflicting popes.

In the early fifteenth century a distinction began to be drawn between papal primacy and papal supremacy. By the thirteenth century the idea was well established that the pope held the *plenitudo potestatis*, the 'fullness of power', but in the fourteenth century some canon lawyers argued that it was vested not in the pope but in the church as a whole. In day to day matters the pope should therefore act only after consultation with and with the agreement of the College of Cardinals, and only an ecumenical council should decide important matters of doctrine and practice. The papacy was being attacked from within the church as well as from outside. On the one hand it was being threatened by the rulers of Europe with the development of separate state-controlled churches. On the other hand the College of Cardinals was claiming at least a share in papal power.

In 1408 all the cardinals, the supporters both of the Roman pope and of the Avignon pope, got together and on their own authority summoned a general council of the church to meet at Pisa. It was a practical expedient to try to find a way of healing the division of Western Christendom which had lasted since 1377. The cardinals who summoned the council were not intending to set up their own power in opposition to the papacy. They wanted to put the papacy in order and get back to an undivided church ruled by a universally accepted pope who would combat heresy. The object was first of all to heal the schism, and as soon as the Council of Pisa met in 1409 it deposed both the Roman and the Avignon pope, and the cardinals of both obediences elected a new one. But now Europe had three popes, and all three attempted to exercise papal authority.

The Council of Constance

The pope elected at the Council of Pisa died within a year in suspicious circumstances and was replaced with equally suspicious speed by the cardinal Baldassare Cossa, the leader of a band of mercenary soldiers, who now had himself elected as Pope John XXIII. After considerable political manoeuvring involving the Emperor Sigismund, John XXIII summoned another council, which met at Constance from 1414 until 1418 with a threefold programme of achieving unity in the church, stamping out heresy and promoting reform.

It approached its first task by seeking to dispose of all three popes. Edward Gibbon describes how it was the pope who had summoned the council, John XXIII, who was disposed of first. In 1415 he 'fled, and was brought back a prisoner; the most scandalous charges were suppressed; the vicar of Christ was only accused of piracy, murder, rape, sodomy and incest.' Not surprisingly it was more than five hundred years before a newly-elected pope took the name 'John', and when that did happen, in 1958, the previous John XXIII was written out of history, or consigned to being an anti-pope. It was also in 1415 that the Roman pope, who had already been deposed by the Council of Pisa in 1409, resigned, and in 1417 a new pope was elected. The Avignon papacy continued obstinately until 1429, but from then on, for the next ten years, there was just one pope in Christendom.

The second task, of stamping out heresy, was principally a matter of suppressing John Huss, who had been given a safe-conduct by the emperor to come to the council and put his case. On his arrival he was arrested and imprisoned. The council was determined to assert its own orthodox credentials and the emperor was told that heresy was an ecclesiastical matter of such importance that his safe-conduct was invalidated. Huss was found guilty of heresy and then handed over to the emperor to be burnt. His death made him both a martyr and a national hero, and for the next twenty years the Czechs successfully fought against the combined might of empire and papacy until they agreed a compromise with both in 1436. Huss remains a hero to the Czechs today.

The third task was reform of the church and in particular of the papacy. Some of those who came to the council believed that it was the corruption of the church which had caused the schism rather than the schism which had caused corruption. They talked about the abuses in the church, demanded change and generated widespread discontent. But they entirely failed to solve the problems they had revealed. What was left after the council was dissolved was widespread resentment against the clergy and an unsatisfied demand for reform. More than ever men were aware of what was wrong, and they wanted to see it put right. But the council did little. Its most significant reform was the making of arrangements for future councils to meet at regular intervals.

The end of the Conciliar Movement

The next council, which met at Pavia in 1423, achieved nothing. The Council of Basle, which first met in 1431 and continued until 1439, talked a lot, did little and brought about its own destruction. Faced with an offer by the Byzantine emperor, John VIII Palaeologus, and the Patriarch Joseph of Constantinople to come to Italy to discuss submission to Rome, the council split over the issue of where to negotiate with the Greeks. Pope Eugenius IV and a minority of the council went to Florence in Italy and reached agreement with the Greeks. The majority stayed in Basle, and in 1439 created a new schism by deposing Eugenius IV and setting up Duke Amadeus of Savoy as an alternative pope, Felix V. The councils had come into existence above all to end schism. Creating a new schism which lasted for the next ten years brought the council into disrepute. Its reputation was steadily eroded, Felix V resigned in 1449, and the council then dissolved itself. The Conciliar Movement was wounded irreparably. In 1460 Pope Pius II declared that the conciliar doctrine was a 'pestilent poison' and condemned any future appeal to a general council as heresy and treason. The pope was back in business as an autocratic monarch.

The fall of Constantinople

The union between the Eastern and Western churches negotiated at Florence was scarcely noticed in the West and was repudiated in the East. The division between them had been hardened by the Western conquest of Constantinople in 1204 and was re-affirmed by the failure of the union negotiated by Michael VIII, the first Byzantine emperor of the Palaeologus dynasty, in 1274. Meanwhile, during the thirteenth century, a political upheaval in the steppes of Asia had displaced a nomadic Turkish people known as the Ottomans. Their Sultan Osman, from whom their name is derived, led them into Asia Minor and conquered much of it in the early fourteenth century. In 1352 the Ottomans crossed into Europe and in the second half of the century conquered most of the Balkans. In 1437, with the Ottoman Turks now surrounding and threatening Constantinople, the Emperor John VIII and the Patriarch Joseph of Constantinople travelled to the West to be received into the Roman church, accept union with Rome on behalf of the Orthodox Church and seek help against the Turks. At the beginning of July 1439, a matter of days after the Council of Basle had deposed Pope Eugenius IV, the union was proclaimed.

But yet again, as in 1274, an arrangement for union with the Roman Church by the leaders of the Byzantine Empire in order to buy help from the West met with passionate opposition at home, and this time the union had no practical value. In 1274 it had at least enabled Michael Palaeologus to buy off a possible attack from the West. In 1439 the Emperor John VIII created dissension at home and failed to get the military help he needed. The pope was in no position to provide military assistance and none of the nation states of the West yet felt sufficiently threatened by the Turks to feel it was worth fighting them. The effect of John VIII's action was to weaken the cohesion of Byzantium at a time when it needed to stand firm against the Turk, and in 1453 the Turks took Constantinople. The Roman Empire, which had survived a thousand years longer in the East than in the West, had at last come to an end. The Greek Orthodox Church survived, but it was now under the rule of a Turkish Sultan who made a practice of dealing with his subject peoples through their religious leaders.

The Third Rome

The upheaval in Asia in the early thirteenth century had arisen out of the creation by Genghis Khan of the great confederation known as the Khanate of the Golden Horde, which eventually dominated all the land from the shores of China to Eastern Europe. From 1220 until 1480 the Russian state was under what its people referred to as the Tartar yoke. But the Tartar, or Mongol, Khans ruled from a distance and the Russian Grand Prince Ivan I, the founder of a Russian state based on Moscow rather than Kiev, received from the Great Khan the right to collect the tribute owed to the Mongol overlords. He was responsible for its payment, but in return he was allowed to exercise the Khan's unlimited power over his own subjects. This was the beginning of a Russian state based on the three principles of Autocracy, Orthodoxy and Nationalism.

The submission of the Greek Orthodox Church in 1439 to Rome was seen in Russia as a betrayal, and it gave the Grand Prince reason to see himself as the true defenders of the orthodox faith and then take the title 'Tsar' (from the Latin Caesar), implying imperial authority. In 1472, nearly twenty years after the fall of Constantinople, Tsar Ivan III married Sophia, the niece of the last Byzantine emperor, Constantine XI, and in 1480, as the power of the Khanate of the Golden Horde began to disintegrate, he refused to pay the annual tribute to the Great Khan. He retained the powers which dated from the two hundred and sixty years of the Tartar yoke and merged them with ideas inherited from Byzantium. With the establishment of the patriarchate of Moscow in 1589 it was at last possible to see Moscow as the Third Rome, and over both church and state presided the tsar, the *Samodyerzhavets*, or 'autocrat', with supreme political and ecclesiastical authority. It was a system which lasted until 1917.

Nationalism triumphant

The ideal of monarchs who ruled by the grace of God (*Dei Gratia*), exercising both political and ecclesiastical authority, existed in the West as well. But the West was different. In the East there had always been a tradition of supreme imperial authority. In the West there was a long tradition of conflict between church and state. Theoretical arguments for papal authority had come from the papacy, but power often rested with the lay rulers; and the issue of whether pope or emperor was the senior partner had never been satisfactorily resolved. Now, in the early fourteenth century, the theoretical case was made for the Godly Prince, as both Dante, in his *De Monarchia*, and Marsilio of Padua, in his *Defensor Pacis*, argued in favour of lay rulers having authority in church affairs.

Meanwhile the reform of the church which some had hoped would be promoted by the general councils never happened. The

Babylonish Captivity, the Great Schism and the Conciliar Movement had spread over a century and a half, and the beneficiaries of those troubled years were the rulers of the nation states. In the first half of the fifteenth century many lay rulers acquired increased powers over their churches by negotiation with the pope. That strengthened his position in relation to the councils but weakened his position in Europe as a whole. Once the process had started it continued, and in the second half of the century one state after another, large and small, asserted its autonomy.

The popes found themselves manoeuvring to salvage what they could. It was largely a matter of granting practical concessions in order to retain acceptance of the papacy's theoretical supremacy in the church. In 1478 the pope granted the Spanish monarchy the right to set up the Spanish Inquisition, a system which gave the king control over the religious orders within Spain. Then in 1531 that was extended to give him power over bishops. The inquisitors were responsible directly to the Spanish king and there was no right of appeal to Rome. In 1516, by the Concordat of Bologna, the pope granted the king of France the right to make all appointments to higher ecclesiastical posts in France, and in practice this gave the king control over ecclesiastical property and the opportunity to raise revenue from the church as he pleased. It was only a matter of time before other rulers demanded similar concessions.

Nominalism triumphant

Not only was the centralised papal church losing control of taxation and ecclesiastical appointments. It was also being challenged in the area of doctrine. In the first half of the fourteenth century the grand logical structure of St Thomas Aquinas, with its answer to all theological problems, was challenged and undermined by the Franciscan friar and scholar, William of Ockham, who argued that many of the basic ideas of Christianity could not be proved or demonstrated by logic, but had to be accepted by faith.

Aquinas was a Realist. He accepted the Aristotelian idea that all things have external characteristics, or 'accidents', but underlying those 'accidents' was the true nature of the thing, its 'substance', which it shared with all other things of the same category. Thus, despite variations in colour, weight, speed, smell and so on, every horse was 'really' a horse. It had the 'substance' of horse in common with all other horses. William of Ockham was a Nominalist. He took the view that every individual thing is what it is and no other thing, and where we see a resemblance among several things we choose to call them by the same name. Thus a horse is a horse because we call it a horse – not because it approximates to the ideal of 'horse' and shares the substance, or true nature, of 'horsiness' with a range of other creatures.

This view of things destroys the rational basis of the doctrine of transubstantiation. If bread and wine do not have a 'substance', the bread and wine used in the eucharist cannot rationally be said to change 'substantially' into the actual flesh and blood of Jesus while the 'accidents' remain the same. Nevertheless William of Ockham did not deny the doctrine of transubstantiation. He only argued that it could not be justified rationally; it was a divine mystery which had to be accepted by faith. All the same, once transubstantiation was widely seen as intellectually unsound, it was no very big step from that to the view that the bread and the wine of the eucharist should be seen simply as symbols of the body and blood of Christ, which should be eaten and drunk as an act of remembrance, or *anamnesis*, rather than offered to God by a priest as part of a continuing, or repeated, sacrifice.

The need for reform

In the fifteenth century many people in Europe were yearning for reform, which is not the same thing as suggesting that they were looking for the Reformation. Reform was always needed in the church, and the pope was the natural leader of a reform movement. In the twelfth century the papacy had encouraged new ideas, new developments and new organisations. By the middle of the fifteenth century, triumphant over the Conciliar Movement, it could have done so again. The development of scholarship meant that more and more men were able to read the scriptures in the original Greek and Hebrew, look at them with new eyes and read new and different messages in them. The papacy had the opportunity to take the lead. It was Lorenzo di Valla, the secretary of Pope Nicholas V (1447-55), who revealed that the *Donation of Constantine* was a forgery and found numerous mistakes in the Latin version of the Bible by St Jerome. At much the same time the first printed books were being published at Mainz. By the end of the century there were more than two hundred printing presses at work in Western Europe. The opportunities were enormous.

But the papacy plunged into the local politics of Italy, manoeuvring for practical advantage. Popes such as Alexander VI (1492-1503), the notorious Rodrigo Borgia, lived publicly scandalous lives, openly flouting the requirement for celibacy. Julius II (1503-13) made himself a reputation as a soldier. Leo X (1513-21) and Clement VII (1523-34) pursued the interests of the Medici family. Simony flourished, with ecclesiastical posts being created in order to sell them. Nepotism flourished, with posts as cardinals being found for the illegitimate sons of popes. Pluralism and absenteeism flourished as well, with cardinals holding multiple bishoprics, abbacies and priories, most of which they never visited. The corruption of the church was at its worst at the top. The papacy urgently needed to put its own house in order. There was no sign that it was likely to do so.

Chapter 15

Reformation, Counter-Reformation and War

The idea of reformation

The problem facing Western Europe by the sixteenth century was that Christianity had taken root so strongly over the previous thousand years that many people were shocked by the failings of the church and wanted reform. The church had very impressive administrative and legal systems. But too many of the individuals operating it were corrupt. What was wanted was a moral reformation. There was a yearning back to the idea of a past in which holy saints and martyrs, with pure hearts and devotion to the Lord, had set an example from which in recent times men had turned away. Now priests, when offering the sacraments, seemed to stand as an obstacle between the people and God. Similarly, the schoolmen stood between an increasingly literate population and the gospels, which many people now wanted to read for themselves.

The idea of reformation was essentially a matter of looking back and seeking to recover the virtues of a former age. It was seldom revolutionary – at least to begin with. It was far more a yearning for the church to be something better and nobler than it had become. But there was no agreement about how to tackle the problems in the church. For example, if priests ought to be celibate, then it was a scandal for large numbers of them to be living with women. But if marriage was a holy and blessed state for laymen, then perhaps the same should apply to the clergy.

Desiderius Erasmus

For centuries the Western church had sought to stamp out clerical marriage, but by the end of the fifteenth century perhaps as many as half the clergy of Western Europe had unofficial wives, or concubines, and often children as well. One of these illegitimate children, born probably in 1466, was the second son of a Dutch priest and a young woman who took in washing to supplement the family income, and is known to the world as Desiderius Erasmus. He became a distinguished scholar and his writings, such as the satire *The Praise of Folly*, made him one of the most influential figures in the movement later referred to as the Reformation. He looked forward to a thorough reform of society, with men of goodwill throughout Christendom uniting to root out corruption and create a better world. He wanted to recover the purity of the Christian message and saw pilgrimages, spurious relics, the selling of indulgences and the saying of innumerable masses for the dead as part of a mechanical and legalistic approach to religion, which was exactly what Christ had inveighed against so vehemently.

Erasmus came to distrust theology and asked if it might not be possible 'to have fellowship with the Father, Son and Holy Spirit, without being able to explain philosophically the distinction between them.' He wanted to reduce theology to a minimum. Christians needed to live at peace with one another, but he believed that would only be possible if 'we define as little as possible.' The church had got used to providing an authoritarian answer to every question. It was not what Jesus had done, and Erasmus's study of the New Testament made that clear. Such agnosticism was not acceptable to the papacy, which wanted acceptance of its authority. But nor was it acceptable to the other leading reformers, who wanted assurance of truth rather than increase of uncertainty. Erasmus had hoped for a consensus of all right-thinking men to build a better world, with abuses corrected and mutual understanding. Instead Europe divided itself into armed camps. Both sides were sure they were right and fought God's battles with human weapons. Erasmus continued to seek reform and reconciliation and never broke with the traditional church. But before he died in 1536, when he was about seventy and the Protestant Reformation was well advanced, he asked to be buried in the Protestant cathedral at Basle. A decade later Pope Paul III denounced him as 'the leader of all the heretics' and called for all his published works to be burnt.

The problem of indulgences

The issue which was the trigger for what came to be known as the Reformation was the sale of indulgences, which raised not only moral but also theological problems. People were being promised remission from the pains of purgatory in return for a cash payment. Purgatory was a place where, after death, people were purged of their sins before receiving the benefits of heaven. It was claimed that the *plenitudo potestatis*, the 'fullness of power', of the pope gave him the authority to reduce the pains of purgatory for any individual – or even remit them entirely. It is possible to see this as originating in a spirit of Christian charity. If the pope had full power, then surely it was right to use that power to free repentant sinners from the pains of purgatory. So people bought indulgences from their confessor on their deathbeds and the papacy used the sale of indulgences to raise money. Once the sale of indulgences had gone that far, it was argued, why not extend it? And why confine it to the living? If the pope had full power, the fact that someone had died without repenting of his sins was not an insuperable obstacle. All over Christendom Christians wanted the assurance of salvation, for themselves and for those whom they loved, including close relations who had died; and the pope was empowered to provide it.

What is more, the pope did not only bear responsibility for the salvation of Christian souls, which could be provided by granting indulgences; he was also responsible for the care of the church throughout the world and could use the sale of indulgences to pay for its expenses. Thus when Pope Julius II wanted to raise money for the rebuilding of St Peter's in Rome, which began in 1506, indulgence salesmen known as pardoners peddled their wares all round Europe with such slogans as, 'As soon as the coin in the coffer rings, the soul from purgatory springs.'

A few years later a German prince, Albert of Brandenburg, borrowed a large sum of money from the great banking house of Fugger in Augsburg to pay the pope for letting him break ecclesiastical law and hold two archbishoprics and a bishopric at the age of only twenty-four. He then proclaimed a sale of indulgences, ostensibly to help pay for the rebuilding of St. Peter's, Rome, but with half of the proceeds going to pay off his own debts.

Martin Luther

The consequent preaching of indulgences provoked a thirty-four year old member of the Augustinian Order, Martin Luther, who was Professor of Holy Scripture at the University of Wittenberg, to write out ninety-five theses and fix them to the door of the castle church at Wittenberg with an announcement that he was ready to defend them in public disputation, a normal academic practice at that time. Luther at this stage believed, or claimed to believe, that the pope would disapprove of the sale of indulgences if only he knew about it.

In recent years Luther had been working on and thinking about a doctrine of salvation. The question which dominated his thinking was *Wie krieg' ich einen barmherzigen Gott?* (How can I find a merciful God?). Later in life he looked back to a time when he was reading St. Paul's letter to the Romans and was overwhelmed by the importance of the assertion in verse 17 of the first chapter that 'the just shall live by faith.' That he saw as a key thought of immense significance. God could not be placated by good works, by burnt offerings, by payments, or by any other human acts. Rather He offered salvation freely to those who had faith in him. It seemed clear to Luther that his own views were to be found in the Bible, in the writings of St. Augustine and indeed in the main stream of Christian teaching down the ages. Somehow the church had strayed away from it. Luther believed he was teaching something which was central to the Christian faith. The selling of indulgences revealed how far the church had drifted away from that faith, to which it needed to be brought back.

The Diet of Worms of 1521

When Luther's attack on indulgences was reported to Rome, Pope Leo X thought it a trivial matter and told the head of the Augustinian Order to keep Luther quiet. But the effect of this was that the argument ceased to be one primarily about indulgences and came to be a conflict over the central issue of the power of the papacy. That was not the issue over which Luther had first stood and fought; but when he was instructed by a papal legate to retract his arguments against indulgences, he refused. His study of the Bible convinced him that indulgences were wrong, but the justification of indulgences rested on the authority of the pope, so Luther now found that if he was to continue to oppose indulgences he necessarily had to deny the authority of the pope, who was justifying them. Given a choice between the authority of the pope and the authority of a General Council, Luther preferred a General Council. Given a choice between the authority of a General Council and the authority of scripture, Luther preferred the scriptures. What is more, he saw the church as consisting of a holy priesthood of all believers (*1 Peter 2. 5 and 9*), and if the senior clergy could not be relied on to produce reformation, then Luther saw it as the duty of the senior laymen, the princes, to do that.

In 1520 the papacy issued a bull condemning Luther's propositions as heretical and Luther reacted by burning the papal bull publicly. The following year, when asked to recant at the imperial Diet of Worms, he replied, 'Unless I am proved wrong by scriptures or by evident reason, then I am a prisoner in conscience to the word of God. I cannot retract and I will not retract. To go against conscience is neither safe nor right. God help me. Amen.'

Protestantism

Martin Luther now translated the Bible into German so that all Germans could read and know it. Then in 1529 a group of German princes who were in sympathy with Luther's attitude delivered a protest to the emperor, who supported Rome. They formed a Protestant League (from which the term 'Protestantism' is derived), which was directed against both imperial and papal authority and thus inevitably drove the emperor and pope closer together.

In those states and cities of Germany where the princes supported reform a German Bible, once it was printed, was placed in church pulpits, and services were conducted in a new way, with the word of God read in the common tongue and eventually with Lutheran hymns to sing. Priests were allowed to marry and it became usual for them to preach sermons in church. Luther and those who led the worship in Lutheran churches did not see themselves as founding a new church. They saw themselves as part of the congregation of saints which had existed for centuries. They were engaged in reforming the church to rid it of abuses and restore it to conformity with Holy Scripture. Luther believed and taught that the bread and the wine of the eucharist were the body and blood of Jesus. He did not believe in transubstantiation, but he most certainly held fast to a doctrine of the real presence of God in the sacrament. None of this involved a need for a breach with the rest of the holy catholic church. But there was, he believed, a need for the rest of the church to join in the process of reformation.

Luther died in 1546, increasingly unable to control the changes he had begun. He had been profoundly conservative in his approach to reform. He had no wish to change anything other than that which needed to be reformed because it was corrupt, and his central belief, the doctrine of salvation by faith, was firmly rooted in the teaching of St Paul.

The Third Way

Under these circumstances one is entitled to wonder why the so-called Reformation happened. The church was *semper reformanda*, 'always in need of reform', and during Luther's lifetime men on both sides of the religious divide were working for compromise – a possible 'Third Way.' Cardinal Contarini, who was sympathetic to Luther's teaching on justification by faith, and the Lutheran layman Philip Melanchthon met for a series of talks in 1538-41 and found they had a lot of common ground. This was very much in line with the hopes of Erasmus, who above all wanted goodwill, with a minimum of theology, so that Christians would tolerate differences of opinion, preferably with understanding. Erasmus had believed that a moral transformation of the church was needed so that it could lead men towards a more Christian society. But the weakness of this approach was that men of goodwill could go on for ever seeking reform, toleration and understanding, while corrupt and self-seeking men continued to control the church and manipulate it in their own interest, and meanwhile the underlying doctrinal problems remained unresolved.

Luther believed that it was only on a basis of sound theology that one could hope to build a truly Christian society. Faith had to come first, and salvation was by faith alone. The problem with this was that it led to conflict. Luther not only condemned corruption, but he also fought for truth, and the outcome was the division of the church. Erasmus and Luther both believed in the need to overcome Evil with Good, but they had entirely different approaches to how to do that. The Erasmian approach, which looks so attractive at the beginning of the third millennium, did not succeed in the sixteenth century. Instead Luther's zeal for reform combined with a long drawn-out failure of the papacy to appreciate the need for reform to produce conflict for tens and even hundreds of years. In the 1560s the Catholic humanist, George Cassander, expressed clearly and beautifully an ideal for reconciliation: 'In essentials, unity; in inessentials, liberty; in everything, charity.' Few were able to adopt that attitude, for men always find it difficult to agree on what is essential and what is not.

Huldreich Zwingli

Erasmus and Luther could only have had so great an impact because in the early sixteenth century society was going through an upheaval which threw up a number of individuals with reforming views. One of these was Huldreich Zwingli, a Swiss priest whose ideas involved a more fundamental shift from the traditional position of the official church. Whereas Luther believed that one should do and believe nothing contrary to scripture, Zwingli believed that one should do and believe nothing which scripture had not clearly sanctioned. While Luther continued to believe in the real presence of God in the sacraments, Zwingli took the view that the bread and the wine were *nuda signa*, 'bare signs', to remind us of Christ's death on the cross. Jesus had said 'I am the way, the truth, the light', but no one expected statements of that sort to be interpreted literally. He had also said 'This is my body' and 'This is my blood', but there was no reason to take those words literally either. The difficulty with this is that it involves an issue of interpretation, and that in turn raises the question of whether the authority for deciding such matters lay with the church or with holy scripture or with the Holy Spirit working through conscience. If one did not have a clearly recognised authority, such as the pope, then people might interpret the scripture in different ways and their consciences might lead them in quite different directions. The strength of the papal position was that the papacy could be seen as the one true and reliable source of authority.

John Calvin

In 1536, the year Erasmus died, five years after the death of Zwingli and ten years before the death of Luther, the other great early reformer, John Calvin, published *The Institutes of the Christian Religion*. Calvin was a Frenchman who eventually settled in Geneva and believed that it was necessary to look closely at the New Testament in order to produce a reformed church modelled on the practices of the primitive church. While Luther wanted reform in the sense of getting rid of abuses, Calvin believed that it was necessary to undertake a fundamental reorganisation in order to imitate the church of the apostles. While Luther set out to remedy corruption, Calvin set out to enforce holiness. He wrote clearly, was a brilliant organiser, and both his theology and his system of church organisation were based on scripture. The theological ideas came to be known as Calvinism. Like St Augustine Calvin believed above all in the absolute sovereignty of God and, also like St Augustine, he therefore emphasised the doctrine of predestination. God had pre-ordained or pre-destined everything from the beginning. He had chosen some men for salvation and others for damnation, and His divine purpose was not open to question. Calvin also devised the system of church government which came to be known as Presbyterianism. This provided for the people to elect elders, or deacons, who in turn would approve the appointment of ministers, or presbyters. These presbyters governed the church and the conduct of society, dealing with social problems and overseeing the behaviour and beliefs of its members.

The clarity of Calvin's teaching and the efficiency of the organisational structure he devised provided people with the certainty which many of them wanted, and for the next hundred years or so the Calvinists were the most powerful force in Protestantism. Luther had rebelled against papal authority and proclaimed his faith in a merciful God. Calvin rebelled against both Catholicism and Lutheranism and presented a clear picture of an awsome and terrifying God who had to be obeyed.

The division of Protestantism

The Reformation moved in two different directions. In the Protestant principalities of North Germany and in the kingdoms of Denmark and Sweden the movement for reform was protected by the rulers and was essentially Lutheran in tone. Lutheranism depended on the goodwill of a Godly Prince and could not take root where the ruler was opposed to reform. The German states were divided between the Lutheran and Catholic churches. Eventually, after years of conflict, agreement was reached in 1555 on the principle *cuius regio eius religio* (literally 'of whom the rule, of him the religion'), the idea that each principality would follow the religion of its ruler. But toleration was still unthinkable, and neither Lutherans nor Catholics tolerated Calvinists.

Calvinism took root in a number of countries where there was no Godly Prince to lead a Lutheran Reformation. It established itself in several Swiss cantons, in much of France, in Scotland and in the Netherlands. Wherever the Calvinist system of church government came to be established, Calvinist doctrine necessarily followed. In other territories where the Calvinist system of church government was never established Calvinist theology nevertheless infiltrated the minds and the teaching of many reformers.

Lutherans and Calvinists were as much divided against each other as against Catholics. Lutheran states allowed neither the Catholic mass nor Calvinist worship, and the disciplinary bodies of Calvinist churches, which took Calvin's view that the sacraments were certain, sure and effective signs of the Grace of God, would take action just as much against someone who held the Lutheran doctrine of the real presence of God, as they would against someone who held the Catholic doctrine of transubstantiation. Both were seen as vain superstition.

Dissent and persecution

Perhaps the greatest problem with Protestantism was its tendency to produce a proliferation of sects. One important group of radical reformers took the view that it was wrong to baptise small infants into the Christian community, since becoming a Christian involved having a personal faith, which was impossible for a baby. Thus an adult choosing to follow Christ would need to be baptised again, and since the Greek prefix *ana* can be used to mean 'again', they were known as Anabaptists. In time, when members of their community who had not been baptised as infants accepted baptism as adults, they came to be known as Baptists rather than as Anabaptists. Their social and political attitudes were often radical, and they were persecuted by all lay rulers and opposed by Catholics, Lutherans and Calvinists alike. They therefore often had to meet in secret, and their beliefs and practices varied from place to place. But they had in common a fundamentalist and even literal approach to the scriptures, and their ideas spread. Persecution led to emigration and the first Baptist congregation in America was formed at Providence, Rhode Island, in 1639.

Other reformers took the view that the church should be made up of independent congregations of Christians. It should not be either an international organisation controlled from Rome or a national institution run by king and bishops. Instead each separate community should gather together for worship independently, forming its own congregation and appointing its own ministers. From this derived the English Independents of the seventeenth century and then the Congregationalist churches, which, while not Presbyterian in their organisation, were nevertheless Calvinist in their theology.

The Counter-Reformation

By the time most of Northwest Europe had embraced Protestantism a movement usually called the Counter-Reformation was developing. That name implies that it was a reaction against the Reformation, and in part it was. But it can also be seen as a parallel movement for reform, in which similar developments to those happening in the Protestant churches were also happening in the Catholic church. New religious orders were founded to meet contemporary needs. The Capuchins, a reformed order of Franciscans, came into existence in 1528 to care for the needy and became particularly successful as popular evangelists and as missionaries. Even more important was the Society of Jesus, founded in 1534 by a Basque soldier, Ignatius Loyola, who gathered a number of companions around him and encouraged them to lead lives of rigorous, Biblically based self-discipline. Each Jesuit abandoned himself to obedience and was 'a stick in the hands of his superior', ultimately at the disposal of the pope. They were to take a large part in Roman Catholic missionary activity.

By the 1540s the papacy was taking Protestantism seriously and in 1542 it established its own Inquisition, the Holy Office, to stamp out heresy. Then, despite residual concerns about the Conciliar Movement, a great council was summoned to meet in 1545 at Trent in the Hapsburg lands of North Italy, and its sessions continued every few years until 1563. Considering how long it continued, it may seem to have achieved little. It issued a decree requiring bishops to set up seminaries for training priests, it produced a new catechism for the education of the young and it maintained a traditional line on theological issues, insisting, for example, that the bread and wine in the eucharist become *veriter, realiter, substantialiter* ('truly, really and substantially') the actual body and blood of the living Christ when they are consecrated.

But the principal aim of the Council of Trent had been to strengthen the papacy's authority in the church, and in that it succeeded. While it was meeting the whole climate at Rome changed, the conciliatory approach of Cardinal Contarini was put aside, and the prestige of the papacy grew significantly. One particularly significant appointment was that of an austere Dominican friar, Michele Ghislieri, to preside over the Holy Office from 1551 onwards. Effectively he was the Grand Inquisitor for the next fifteen years, and then in 1566 he was chosen to be pope and reigned as Pius V. He aimed to root out heresy, and when Protestants were caught they were burnt. He punished immorality in Rome in much the same way as Calvin punished it in Geneva. Prostitutes were expelled from the city. Simony was ruthlessly punished. Priests were required to be celibate and to live and work in their own parishes. He limited the sale of indulgences. In 1568 the Congregation for the Conversion of Infidels was set up. In 1570 an *Index of Forbidden Books* was drawn up for the first time. He proclaimed the excommunication and deposition of Queen Elizabeth of England. Later he was himself declared a saint – the first pope since the thirteenth century to be canonised.

Persecution

The age of hunting heretics was also the age of persecuting Jews. Intolerance was especially strong in Spain. With the fall of Granada in 1492 the Muslims were finally defeated and driven out of Spain. The Spaniards went on to drive out Jews and then Protestants. Persecution of both flourished, with the Spanish Inquisition raising money by confiscating the property of its victims, using torture to secure convictions and paying informers to provide more victims.

The persecution of Jews and heretics was accompanied by the persecution of women perceived to be witches. Witch-hunting, which, contrary to common belief, had been unusual in the so-called Middle Ages, effectively began in 1468, when the papacy authorised torture to root out witches and generate accusations and confessions. It was stimulated further by the publication in 1487 of *Malleus Maleficarum*, 'The Hammer of Witches', by two

Dominicans. Calvinists soon came to be as zealous as Catholics in their zeal for seeking out and killing those they believed to be witches, and they systematically hunted them, both in Europe and in the New World. The more Catholics and Protestants feared and hated each other, the more they burnt witches.

The Wars of Religion

Another expression of the bitter division of Europe in the sixteenth and seventeenth centuries was warfare. Much of the fighting involved religious issues, but it always involved other issues as well and is unintelligible in purely religious terms. In 1527 Rome was sacked by Lutheran soldiers fighting for the Catholic Hapsburg Emperor Charles V, who now held the pope prisoner. In 1531 Zwingli died carrying the banner of Zurich as a military chaplain when Zurich was fighting the Catholic cantons of Switzerland. In Scotland Calvinism took root against the opposition of its Catholic Queen Mary, who in 1567 was forced to abdicate. In France the monarchy remained Catholic, so Lutheranism was not a possible option, but Calvinism spread rapidly and widely. The country came to be bitterly divided between Catholics and Calvinists, who were known as Huguenots, and in the second half of the sixteenth century there was a succession of civil wars. Calvinism also spread to the Netherlands, which was ruled by Catholic Spain, and that resulted in a rebellion which was both a war of independence and a religious war. By the end of it the Netherlands was divided into a Catholic area in the south, which the Spanish armies were able to hold and which two centuries later became the kingdom of Belgium, and a Protestant Calvinist republic in the north, which was able to secure a tenuous independence as the Dutch Republic in 1609 and international recognition in 1648.

The last of the so-called Wars of Religion in Europe ravaged the Holy Roman Empire for thirty years in the first half of the seventeenth century and involved other European countries from Sweden to France. It began in 1618 when the Czechs chose as their king the Protestant ruler of the Rhineland rather than the Catholic and Hapsburg heir to the Empire. In its final stage

Catholic France, whose chief minister was Cardinal Richelieu, led the Protestant side.

Toleration

The principle of toleration, which eventually emerged from the conflict, was no more the intention of the Protestant reformers than of the papacy. France was the first country where toleration was enshrined in law. In 1589, after years of warfare, a Huguenot, King Henry of Navarre, had succeeded to the throne of France. To establish his authority he needed to adopt the Catholic faith, and there is a tradition that he said *Paris vaut bien une mess*, 'Paris is well worth a mass', before being crowned in 1594. In 1598 he published the Edict of Nantes offering toleration to the Protestants, and after that, for nearly a hundred years, until 1685, it was possible for a Frenchman to be both a Protestant and a loyal subject of the crown. The Treaty of Westphalia, which ended the Thirty Years' War in 1648, also provided a considerable measure of freedom of religion, not because of a general belief in toleration but rather because Europe was exhausted. Catholics and Protestants had been killing each other for too long. Toleration was a practical expedient for avoiding continued bloodshed.

Chapter 16

The *ecclesia Anglicana*

The King's Great Matter

The English Church, or *ecclesia Anglicana*, was described by Archbishop Hubert Walter in the reign of King John as 'that part of the western church which the Most High placed in England.' At the head of both church and state was the king. Next in order of precedence, before any of the lay barons, was the archbishop of Canterbury. The spiritual authority of the pope, the bishop of Rome, was recognised, but it had been made clear by William the Conqueror that papal representatives and letters could not be received in England without the king's permission. The king was sovereign and church and state were one. During most of the so-called Middle Ages crown and church collaborated. Not always. When Archbishop Thomas Becket stood up to King Henry II over the rights of the see of Canterbury, he was killed in his own cathedral. But usually they did. When two archbishops of Canterbury were assassinated in the fourteenth century, it was not because of any conflict between the church and the king, but because they were seen as agents of the crown. By then something like a quarter of all the land of the kingdom was in the hands of the church. The king and his magnates, the pope and the bishops were all increasingly seen as involved in a conspiracy to exploit ordinary people.

Eventually, at a time when Luther and Zwingli, though not yet Calvin, had already challenged the pope's authority in Europe,

Henry VIII wanted Pope Clement VII to annul his marriage to Catherine of Aragon on the grounds that it was incestuous, in that she had previously been married to his elder brother, Arthur. He also wanted to marry Anne Boleyn. It was the sort of issue on which kings and popes usually found they could reach an accommodation. But this case was intractable. In 1527 the armies of the Emperor Charles V had taken the pope captive, and since Charles was the nephew of Catherine of Aragon, whom Henry no longer wanted as his wife, Clement VII could not grant Henry his wish without bitterly offending his captor. In 1529 Henry summoned a parliament and introduced a number of measures to put pressure on the pope and assert his own authority. In January of 1531 all the clergy of England were charged with the offence of administering Roman canon law in their courts, contrary to the rights and privileges of the English crown. The Convocations of both Canterbury and York bought their forgiveness with substantial sums of money and were then forced by the King to recognise him as Head of the Church – its 'especial protector and only and supreme Lord.' This pressure had no effect in Rome. Nor did an Act of 1532 which, by restricting the payment of 'annates' to Rome, warned the pope that his ecclesiastical revenues from England were under threat. So early in 1533 the king, at last ignoring papal authority, secretly married Anne Boleyn to ensure the legitimacy of the child she was carrying. Later in the same year she was crowned Queen.

The Act of Supremacy

It was also in 1533 that an Act in Restraint of Appeals was passed, banning legal appeals to Rome and also declaring that 'this realm of England is an Empire', thus asserting the supreme authority of the king 'next to God' in all matters spiritual and temporal. Early in 1534 another act finally abolished the payment of 'annates' and transferred any other former or surviving legal rights of the pope in England to the Crown. Then near the end of the year an Act of Supremacy declared that the king was 'the only and supreme head in earth of the Church of England.' In 1535 two opponents of royal supremacy, Bishop John Fisher of Rochester and Sir Thomas

More, the former Chancellor, were beheaded. But men like Fisher and More were in a tiny minority. Most of the higher clergy accepted the idea of royal supremacy. It was Henry, not the pope, whom God had ordained to rule as king of England, and there was no generally accepted view of the supreme authority of the bishop of Rome over all aspects of the English church. Even Thomas More, who died because he could not accept the extent to which Henry had exalted his own authority over that of the universal church, saw the pope as the servant of the church rather than its master and had declared, 'Yet never held I the pope above a General Council.'

Thus far the Henrician reformation in England had been relatively limited in scope and was largely a matter of transferring theoretical authority to a king who was anxious to be seen not as a reformer but as a good catholic and Defender of the Faith, a title which had been granted to him by Pope Leo X in 1521 and which in 1543 was attached to him and his successors in perpetuity by an act of parliament. So far the issues were personal and political rather than religious, and the victor was the person with power on the spot. Whatever the theoretical claims of the pope, power in England lay with the king.

The Dissolution of the Monasteries

In the mid-1530s he prepared to use that power more vigorously. In 1535 the king's secretary, Thomas Cromwell, or his representatives, visited a number of monasteries, many of which had property well beyond the needs of the few surviving monks. By an Act of 1536 the smaller monasteries were dissolved and by another Act of the same year the Court of the Augmentations of the Revenues of the King's Crown was set up to receive the income from these acquisitions. Towards the end of 1537 some of the larger houses began to dissolve themselves and surrender their property to the king rather than wait for action to be taken against them. Step by step they all went, their lands sold to those with money to buy them. Thus a new class of landed gentry with a vested interest in the dissolution of the monasteries was created and the crown acquired a vast new source of revenue. Some of this wealth went to found new bishoprics and some to found or re-found Oxford and Cambridge colleges. But most of it disappeared into the bottomless pit of funding Henry's pointless, expensive and unsuccessful wars with France. Up to the time Henry died in 1547, one year after Martin Luther, it is difficult to see much in common between the essentially political Henrician reformation in England and the essentially religious and moral reformation which Martin Luther had led in Germany.

Thomas Cranmer

But reforming and Protestant ideas were taking root. The first English version of the New Testament by William Tyndale had been printed at Worms in 1526 and in 1535 Miles Coverdale produced an English translation of the complete Bible. Meanwhile reformers were coming into positions of influence. One of the first and most important of them to be elevated to a position of authority was Thomas Cranmer, a quiet and retiring Cambridge academic who believed in the Lutheran doctrine of the Godly Prince: that it was the duty of the king's subjects to accept royal authority as coming from God. Cranmer was employed by Henry to help over the matter of the annulment of his marriage to Catherine of Aragon and he was subsequently appointed to be the king's ambassador to the Emperor Charles V. While abroad Cranmer secretly married the niece of a Lutheran theologian and shortly afterwards in 1532 was appointed archbishop of Canterbury. He was to play a leading part in the reform of the English church, and before the end of the decade a Bible based on Tyndale and Coverdale was placed in every parish church in the country.

The king, having divorced Catherine of Aragon, executed Anne Boleyn for adultery and lost his third wife, Jane Seymour, to puerperal fever shortly after the birth of his heir, later Edward VI. Henry then entered into an alliance with the Protestant princes of Germany, and to cement the alliance agreed to marry the Princess Anne of Cleves. Both the alliance and the marriage were short lived. In 1539 the king had parliament pass the Act of Six Articles, which was a clear attempt to block any movement towards reform of a Protestant nature, upheld the doctrine of transubstantiation and insisted on the need for the celibacy of the clergy. Cranmer was enough of a reformer to oppose it in the House of Lords, but he was sufficiently committed to the Doctrine of the Godly Prince to accept it, at least publicly, if the King insisted. He was also a conscientious, thoughtful and honest man, whose own ideas were developing in the light of the theological controversies of the time. He had come to believe in the Lutheran doctrine of justification by faith alone, he did not believe in the doctrine of transubstantiation, despite its royal, as well as papal, authentication, and he did not, of course, accept the need for clerical celibacy. Here can be seen in an acute form the central problem which faced so many of the early Protestants. Where in the end did authority lie? If not with the Pope, then was it with the church as a whole? But if the church was disunited, where then? With a Godly Prince? And if the prince held views contrary to scripture, should one still accept his authority? That was the problem, and there was no easy answer.

The Edwardian Reformation

In 1547, when Henry VIII died, the natural direction for the nation to take was towards reform and Protestantism. The new king was the nine year old Edward VI, son of Jane Seymour, Henry's third wife. He had been brought up with Protestant tutors, and those who ruled as regents on his behalf were Protestants. Instructions were issued for the gospels and epistles to be read in church in English; the Act of Six Articles was repealed; orders were issued first of all for destroying, and then removing, images from churches; in 1549 a new Book of Common Prayer, the work of Archbishop Cranmer, was introduced.

Cranmer had been working for years on an English liturgy which was to be in line with Lutheran reforming principles. The aim was to have services which were readily intelligible to the congregation, who would be active participants rather than mere spectators. The 1549 prayer book was not so much a revolution as a carefully crafted reform of the traditional liturgy, making it simpler and also, because it was in English, intelligible.

215

The traditionalists felt the changes went too far. The reformers believed they did not go far enough and as soon as the book was published sought its revision. They disliked the way it was so clearly based on English mediaeval liturgies. They disliked its traditional atmosphere and the formal nature of the prayers. They objected to the practice of kneeling to receive communion, and they objected to the sign of the cross in baptism and the use of the ring in marriage. Above all they disliked those things which could be interpreted as supporting the doctrine of transubstantiation. On this last point Cranmer agreed to make a change. In the revised version of the prayer book published in 1552 the altar, which symbolised the idea of a sacrifice, was replaced by a table at which the faithful met to remember their Lord. Most significantly a different formula was used at the administration of holy communion. The sentence in the 1549 prayer book was, 'The body of our Lord Jesus Christ which was given for thee, preserve thy body and soul unto ever lasting life.' This was compatible with both the Roman doctrine of transubstantiation and the Lutheran doctrine of the real presence. The 1552 prayer book moved towards the views of the Swiss reformers by substituting the words, 'Take and eat this in remembrance that Christ died for thee, and feed on him in thy heart by faith with thanksgiving.' The aim was to make it clear that the eucharist, or thanksgiving, was a memorial of a sacrifice made once and for all time on the cross and not a re-enactment of that sacrifice on an altar every time the bread and the wine were consecrated. Moreover, although Cranmer insisted on keeping the practice of kneeling at communion, he inserted what is known as the Black Rubric, which declared that no adoration of any real presence of God was intended by that kneeling.

These were matters of immense importance to a relatively small number of educated clergy and laymen. But they did not have any great significance for most of the population, who according to their individual temperaments and in the light of their experience either approved or disapproved of the dissolution of the monasteries, either liked or disliked the substitution of English for Latin in the liturgy and were either pleased or displeased by the removal of images from churches. In the early 1550s many of the landowning class had an interest in keeping the lands they had acquired from the dissolution of the monasteries, and a minority of intellectuals wanted to push the Protestant reformation further and faster, but the mass of the population seem to have been rather uncomfortable with all the changes imposed on them. Much was still uncertain, and throughout Edward's reign thought was free, debate was open and no-one was executed for his theological opinions. But had Edward lived, it would probably have taken a long while for England to adjust to Protestantism.

'Bloody Mary'

In the event he died when only fifteen and was succeeded by his elder sister, Mary, the daughter of Catherine of Aragon. By a strange irony it was she who, by her zeal to restore the Catholic faith and the authority of the pope, turned England into a Protestant country. Mary's legitimacy and her right to the succession depended theoretically on the Catholic view that Henry's marriage to Catherine of Aragon had always been lawful, and that Mary could not be bastardised by the retrospective annulment of the marriage. Similarly the legitimacy of her young half-sister, Elizabeth, depended on the Protestant view that the annulment of Henry's marriage to Catherine of Aragon was lawful, as was Henry's subsequent marriage to Anne Boleyn, the mother of Elizabeth. In practice, when it came to the issue of succession, the English nation adopted a pragmatic attitude which ignored both the Protestant and Catholic views on marriage and divorce. Henry's only male heir, his youngest child Edward, was the first to succeed him. When Edward died six years later, in 1553, he was succeeded by the elder of his two half-sisters, Mary, and when Mary died five years after that, she was succeeded by her younger half-sister, Elizabeth.

At her coronation Mary promised to maintain the rights of the Holy See. She required parliament to repeal the reforming legislation of the reign of her brother. She required the Convocation of Canterbury to declare that the doctrine of transubstantiation was true. Several bishops, including Thomas Cranmer, the archbishop of Canterbury, were imprisoned. Two thousand clergy were ejected from their livings because they had married. The papal legate, Reginald Pole, was appointed archbishop of Canterbury, and on his arrival in England in 1554 the members of parliament and the Convocation of Canterbury had to submit to him and receive absolution. Statutes against heresy were re-established and in 1555 the process of burning Protestant heretics began. It was not a matter of executing notorious criminals or fanatics. It was a matter of the systematic destruction of godly and conscientious men who had been the leaders of the church. Bishops Ridley and Latimer were burnt together at Oxford in 1555. Archbishop Cranmer was burnt in 1556.

The accession of Mary was a real problem for a conscientious theologian such as Cranmer, who believed in the doctrine of the Godly Prince and in the need to submit to the requirements of a sovereign ordained by God. His own views had shifted in the direction of reform, though he was, except in eucharistic theology, more a Lutheran than a Calvinist and thus was regarded as too much of a traditionalist by many of his fellow reformers. He had assumed that one could rely on royal authority to root out corruption in the church. Now the royal authority in which he believed required him to accept the authority of the pope. He was a scholarly and good man in his late sixties, fearful for his life and humiliated by the position in which he had been placed by a monarch whom he wanted to serve. In the end, in fear and under pressure, he recanted his beliefs, but then at the last moment recanted his recantation and, as he burnt, tied to a stake, held his hand in the flames to burn first because it had signed the recantation of which he was ashamed. There has seldom been a more striking example of a martyr who clearly did not seek martyrdom and satisfied St Augustine's condition that an essential qualification for martyrdom was that one should have tried to avoid it. The killing of men such as Cranmer came to be a source of serious concern throughout a nation which might otherwise have been content to drift back towards Catholicism, so long as it was not accompanied by violence, and so long as those who had benefited from the dissolution of the monasteries were not deprived of their lands.

The Spanish Ambassador saw the danger to the Catholic cause. He wrote back to Spain about how the burnings provoked the sympathy of the crowds and recommended that, if executions were needed, they should be done secretly rather than publicly. But Queen Mary, like her father, was driven by an uncomfortable and demanding conscience, and nothing would turn her from the task of cleansing her realm from the contamination of Protestant heresy. As the Protestant martyrs burned the minds of Englishmen associated the bloodshed with tyranny and with Rome. Even those who had been inclined to see the new-fangled Protestant ideas as an interference with cherished tradition, and the destruction of church decorations an unnecessary irreverence, now feared Rome. If the queen and her unpopular husband, King Philip II of Spain, had an heir, Catholic tyranny could reach on into a distant future. But Mary never had a baby and in 1558, still a relatively young woman of forty-two, she died.

Elizabeth

Mary was succeeded by her half-sister Elizabeth, who was still only twenty-five when she came to the throne. Her mother, Anne Boleyn, had been executed by her father, she had seen the swing to Protestantism in the reign of her young half-brother Edward, and she had seen the swing back to Roman Catholicism in the reign of her older half-sister Mary, by whom she had been imprisoned. She had lived in fear of her life. The circumstances of her birth meant that she must be a Protestant, but she had seen enough of politics to know that she must also move with care. There is no certainty about her own religious position, but shortly after coming to the throne she told the Spanish Ambassador that she intended to restore religion as it had been towards the end of her father's reign. In most areas her own position was probably a fairly traditional one. She saw her country as part of the catholic, or universal, church, but a part which did not acknowledge the authority of the bishop of Rome. She accepted the idea of royal supremacy, but saw it as imposing a public responsibility on her rather than providing an opportunity to give expression to her personal beliefs. She may have believed in the real presence of God in the sacraments, but probably not in the doctrine of transubstantiation. An indication of her position on the important question of eucharistic theology is given in a brief and ambiguous poem which is attributed to her: 'His was the word that spake it. He took the bread and brake it, And what his words do make it, That I believe and take it.' It is one of the best short statements on eucharistic theology ever made.

Unlike many contemporary rulers she had to take account of parliament. But when it offered her the title of Supreme Head of the Church of England, she refused it and chose to be the Supreme Governor of the Church instead. It was an important distinction, for it was less presumptuous but left her with the reality of such power as it was possible to wield.

The Anglican *via media*

Elizabeth had no wish to 'make windows into men's souls' and avoided burning heretics. But almost all her subjects were agreed on the need for uniformity, in the sense that there should be one national church for all. Where they differed was over what form that church should take. So, because everyone expected it, an Act of Uniformity was passed in 1559 and the Prayer Book was re-issued. Mostly it was the same as the Prayer Book of 1552, which in turn was very largely the same as that of 1549. But there were significant changes. The Black Rubric, denying the real presence of God in the sacrament, was omitted. The sentence used in 1552 at the administration of communion was now preceded by the 1549 sentence, so that the whole formula ran together thus: 'The body of our Lord Jesus Christ which was given for thee, preserve thy body and soul unto everlasting life. Take and eat this in remembrance that Christ died for thee, and feed on him in thy heart by faith with thanksgiving.' The first sentence is entirely acceptable to those who believe in the real presence, or even in transubstantiation, and there is no reason for them to object to the second sentence. For someone who adopts a Zwinglian or Calvinist position on eucharistic theology the first sentence can be seen as entirely metaphorical and the second sentence affirms the symbolic nature of the consecrated elements. Ideally those two sentences would satisfy everyone and Zwinglian and Catholic, Lutheran and Calvinist would all now happily worship together.

Popish plots

Those who drafted the 1559 Act of Uniformity had done all they could to make it generally acceptable, but it did require both clergy and laity to accept the authority of the Church of England and attend its services. Most people did, some because they had always expected to go to church on Sundays and the parish church was the only one to which they could conveniently go. But those who wished to be loyal to the pope in religious matters had to compromise with their consciences if they were also to be loyal subjects of the queen. The biblical story of how the heart of Naaman the Syrian was with the God of Israel when he bowed down to worship in the house of Rimmon (*2 Kings 5.18*) reassured many Roman Catholics that they could be physically present at what they saw as the heretical services of the Church of England, so long as in their hearts they remained faithful to the religion of Rome.

Pope Pius V made it more difficult. In 1570 he excommunicated Elizabeth and declared her deposed. Shortly afterwards, in August of 1572, the Massacre of St Bartholomew's Day in France, when thousands of Calvinists, or Huguenots, were slaughtered, including almost all of their leaders, produced an influx of Huguenot refugees into England with stories of Catholic atrocities. Pius V's successor, Gregory XIII, celebrated the massacre and soon was pursuing plans for the invasion of England. When those plans came to nothing, he encouraged the assassination of the English 'Jezebel', with the aim of replacing her with Mary Queen of Scots. There then was a succession of terrorist plots. In 1580 two potential assassins, who wrote to Rome because they were worried that in killing the queen they would incur sin, received a reply from the Pope's secretary reassuring them that 'whosoever sends her out of the world with the pious intention of doing God's service, not only does not sin but gains merit.'

In 1588, with Mary of Scots dead the previous year, the might of Spain was directed towards overthrowing Elizabeth. The Spanish Armada, which was to have landed Spanish troops in England, was overwhelmingly defeated, but it left behind it a fear of the unholy trinity of Popery, Tyranny and Spain. Then in 1605, two years after Elizabeth's death, there was perhaps the largest-scale terrorist plot in history. A group of Roman Catholics planned to blow up the Palace of Westminster while King James I and all the members of the House of Lords and the House of Commons were gathered together, and use the succeeding chaos to seize power and return England to allegiance to Rome. The echoes of the Gunpowder Plot and the answering cries of 'No Popery!' rang down the following centuries. The bonfires lit by Queen Mary may have turned England into a Protestant country. The Pope and the King of Spain between them ensured that England became vehemently anti-papal.

Puritanism

If Queen Elizabeth could not satisfy all her Roman Catholic subjects, perhaps she could find a way to satisfy most Protestants. But those who had returned from exile in Geneva wanted Calvinist theology and a purified church with a Presbyterian structure. The reformed English church, which had retained the threefold ministry of bishops, priests and deacons, did not satisfy them. Most remained within the Church of England, were known as Puritans, and sought to reform the church in a Calvinist direction from within. But some found it impossible to tolerate the liturgy of the Prayer Book, even though the liturgy was now in English rather than in 'a tongue not understanded of the people' (Article XXIV of the *Articles of Religion* in the Prayer Book), and even though the internal decoration of churches was generally simpler than it had been. They saw the sign of the cross in baptism and the use of the ring in the marriage service as vain superstition. They felt obliged to worship separately, and even secretly, and were known in the seventeenth century as Independents and later as Congregationalists. Meanwhile the Baptists could live neither with the idea of an established church nor, of course, the practice of infant baptism. Some fled abroad, for example to the Netherlands, or eventually to the New World.

Civil War and after

England had experienced the elements of the European Reformation in a strange sequence. The Henrician Reformation confirmed that the *ecclesia Anglicana* was a national church. While the reality of power had long been with the king, now theoretical authority was transferred to him as well. In the reign of Edward VI the English church accepted the Reformation. Under Mary it experienced the Counter-Reformation in its fiercest form. Under Elizabeth it reverted to being a national church, though not a state church on the Lutheran model. Then, in the seventeenth century, as in Europe, a mixture of political and religious conflicts culminated in warfare. When England plunged into civil war in the 1640s, the struggle was over the two great issues of religion and the constitution. And, as is the way with conflict, it tended to polarise the opponents. Both sides agreed in principle that government should be by king and parliament working together, but when the battle lines were drawn they were drawn between the supporters of the king and the supporters of parliament. Most men on both sides wanted to retain the established Church of England. But the parliament side came to be dominated, in the words of Oliver Cromwell, by 'men who had the fear of the Lord about them and made some conscience of what they did'; and many of the leaders of the parliamentary army were, like him, Puritans and Independents who made the so-called 'Presbyterian' element in parliament look moderate. Meanwhile the Royalist cause came to be associated with the more traditional and catholic wing of the Church of England, and King Charles I numbered among his supporters some who were self-avowed Roman Catholics.

The victory of parliament, or rather of parliament's army, led to the execution of the king and the dominance of Puritanism. Then the restoration of Charles II in 1660, eleven years after his father's execution, led to the restoration of the bishops and a return to the use of an essentially Cranmerian prayer book in church services. But by then England, like the rest of Europe, was worn down by more than a century of ecclesiastical conflict and people were more prepared than in the past to tolerate dissent, not so much because they believed in toleration as because the nation had exhausted itself with its intolerance and the determination of each extreme to root out opinions to which it was opposed. Catholics who accepted the authority of the pope were now more willing than in the past to live as loyal servants of a Protestant king. Congregationalists and Baptists were more prepared than they had been to live and worship in their own ways without seeking to impose their views on the rest of the nation.

The Church of England

By now the Church of England was a broad church which included traditional catholics, so long as they had no allegiance to the pope, and many whose theology was essentially Calvinist, so long as they felt no need to insist on a Presbyterian structure of church government. Many people were devoted to their reformed English church with its Book of Common Prayer, its services of Matins and Evensong derived from medieval monastic services, its country parsons and its acknowledgement of the authority of the monarch. It was similar to the Lutheran churches of the North in that it was the church of a nation, reformed under the monarchy, and very largely retaining the dioceses and parishes, and also the ministry, of the late medieval church. But if England was to be a nation in which an educated priest in every parish could not only celebrate the eucharist but also preach intelligently, and if the members of his congregation were to understand what he said and live lives affected by the teachings of Christ, there was still a long way to go.

Section 6
The Modern World
(the 1660s to 2000 AD)

Chapter 17

Mission and Division

The church militant

There were three main developments in the Christian Church in Europe during the centuries after the period of the Reformation. One was the attempt to evangelise the world beyond Europe. Another was the tendency of the Protestant churches to divide into ever more sub-divisions. The third was a change in the way in which the papacy came to be perceived by both Catholics and Protestants – from a corrupt and embarrassing monarchy to an institution with significant spiritual authority.

The movement towards world-wide mission effectively began with Portuguese and Spanish exploration. In 1487 Portuguese explorers had reached the southernmost tip of Africa, and in 1492 Christopher Columbus, in the service of Spain, had sailed west and reached what came to be called the West Indies. The following year, 1493, the notorious Renaissance Pope Alexander VI, Rodrigo Borgia, drew a line down the middle of the Atlantic, dividing the unknown world between the Spanish and the Portuguese, and giving the kings of Spain and Portugal responsibility for bringing Christianity to their new territories.

Missionary activity went hand in hand with conquest and settlement. Whereas in the first millennium Christian missionaries had often faced barbarians with faith in their risen Lord and preaching the gospel of love, so that by the end of that millennium Christianity embraced most of what is now Europe, in the second millennium missionary activity was often accompanied by force. There is something distasteful about the reign of the Prince of Peace being advanced with the crossbow, the musket or the repeating rifle, and the destruction of the Aztec and Inca civilisations by the Spanish *conquistadores* and the subsequent imposition of Christianity on the native peoples of the area is a striking early example of conversion by conquest.

The Jesuit missions

There were genuine attempts to spread the Kingdom of Heaven through the world by peaceful means, and the Society of Jesus, which had been formed in 1534 and is more commonly known as the Jesuits, took the lead in that. In Paraguay, for example, they established large settlements where they provided tens of thousands of the native people with a peaceful and settled life, with land to cultivate, elementary education, and churches in which the Christian festivals were splendidly celebrated. The communities were well ordered and run by the Jesuits in a manner in which beneficent and efficient schoolteachers might run a school. They cared for their charges, but the dividing line between teacher and taught was absolutely clear and there was no question of any of the native people joining the order or becoming priests.

The Jesuits were also to be found in Japan, China and India, and in the Spice Islands of Southeast Asia. One of the most important of their missionaries, St Francis Xavier, had appreciated when he came into contact with the Japanese in the middle of the sixteenth century, that the task of Christian mission was not to sweep away all that had gone before and replace it with Christianity, but instead to recognise what was good and admirable in a different civilisation and trust the teaching of the gospel to transform it into something even better. But early success was followed by disaster. In the early years of the seventeenth century the Japanese, fearing colonisation, exterminated both foreign and native Christians and closed Japan to European contact for two hundred years.

At about that time, in 1622, Pope Gregory XV established *the Sacred Congregation for the Propagation of the Faith*, commonly known as *the Propaganda*, with the explicit aim of spreading Christianity throughout the world. At first it had a strikingly enlightened policy, which was intended to free missionaries from colonial control and develop an indigenous clergy wherever possible. Thus the Jesuits who established a mission in China during the seventeenth century took pains to understand the language and culture of the Chinese and accepted, and even adopted, a range of Chinese customs, including the honours paid to Confucius and to departed ancestors. But other religious orders challenged their approach, suggesting that they were trying to ingratiate themselves with the Chinese ruling class to avoid persecution. So the Emperor K'ang-Hsi issued a statement making it clear that no worship was involved in the veneration either of Confucius or of ancestors: Confucius was honoured only as a legislator, and the honour paid to departed ancestors was a mark of respect, not worship. The Jesuits appeared to have been very successful, and the future for catholic mission in China looked bright.

The national churches

Meanwhile, back in Europe, the Christian Church was seriously divided. If any religious system had triumphed in the Reformation, it was the national church, and that was just as true in areas where the Roman Catholic Church remained dominant as in Protestant areas. The kings of Portugal, Spain and France all acknowledged the pope as the titular head of the church, but they expected to be masters in their own kingdoms. In France, where the principle of toleration had been enshrined in law by the Edict of Nantes in 1598, that edict was revoked in 1685 by Louis XIV, who established that it was now necessary to be a catholic in order to be a French citizen. There was to be *un roi, une loi, une foi* ('one king, one law, one faith). But it was the king, not the pope, who was supreme, and Louis XVI distanced the French church from Rome and aimed to turn it into a department of state within an autocratic monarchy. During the eighteenth century the Catholic monarchs of Spain, Portugal and France all expelled the Jesuits from their own countries, and in 1773, when they threatened to invade the Papal States, Pope Clement XIV gave in to pressure to dissolve the order.

Meanwhile the Lutheran churches in North Germany and Scandinavia were controlled by their local 'Godly Prince', and while Luther had secularised the church, Calvin had clericalised the state, so that Presbyterian churches were the dominant force in the city state of Geneva, in Scotland and in the Netherlands. Perhaps surprisingly the one nation which for a while did not have a national church, from the execution of Charles I in 1649 until 1660, was England. But when Charles II was restored to the throne in 1660, the Church of England was restored as well. On the other side of Europe, in Russia, the Orthodox Church was obedient to the tsars, who during the eighteenth century diverted much of the revenues of Russia's vast monastic estates to the crown.

Protestant divisions

But no longer did the existence of a national church mean that all the people of that nation could be assumed to be members of the national church. In England there were many who either could not give assent to the theological teachings of the established church, or would not conform to its practices, or both. These two groups, the Dissenters and the Nonconformists were in practice the same, and they acquired a sort of second-class status in society: tolerated, but for many years excluded from all public office. There were at first four main denominations of Dissenters: Presbyterians, Congregationalists, Baptists and Quakers. The Presbyterians were Calvinists who wanted but did not have a Presbyterian system of church government. The Congregationalists, who had previously been known as Independents, were also Calvinist in their theology but recognised that, in the absence of a national system of church government of which they could approve, they needed to find a way of operating as separate, or independent, congregations. The Baptists, who were not Calvinist in their theology, differed from the mainstream of the Anglican Church in their insistence on the importance of receiving baptism only when adult and capable of making a commitment to a life of faith in Christ. The other important group was the Quakers, who were distinguished by their commitment to non-violence.

The Protestant Reformation had shifted assumptions in the direction of expecting personal commitment from each believer, and the logical consequence of that was that each believer was entitled to his or her own beliefs. That led in turn to the proliferation of Protestant sects and also to the development of distinctive groups within a church. Thus Pietism, which involved a belief that Christianity should be about the transforming of lives rather than a search for theological correctness, developed in the Lutheran territories of Northern Europe. Pietists attended normal services, but they also met in private houses to study the Bible, pray and join each other in good works. As Lutherans they knew that salvation was 'by faith alone', but their faith led to good works, and Pietism was a shining example of reform at work.

England eventually produced its own brand of Pietism when an energetic clergyman, John Wesley, influenced by the Pietist movement, went round urban areas, which often had a growing population but no church, preaching and attracting large crowds. He believed that 'God willeth all men to be saved', and throughout England he found people eager to hear him preach a gospel of hope and willing to follow his demand that they should live lives with some method in them. He remained an Anglican clergyman, insisted that he would 'live and die a member of the Church of England', and did. But the hierarchy of the established church failed to take advantage of him or of the Methodist movement he started, and when in frustration he took it upon himself in 1784 to ordain ministers to serve the ever-growing Methodist congregations, a breach became inevitable and after his death in1791a new denomination of Methodism came into existence. That in turn broke up bit by bit into Wesleyan Methodists, the

New Connection, Primitive Methodists, and Bible Christians, and an attempt at reunion only produced another group: the United Methodists. Others denominations divided as well, and new ones came into existence.

Within a church there could now be significant differences of belief and practice. Thus in the eighteenth century there developed within the Church of England a group known as Evangelicals. They were austere in their liturgical practices, sympathetic to fellow-evangelical Nonconformists, suspicious of theology, but morally and socially high-minded. They were very influential in middle-class Victorian England. Then in the 1830s there developed an Anglo-Catholic movement, which aimed to get back to the original doctrines and disciplines of the church and was attached to ceremonies and beliefs associated with Catholicism. But most church members were simply members of the Church of England. They had been baptised, might well have been confirmed, would expect to get married in church, and would expect to be buried by the local vicar. Many attended church on Sundays, and even more sent their children to Sunday school. They might well have no very clear theological views, but they gave general assent to central Christian ideas and Christian values. They learnt to live with Anglo-Catholics and Evangelicals, and Anglo-Catholics and Evangelicals managed to live with them and with each other.

Catholic failures abroad

Meanwhile the papacy struggled to assert its authority within the Roman Catholic communion throughout the world, often with disastrous consequences. In 1704 the pope ruled that Chinese Christians should not honour either Confucius or departed ancestors and required them to conform to Roman customs. The Chinese emperor responded by expelling all missionaries other than those willing to continue in the polite and respectful fashion which had characterised relations in the previous century. So bishops and priests had to choose between the requirements of the pope and those of the emperor. Most left, but four bishops and a significant minority of priests remained, continued their work and tried to get Rome to make concessions. The issue dragged on until the middle of the eighteenth century, when Pope Benedict XIV made things even worse by insisting that all local practices must be swept away and everything done in accordance with Roman custom and practice.

Catholic missionaries in Asia suffered from papal interference and from having to impose Roman practices, such as the requirement for all clergy to be celibate and for Latin to be used in the liturgy. They failed to make use of the Bible when teaching about Christianity, and in the Philippines, the one area in the East where the Catholic church succeeded in establishing itself as the majority religion, it was more than three hundred years after the arrival of Catholic missionaries in 1565 before the people acquired a translation into their own language of St Luke's Gospel. But the principal reason for their widespread failure was that the other religions they encountered, such as Islam, Buddhism and Hinduism, had a spiritual strength which made them difficult to displace.

Catholic mission in Africa was largely unsuccessful for rather different reasons. During the seventeenth and eighteenth centuries various Catholic religious orders sent missions to Africa, but few acquired any more than a superficial knowledge of the language spoken by their potential converts, still less an understanding of their customs and culture. There was no real contact of minds, and though many missionaries worked hard in Africa, and many died from illness and from violence, their achievements were few.

Over centuries the Catholic Church had put immense energy and resources into missionary activity, with Jesuits, Capuchins, Dominicans and Franciscans suffering disease, shipwreck and persecution throughout the world. But measured against the effort expended their achievements were small. Even in Paraguay, where the Jesuits had seemed to be so successful, there was a disaster. When the order was dissolved in 1773 and the Jesuits left Paraguay, the missions disintegrated and the Indians returned to the forest. It was the price paid for the failure to develop an indigenous leadership.

Protestantism awakens

While the Catholic Church had attempted to evangelise the world in the seventeenth and eighteenth centuries, the Protestant churches in Europe had done little, being more concerned with survival at home. The Presbyterian and Congregationalist churches, both Calvinist in their theology and committed to an extreme version of the doctrine of predestination, took the view that they could leave the conversion of the heathen to the inscrutable workings of the Almighty. So although the Church of England set up the *Society for Promoting Christian Knowledge* as early as 1698, although the *Society for the Propagation of the Gospel in Foreign Parts* was founded in 1701, and although a group of Danish Pietists launched a Protestant mission to India in the eighteenth century, it was not until the *Baptist Missionary Society* was founded in 1792 that there was a great surge in missionary activity, with the Baptists translating the Bible into as many languages as possible and setting out to convert the world.

For centuries the Orthodox churches had been in no position to engage in mission. The Greek Orthodox Church had survived under Turkish rulers. The Russian Orthodox Church was under the control of the tsarist autocracy, with millions of its members living as serfs, tied to the land. But by the nineteenth century it was the largest Christian community in any country in the world, and after the emancipation of the serfs in 1861, two years before the slaves were freed in the U.S.A., Russia was ready to colonise Asia, and the Russian church was ready to establish itself in Siberia and as far as Alaska.

Meanwhile the English and the Dutch, who had started challenging the sea power of Spain and Portugal as early as the sixteenth century, had built up overseas commercial empires. Eventually, just as Roman Catholicism had accompanied Spanish and Portuguese colonialism and now followed French colonial expansion, and just as the Orthodox Church followed Russian expansion across Asia, so the various Protestant churches accompanied British and Dutch colonialism. The nineteenth century saw a great expansion of missionary activity, with every Christian denomination and every Christian country forming missionary societies. Churches were founded throughout the world, schools were opened, and translations of the Bible were made for every people with whom the missionaries came into contact. Meanwhile Catholics and Protestants of various nationalities disagreed with each other and competed for converts. What they had in common was a view that it was their duty to convert all the peoples of the world to Christianity and also introduce them to western ways. They did so energetically.

Mission problems

Nineteenth century missionary activity was closely and damagingly associated with colonialism, trade, commerce and military force. There was a striking example in 1839, when the British undertook a war in the name of Free Trade to force the Chinese government to allow the East India Company to sell opium to the Chinese. The gunboats which opened up China to the trade in opium also opened it up to the missionary societies. The churches, instead of condemning the war, saw it as an opportunity for evangelism. It was a bad mistake and to the end of the twentieth century Protestant Christianity in China suffered from the way in which it was intruded in the wake of the Opium War.

A related problem was that the missionaries usually remained European in their culture, assuming both that white men were naturally superior to all other races and that men were superior to women. They behaved as if a small number of white male European missionaries would for an indefinite future look after their inevitably backward charges. The idea that men, still less women, with black or brown skins could lead a church of their own was, with few but notable exceptions, foreign to the European way of thinking. At the same time, as communications improved, more and more decisions were taken centrally, in Rome or London or New York, rather than by those on the spot. Thus the church came to be seen by many converts as a collection of competing and centralised administrative organisations, which made rules about conduct and about the liturgy and had authority to settle disputes. Where missionaries appeared to be successful, what was established was not so much a local church, a community of those called to follow Christ, part of the whole Body of Christ throughout the world, but rather a mission station, in which Christian converts were looked after by a missionary.

The French Revolution

Another important development in the nineteenth century was a transformation in the way the papacy was perceived, whether by Catholics or by Protestants. The first step towards that change was the French Revolution, which began in 1789, saw the execution of the Most Christian King, Louis XVI, in 1792, and replaced St Paul's principles of 'faith, hope and love' (1 *Corinthians 13.13*) with the revolutionary principles of *Liberté, Egalité,* and *Fraternité.* The French church was reorganised in line with civil administration. Each diocese was to cover the same area as a civil department and bishops were to be elected by the people. Then, when Napoleon Bonaparte seized power, he decided to make use of the church to provide cohesion in French society and concluded an arrangement with the papacy which lasted from 1801 into the early years of the twentieth century. The pope had to accept the loss of the church's wealth in France, but the nation would pay the stipends of the clergy, who were expected to hold the social fabric of the nation together. The immediate effect was to make the French church even more dependent on the state than it had been under the monarchy. But the long-term effect was exactly the opposite. Step by step, through the upheavals of the nineteenth century, as France moved from one constitution to another, the French church threw off its dependence on the state. Whereas in the past the church and the monarchy had united against papal interference, now the church turned more and more towards Rome for support against the state.

Pius IX and infallibility

By one step after another the papacy was deprived of the temporal power which it had believed to be important if it were to be able to assert its authority in the world. But as it lost its lands and temporal possessions it seemed to acquire a new spiritual authority. The Jesuit Order, which vigorously upheld papal authority, was restored in 1814, and a significant change took place during the pontificate of the remarkable pope who took office in 1846 as Pius IX and reigned for thirty-two years. He had an attractive personality, combining natural presence with great charm, and he came to the papal throne apparently in sympathy with liberalism. But the widespread revolutions of 1848 destroyed his attachment to liberalism and as republicans took over Rome he was forced, at least temporarily, into exile. Then, when the First War of Italian Liberation of 1859-60 deprived him of much of the Papal States, he ranged the Roman Catholic Church not only against liberalism but against modern developments generally. In 1864 he published a *Syllabus of Errors*, condemning liberalism, socialism, communism, the separation of church and state, the freedom of the press, freedom of religion, civil marriage and secular education.

Next he required Roman Catholics to unite against the forces of evil around them. They had to be loyal to his authority, and that authority had to be strengthened. In 1870 he summoned a general council, which is known as the First Vatican Council, and at the end of July the council, attended only by Roman Catholics, proclaimed the Doctrine of Papal Infallibility with near unanimity. Henceforth it was an article of faith of the Roman Catholic Church that if the pope spoke *ex cathedra*, from the throne of St Peter, on a matter of faith or morals, his views were infallibly true, as much as if they had been uttered by God Himself. Back in 1854 Pius IX had already proclaimed the Doctrine of the Immaculate Conception of the Blessed Virgin Mary – the idea that Mary must have been born without sin, because only a sinless womb could possibly carry the incarnate Lord, and although there was no scriptural authority for such a belief, it was now 'altogether necessary for salvation' to believe it.

On 1st August 1870, the day after the proclamation of the Doctrine of Papal Infallibility, war broke out between France and Prussia, and while the attention of Europe was concentrated on the Franco-Prussian War, Italian troops seized Rome, which now became the capital of the new Italian kingdom. The papacy was deprived of its last vestige of temporal sovereignty – at least until 1929, when it acquired sovereignty over the Vatican City State. The pope, so recently proclaimed infallible, now chose to portray himself as 'the prisoner in the Vatican', besieged by the forces of evil, publicly opposed to the various developments of the modern world, deprived of all temporal sovereignty, but still the infallible representative of God on earth. From that position he ruled the Roman Catholic Church throughout the world as a supreme autocrat, rigidly authoritarian, but relying now entirely on moral or spiritual authority rather than on any temporal force or power. Pius IX became something of a martyr in his own lifetime and an object of veneration bordering on worship. Increasingly the pope was seen by Catholics not just as the successor of St Peter but as the representative of God, the Vicar of Christ, on earth. The Holy Spirit moved in him and guided him into all truth.

The struggle for civilisation

Meanwhile the papacy was at enmity with the nation states of late nineteenth century Europe. The pope forbade Catholics to take part in the elections for the parliament of the new Italian kingdom. When, Bismarck, the Chancellor of the new German Empire refused to accept papal interference in appointments to theological faculties in German universities, that led to a conflict known in Germany as the *Kulturkampf*, a 'struggle for civilisation', during which Bismarck, referring back to the Investiture Contest of the eleventh and twelfth centuries, proclaimed that he would not 'go to Canossa.' Meanwhile in France anti-clericalism became an integral part of left-wing politics. Members of Catholic religious orders were forbidden to teach in French schools, numerous religious orders were compulsorily dissolved and all church schools were closed. In 1904 diplomatic relations with the papacy were broken off and in 1905 a law was passed enforcing total separation of church and state. There were to be no more state subsidies and for some years it was only possible for the clergy to make use of church buildings by leasing them from the state.

But papal authority within the Roman church was greater than ever before, and in a world in which the various Protestant denominations were divided among themselves and the Orthodox churches were surviving precariously either under Ottoman rule or under Tsarist autocracy, the claim of the Roman church to be the one true church, while all other denominations were heretics or schismatics, could sound plausible.

Protestantism triumphant

Abroad the Protestant missionary churches seemed remarkably successful by the end of the nineteenth century. Creating indigenous churches was not yet thought to be desirable. Nor was it easy. Necessarily the missionaries passed on something of their own beliefs and practices, and some converts expected and even demanded change in their own way of life and worship. Missionaries built churches in the Gothic style and sang Wesleyan hymns, for example, because that was what they were used to. Many converts expected to share in that. They did not want to worship their new God in their own huts to the music of their own tribal dances.

Nor was it easy to draw a line between what is and is not essential. Whether one stands, sits or kneels to pray is customary – not essential. Repentance for harm done to others and a willingness to forgive harm done to oneself is essential. But it is easier to learn to kneel than to learn to forgive. It is easier to assert belief in theological propositions than to live one's life trusting in God and following the example of Jesus.

With hindsight it seems clear that the Europeans needed to learn to respect local culture and be prepared to learn as well as teach. They needed to plan for local autonomy rather than continue to expect obedience. But few thought like that at the end of the nineteenth century. By then Europe was preparing to take over the world. The white man was sure of his superiority to others races, but he was also conscious of his obligations towards them. He brought with him the potential benefits of European culture, farming methods, engineering and medicine, and all of those reflected the glory of the God whom he worshipped. The

European God, and particularly the Protestant God, had the most powerful guns and the best building techniques and provided the best bridges, railways, irrigation systems, schools and hospitals. There were Protestant missionaries in almost every country in the world and even, in parts of India, a small educated Christian middle class. At the First World Missionary Conference, held in Edinburgh in 1910, it was possible to look forward to 'the evangelising of the world in one generation', and there was an expectation that most of the world would accept Protestant Christianity. It was just a matter of time. 'God is working his purpose out as year succeeds to year,' began a favourite English hymn: 'From utmost east to utmost west, where're man's foot hath trod', it proclaimed (*The English Hymnal, number 548*), 'nearer and nearer draws the time, the time that shall surely be, when the earth shall be filled with the glory of God as the waters cover the sea.'

Chapter 18

The New World

Origins

The most remarkable example of the extension of Christianity beyond Europe in the last centuries of the second millennium, and at the same time the most striking example of the divisions of the Christian Church, was in the area which came to be the United States of America. It was quite different from the missionary activity in other parts of the world. Europeans went to North America not to convert the native people but to settle, and they took their own version of Christianity with them. The first English colony, Virginia, was founded as a commercial venture in 1607 and named retrospectively after the reputedly virgin queen, Elizabeth I. The settlers took with them the teachings and practices of the Church of England, their services were in accordance with the English prayer book, and for a century church attendance was theoretically compulsory. But there was no effective central control, and before long the settlers decided for themselves how they would worship and, indeed, whether or not they would attend church at all.

Meanwhile new settlements were established further north by other members of the Church of England who were escaping to what they called New England from the harassment and problems of life in Europe in the seventeenth century. They wanted to set up a purified version of the church, and just as the European reformers of the early sixteenth century wanted to free the church from corruption rather than break away from it, so these Puritans wanted reform rather than schism. They fled to the Americas to build 'a City on a Hill' which would shine as an example of a free society in which individuals would live godly lives in accordance with the teachings of the gospels and in a reformed church.

The theology they took with them was Calvinist, with its emphasis on predetermination to salvation or damnation, and those who saw themselves as saints elected to salvation aimed to establish an ideal society in the colony of Massachusetts and decide how it should be ruled. But Calvinist theology did not sit easily with a yearning for freedom, and in 1691 the people of Massachusetts exercised their freedom by deciding that ownership of property rather than church membership should give a man the right to vote.

Freedom

The freedom which the early settlers believed would enable godly religion to flourish became the dominant ideal of American life and it combined with the so-called Protestant work ethic to bring prosperity. But freedom and prosperity bring problems with them, and early in the eighteenth century the Puritan scholar Cotton Mather wrote about the righteous aims of the great religious experiment and about its subsequent failures that '*Religion* brought forth *Prosperity*, and the *daughter* destroyed the *mother*.'

The atmosphere of freedom which allowed differences of opinion to flourish had led in the 1630s to the founding of Rhode Island as 'a settlement for persons distressed for conscience', such as Baptists and Quakers, and to the establishment of a new colony of Maryland north of Virginia, where Roman Catholics were tolerated. Then in 1681 King Charles II of England granted to the Quaker William Penn, in settlement of a debt, the vast tract of land north of Maryland and south of New England which became Pennsylvania, and there its charter of 1701 established that no-one was 'at any time to be compelled to frequent or maintain any religious worship, place or ministry whatever, contrary to his or her mind.' The foundations were being laid for the wide variety of religious practice which was to be the pattern in America.

The desire for freedom led inexorably to the Declaration of Independence of 1776, with its resounding assertion that all men are born equal, with a right to 'life, liberty and the pursuit of happiness', and thence to rebellion against the British crown and to a war which was successfully concluded in 1782. When the constitution of the newly independent United States of America was drawn up in 1787, it provided that 'no religious test shall ever be required as a qualification to any office or public trust', and the first amendment to the constitution, passed by the House of Representatives in 1789, declared that 'Congress shall make no law respecting an establishment of religion, or prohibiting the free exercise thereof.' At first sight these measures may appear to be opposed to religion. Not so. They were an assertion that freedom and religious faith are compatible, and they were based on an assumption that freely chosen religious faith would underpin democratic institutions and a society with high moral standards.

The Great Awakening

The principal denominations of the colonial years were the Anglicans, the Presbyterians and the Congregationalists, but other denominations were free to establish themselves and develop, and the Baptists and Methodists flourished as new immigrants opened up the West. As the colonies of the eastern seaboard developed and the population grew, new immigrants set off westwards to find land for themselves and farm it. At first there was little or no organized religion in these new lands, life was hard and in the early eighteenth century religion appeared to be in decline. But then in the 1740s came what is known as the Great Awakening, a religious revival spread by word of mouth which was little to do with doctrine but much to do with living a simple and holy life.

A Congregationalist minister in Massachusetts, Jonathan Edwards, was influenced by what he heard, and was renowned in his own time for his impressive and influential preaching. But his long-term importance lies in his work as a theologian who re-thought the Calvinist doctrine of predestination. He shifted the emphasis in his sermons from God's anger towards sinful men to the idea that God's love radiated such goodness and beauty that even 'persons of mean capabilities and advantages' could love beauty in all its varied forms and, loving beauty, could worship the God of Love. His sermons were published and widely disseminated, and meanwhile numerous preachers told their congregations that God's saving grace was open to all and called on them to be converted and 'new born' to a life in Christ – and increasingly the preachers were Baptist and Methodist ministers.

The principal theological idea that the Baptists clung to was that a person had to 'come to faith' as an adult before being baptized. The distinctive theological position of the Methodists was that God offered salvation to all, but it was up to each individual to accept it. These ideas combined as Americans pushed westwards, and there were recurrent bursts of revivalist fervor. The rigidities of Calvinist doctrine were less well suited to this environment than was the fervor of Baptists and Methodist preachers, who, in a wild and violent society, exhorted men to repent, praise the Lord, give thanks for His goodness and the gift of salvation, support their neighbours when in need and ask for God's blessing and protection. There was usually little theological content to the preaching, and the emphasis on personal salvation was accompanied by a neglect of those issues raised in the gospels to do with wealth and poverty and the use and abuse of power. It ignored the ways in which faith might be expected to bear fruit in society, and meanwhile a society was being created in which men and women worshipped their Lord and Saviour, while some killed native Americans to make way for farms, railways and mines, others exploited black slaves to grow cotton, and most adopted the values of consumerism.

'Red Indians'

When the constitution was drawn up, with its magnificent assertion about the equality of all humankind, two great problems

242

remained unresolved. One was how native Americans should be treated. The other related to the use of 'negroes' imported from Africa as slaves. The wording of the constitution inevitably led some Christians to seek a resolution of both problems, for the moral issues raised were disturbing. But the practical difficulties were great. In the case of the native Americans the issue was postponed while the West was opened up. In the case of slavery it would have been impossible to get the agreement of the southern states to join the Union if the issue had been faced head on, so it was avoided.

Back in the early seventeenth century there had been some idea of spreading Christianity to those thought of as 'Red Indians', but the native American people were used to a nomadic life roaming the prairie and hunting buffalo. They had their own families, valued their tribal and religious traditions, and could not accept the widespread belief of white men that it was possible to 'own' land. They saw the arrival of white settlers as a threat, and the settlers did little to understand them and their way of life. To the settlers their own drive westwards was justified by the Calvinist idea that God was working his purpose out in history and had provided 'God's own people' with a 'manifest destiny' to colonize the American continent from the Atlantic to the Pacific. In the nineteenth century, as more and more Americans went west to find land and farm it, they often found 'Red Indians' in the way, so they killed most of them and confined the rest in reservations. Understandably the native Americans did not find the white man's religion attractive.

It was not until the twentieth century, in 1907, that the tract of land north of Texas known as 'Indian Territory' was incorporated into the Union as the state of Oklahoma. Then in 1920 'Red Indians' were at last recognized as American citizens, and from the 1960s onwards they were referred to as 'Native Americans.' Only then did a Native American Church begin to emerge.

'Negro' slaves

The story of the relationship between the settlers and the black men and women who were imported into America as slaves is similarly sad, but entirely different. As early as 1619 Sir George Yeardley, the governor of the new fragile colony of Virginia, bought from a Dutch ship twenty 'negroes' to be 'indentured servants' on his tobacco plantation, and thus began the 'peculiar institution' of slavery in the southern colonies. For the next two and a half centuries the south somehow combined the development of democracy and the operation of democratic institutions for white men with the keeping of black slaves. Thomas Jefferson, the chief author of the Declaration of Independence and later President of the Union, wrote, when considering the position of slaves in America, that he trembled for his country when he reflected that 'God is just.' But he kept slaves himself and he could see no solution to the problem.

In 1808 Congress, the legislative body of the Union, declared illegal the importation of slaves into the U.S.A. But it had little authority over the internal affairs of the various states, and the economy of the South was by then dependent on slaves for the production of cotton. The churches of the North were opposed to slavery, but the churches of the South defended it. So, with the rare exception of the Episcopal Church, they split. The Christian church in America came to be divided in three ways: into different denominations, into separate black and white congregations, and between North and South.

By the early nineteenth century there were millions of slaves who had been imported from Africa to work on the cotton plantations of the South. Their tribal and family attachments, their languages and culture were destroyed. The Christianity of their masters was imposed on them. The Baptist and Methodist churches of the South justified slavery by reference to the Bible, and ministers regularly reminded the slaves of St Paul's exhortation that slaves should obey their masters as if they were serving Christ himself (*Ephesians 6.5*).

But black congregations often interpreted the Bible differently. They heard of the deliverance of the Children of Israel from the bondage in Egypt described in the *Book of Exodus*, and they heard the good news of a new deliverance from bondage by Jesus's death upon the cross. They found comfort in the music and words

244

of so-called 'negro spirituals' in which, for example, Moses could 'tell ol' Pharaoh to let my people go', and they placed their own interpretation on St Paul's assertion that there was no longer 'Jew nor Greek, slave nor free, male nor female – you are all one in Christ Jesus' (*Galatians 3.28*).

Things came to a head over the issue of extending slavery into the new lands to the west. The great principle on which everyone was agreed was Liberty. The North justified its opposition to the extension of slavery westwards by appealing to the principle of Liberty. The South appealed to the same principle to justify its right to secede from the Union. In 1863, in the middle of the American Civil War of 1861-65, in which there was terrible suffering and loss of life on both sides, all slaves in the U.S.A. were at last freed. It was the most important step since independence towards the ideal of a society in which everyone was free. But it was to be another century before the black population had civil rights on the same terms as white people. Meanwhile Americans lived with the problems left over from the war. President Abraham Lincoln called for reconciliation, but he was assassinated in 1865. The North, having won the war, neglected the South. Its economy fell apart, the abolition of slavery was followed by a century of racism in the southern states, and legislation ensured discrimination against 'niggers', who found it difficult to get an education, or be enrolled as voters, or to use facilities which were reserved for 'Whites Only.'

Religious diversity

Meanwhile religious life in America grew ever more diverse. Every brand of Christianity in Europe was imported into the U.S.A. Many Jews and some Muslims came as well, and numerous new Christian, semi-Christian and non-Christian groups were founded.

The Disciples of Christ developed on the frontier in the early nineteenth century, hoping for the unity of all believers and wanting everyone to read the New Testament 'as if no mortal man had seen it before.' In practice they turned into another denomination, and one of the largest in the U.S.A.

The Church of Jesus Christ of Latter-Day Saints, founded in 1827 and better known as the *Mormons*, sought to create an ideal society on earth, grew by a combination of effective communal farming and the practice of polygamy, and settled in the western territory of Utah, which became one of the states of the union in 1896 after the Mormons had abandoned polygamy.

The Adventists, who in the 1840s looked for the second coming, or advent, of Christ, decided that the delay was God's punishment for failing to worship him on the Sabbath, so they became *Seventh Day Adventists*.

Christian Scientists, established from 1863 onwards in Boston, saw God as the only reality and taught that illness and pain are illusions which a person has to recognize as such in order to be healed.

Zion's Watch Tower Society, founded in 1884, also looked for the imminent second coming of Christ and from the 1930s took to calling themselves *Jehovah's Witnesses* to distance themselves from Trinitarian Christianity.

Unitarianism also developed in the nineteenth century. Its roots were in the rationalism of the eighteenth century, and Unitarians taught that men and women were too good to be damned. So they threw off the heritage of Calvinist predestination and at the same time discarded the doctrine of the Trinity and sought salvation through Reason.

Universalism was, in a sense, an extension of the Methodist view that salvation is open to all and that God wills all men to be saved. While Unitarians thought humankind too good to be damned, Universalists thought God too good to damn them. The Unitarians, generally well educated town-dwellers on the eastern seaboard, and the Universalists, more often poorly educated country folk, had reached much the same conclusions while travelling by different routes in different social conditions. Unsurprisingly the two groups tended to merge.

Roman Catholicism and Fundamentalism

At the same time the number of Roman Catholics was growing. During the War of Independence of 1776 – 82 there were no more than 25,000 Catholics in the U.S.A. But the Irish potato famine of 1845-6, widespread European poverty and the failure of the 1848 revolutions in Europe produced an influx of Irish, Italian and German Catholics, and others from central Europe. Many settled in towns on the eastern seaboard, such as Boston and New York, where they had to cope with anti-Catholic propaganda, anti-Catholic riots and the Protestant prejudice that they were all dirty, superstitious, criminal and idle. But the Catholic church was well organized, and its leaders were soon vigorously involved in American political life. They supported the Union's foreign policy and did all they could to ensure that Catholics were at home with the democratic institutions of the New World. By the time of the outbreak of the civil war in 1861 they were the largest single denomination in the U.S.A. There was also a strong progressive element in American Catholicism. Just as the social and political climate of America had produced a less harsh version of Calvinism, so it also produced a less authoritarian version of Catholicism.

But some Protestants saw their ideal of a free Protestant society threatened by Catholic immigration, and the strength and apparent unity of Roman Catholicism, combined with the disintegration of Protestantism into numberless sects, decided some Protestants who thought of themselves as 'evangelicals' to seek their own form of unity. In 1895 they met at a Bible Conference at Niagara and drew up a statement of what they saw as the 'five fundamentals of the Christian religion': the Bible is the Word of God and cannot err; Jesus is God; he was born of a virgin; he suffered and was punished on the cross as a substitute for sinful mankind; Christians should expect his imminent return in glory to bring about the bodily resurrection of those of the dead who have been saved. Those were the 'fundamentals'; anyone who did not assent to them was not a true Christian.

The term 'fundamentalist' came in time to be associated with a range of other beliefs, and in particular with the idea that every word of the Bible was literally true. Few Christians who actually read the Bible believe that, but just as the Roman church sought to draw a line between those who can and cannot count as

Christian, so did the evangelicals. Similarly, just as many American Roman Catholics, including priests and even bishops, did not accept all the teachings and practices which the pope tried to impose on them, many, even most, Protestants did not accept all the teachings which evangelical 'fundamentalists' tried to impose on them. There can have been no society on earth where the diversity of religious belief was so great, while at the same time there was a substantial measure of social cohesion.

Religion and Democracy

The social cohesion did not extend to relations between black and white members of society. Discrimination against black people continued and was made worse by theories apparently justifying racial segregation which developed towards the end of the nineteenth century in the wake of the publication in 1859 of *The Origin of Species by means of Natural Selection* by an Englishman, Charles Darwin. It was in the light of those theories, which arose out of a mistaken understanding of Darwin's ideas, that in 1894 a judgement in the United States Supreme Court allowed for 'separate but equal' facilities for blacks, with the consequence that even in the North churches which had condemned slavery and rejoiced in its abolition nevertheless adopted segregationist policies and separated black and white congregations.

It was not until 1955 that a civil rights movement began, aiming to end segregation. Before long it was led by the black Baptist minister, Martin Luther King, who advocated peaceful protest and in 1963 told the American people in an oration which echoed round the world that he had a dream of a future in which his children would 'be judged not by the color of their skins but by their character.' This was followed by the passing of the Civil Rights Acts of 1964, which gave the black population the same civil rights as white people. It was also followed by the assassination of Martin Luther King in 1968.

For all the divisions of the American churches, and for all the prejudice in American society, which often extended not only to 'niggers' and 'red Indians' but also, for example, to Catholics, Jews, Irish, Poles and Hispanics, there was almost universal recognition of the importance of morality, democracy and religion, and since 1865 the currency of the USA had proclaimed to all that *In God We Trust*. The President through most of the 1950s, Dwight D. Eisenhower, summed up a widespread view when he said, 'Our government makes no sense unless it is founded on a deeply felt religious faith – and I don't care what it is.' Like many Americans he cared that the U.S.A. should be a decent society in which people generally behaved well towards each other without intrusive control by the forces of government.

Progress towards a more just and fair society and towards an intellectually respectable Christian Church was slow. But not all American religion was either irrational or emotional or both. As early as the eighteenth century many Christians on the more settled eastern seaboard had found distasteful what they saw as the crude emotionalism of uneducated preachers. They preferred a calmer and more intellectual approach to religion, which in time led to what is described as 'liberalism' – something which, as its name implies, fits well with the American attachment to Liberty and was increasingly influential.

'Creationism'

An important area where the evangelical 'fundamentalists' and the 'liberals' were at loggerheads was over the teaching in schools about how various forms of life came into existence. Darwin, in *The Origin of Species,* had revealed a process which did not need the direct intervention of a Creator. If an animal could run faster, reach higher or even co-operate better than most of its fellows, that gave it an advantage which, in particular circumstances, enabled it to survive and breed and thus pass on its distinctive characteristics to its descendants. Thus all living creatures evolved. Some species became extinct. New species came into existence. There was no need for 'intelligent design'.

That was seen as particularly objectionable in the southern states of the United States, where a literal interpretation on the Bible was widespread and where it was believed that the world and everything in it was created in six days. But opposition to 'Darwinism' also arose from the fact that the idea of 'the survival of the fittest' was widely seen as a justification for oppression. Some businessmen saw it as an excuse for exploiting their workers. Karl Marx saw it as the biological counterpart to class struggle and wanted to dedicate the English edition of *Capital* to Darwin. The German General Staff of 1914 saw war as a 'biological necessity' and believed that the German *Herrenvolk* would defeat all lesser peoples and come to dominate the world. That was a long way from Darwin's view that some species developed and survived because they were particularly colourful or small or co-operative.

In a climate of biblical fundamentalism and understandable distaste for what was seen as 'Darwinism' several of the southern states passed laws in the early 1920s requiring 'Creationism' rather than 'Darwinism' to be taught in their schools. In reaction the American Civil Liberties Union in 1925 provoked the trial in Tennessee of a teacher who had taught about evolution. The intention was to appeal to a higher court against the inevitable guilty verdict and have the law declared unconstitutional. The lawyer and politician William Jennings Bryan, who had long been an advocate of popular causes on behalf of the poor, acted as prosecutor and inevitably won the case. In terms of the law of Tennessee the teacher was clearly guilty. But the conviction was quashed over a technicality of Tennessee law that the $100 fine should have been set by the jury rather than the judge, and the consequence was that it was impossible to challenge the law in a higher court. Thus the anti-evolutionary statutes remained part of the law of several southern states for decades. They were not enforced, but they remained a threat to any biology teacher who was inclined to step out of line. The issue was only settled in 1988, when a judgement of the Supreme Court of the U.S.A. declared it to be a violation of the first amendment to the constitution to require the teaching of 'Creationism' in schools.

The 'religious right'

Meanwhile many American films and television programmes in the second half of the twentieth century gave the impression of a society dominated by corruption, crime and consumerism. The ideal of Liberty had apparently degenerated into license, and fear of a moral malaise at home and the threat of Communism from abroad produced the rise of the 'religious right.' In the so-called Baptist Bible Belt of the South evangelicals defended the constitutional right of citizens to carry guns, opposed public expenditure on health care, and advocated avoiding sex education, which was seen as leading to undesirable sexual freedom. They found that they had quite a lot in common with conservative Roman Catholics, who shared their opposition to abortion, homosexuality and any scientific research which involved human embryos. This sharing of ideas created what came to be described as a 'Christian Coalition', which did much to help right-wing politicians to power. Evangelical preachers on prime time television attacked pornography, feminism, drug use and the high rate of divorce and called for conversions and cash donations. The audiences were numbered in millions; their cash donations ran into hundreds of millions of dollars. But a succession of financial and sexual scandals brought television evangelism into disrepute, and most Americans were better educated and more sensible than the television evangelists seemed to assume.

'One nation under God'

For all the prejudice and violence which had stained American history, the achievements of the long-standing alliance of religion, liberty and commercial enterprise had been so great that through much of the world the U.S.A. was seen as a land of freedom and opportunity. Prejudice was in retreat. In 1960 the Americans elected an Irish American Catholic, John F. Kennedy, as President. In 2008 they elected as President a man of mixed race: Barack Hussein Obama. American universities led the world of scholarship, and more and more young Americans were receiving a good quality education. Scientists and theologians discussed with each other the relationship between science and religion. Biblical criticism and theology flourished, and from the Union Theological Seminary in New York had come the work of Reinhold Niebuhr and Paul Tillich. Before the end of the century the small but influential Episcopal Church had elected both a woman and a homosexual as bishops. The range of religious beliefs in the United States was vast. But 'middle America' was an altogether pleasanter place than the picture so often presented on films and television, and above all Americans could discuss religious and moral issues in a climate of freedom. Christians and Jews, Muslims and Hindus, agnostics and even atheists knew that they lived in 'one nation under God', and that the supreme characteristic of American religion was a common belief in the importance of toleration and democracy.

Chapter 19

The Dark Night of the European Churches

Protestant success

By the twentieth century Protestantism was successful in much of the world. It had spread though the multifarious colonies and self-governing dominions of the British Empire. In the U.S.A., which had fulfilled its 'manifest destiny' to conquer the West, Protestantism was still the predominant religious force, though it took many different forms. In the recently united German Empire Lutheranism was the principal religion. It was also the state religion of each of the Scandinavian kingdoms. All these nations, British, American, German and Scandinavian, were engaged in world-wide missionary activity, much of it evangelical and non-denominational. Protestantism, together with the Protestant work ethic, seemed to have produced material success. It had also produced a sense of moral superiority to the rest of mankind.

The Papacy against Modernism

The Roman Catholic church, on the other hand, was on the defensive. The policy of opposition to all things modern which had been set out by Pius IX in the *Syllabus of Errors* of 1864 continued and, if anything, intensified with the election of Pius X in 1903. The pope continued to live as 'the prisoner in the Vatican', though in practice he was far less cut off from the world than it appeared. Instead of adopting the position that its kingdom was 'not of this world', the papacy engaged in one country after another, such as Italy, France and Germany, in political activity to support the forces of conservatism with the aim of maintaining the institution of the Roman Catholic Church and in particular the papacy. The church, which had begun as the means for spreading the Kingdom of Heaven on earth, had somehow become the end. Instead of existing to transform the world through 'faith and hope and love' (*1 Corinthians 13.13*), it was now more and more involved in manipulating the world in order to save itself. There was, in a sense, an institutional loss of faith.

Pius X opposed Liberalism, Socialism, Republicanism and Democracy. He saw Protestantism as a step towards atheism. He was devoted to relics and the cults of the saints and was obscurantist in his approach to science and other aspects of modern scholarship. He particularly feared biblical criticism and, even more, ecclesiastical history, since among Catholic scholars it was particularly the ecclesiastical historians who had been opposed to the promulgation of the Doctrine of Papal Infallibility. He appeared paranoid about the idea of a great international conspiracy to destroy the papacy and the Catholic Church. His condemnation of all things modern was followed by persecution of clergy and scholars whose views were suspect. Bishops, priests and teachers had to take an anti-modernist oath. Anyone who did not conform suffered penalties ranging from obscurity to excommunication. Information was lodged against suspects, who often knew nothing of what they were charged with and whose careers were unaccountably blighted. One young seminarian of the time, Angelo Roncalli, survived the anti-modernist terror and rose to be the patriarch of Venice, but he was only able to see the information lodged against him in his Holy Office file when he was elected pope in 1958.

Roman Catholicism world-wide

Nevertheless in the early twentieth century there were millions of pious and faithful Catholics throughout the world who accepted the authority of the pope and were devoted to the institution of the papacy. Priests celebrated the eucharist, which was generally referred to in the Roman communion as Mass, and they cared for their parishioners. Many members of the ruling class in countries such as France and Italy were still loyal Catholics. So were millions of the poor and illiterate, whether in Ireland or Spain, Latin America, the Philippines or Indo-China, and there were substantial numbers of Catholics scattered through the Protestant nations of the world. For the Irish Roman Catholicism was a badge of defiance of their Protestant English rulers. For the Poles Roman Catholicism was a badge of defiance of their Orthodox Russian rulers. The Roman Catholic Church was clearly now the poor relation of its prosperous Protestant brethren, but increasingly and in many areas of the world it was seen as being on the side of the poor and the oppressed.

One area where Roman Catholicism was deeply embedded was Latin America, and there a significant change was taking place. In the early nineteenth century a series of rebellions against Spanish power had established a number of independent republics. There were eventually eighteen Latin American Spanish-speaking republics, each of them usually ruled by a military strong-man, or *caudillo*. Government was authoritative and conservative, strongly influenced by the 'sacred triangle' of the great landowners, the army leaders and the hierarchy of the Roman Catholic Church. But the clergy were no longer all members of the Spanish or Portuguese ruling elite. Many poor priests identified with ordinary people; some had even led rebellions. Things were not so very different from Western Europe in the later Middle Ages.

The Orthodox Church

Meanwhile the Orthodox Church remained largely cut off from the rest of Christendom. It inhabited a world which was strange and unintelligible to Protestant and Catholic alike. But as Turkish rule was driven back in the Balkans during the nineteenth century, independent states emerged with populations which were predominantly Orthodox: Serbia, Greece, Romania and Bulgaria. Constantinople, however, the Second Rome, now known as Istanbul, remained under Turkish rule, so by the early twentieth century the focal point of the Orthodox world was in Russia.

Moscow had adopted the status of the Third Rome when the patriarchate of Moscow was established in 1589. But early in the eighteenth century Tsar Peter the Great, as part of his policy of Westernisation, imposed his own authority over the church, which henceforth had less control over its own affairs than the Orthodox churches had within the territory ruled by the Ottoman Turks. The church remained an important element in the lives of Russian people. Traditional and unchanging theological ideas and a rich liturgy of ceremony and music which could be remembered by illiterate peasants came to be embedded in the lives of millions of people. A tradition of spirituality survived, particularly in monasteries. One element in that was the regular repetition of the so-called Jesus Prayer, 'Lord Jesus Christ, Son of God, be merciful to me a sinner.' That produced a controversy in the early twentieth century which in a small way was not unlike the iconoclast controversy of the eighth and ninth centuries. Russian monks who were devotees of the Jesus Prayer and lived in monasteries on Mount Athos in northeast Greece, argued that the name of Jesus was divine and that perpetual invocation of it led to communion with God. This *onamatoxy*, or praise of the name, was condemned as *onamatolatry*, or idolisation of the name, first by the patriarch of Constantinople and then by the Holy Synod in St Petersburg. The argument dragged on and in 1913 was settled, as so often in the past, by force. The Tsar's government sent a gunboat to Mount Athos and deported some hundreds of Russian monks guilty of *onamatolatry* back to Russia.

Christian civilisation

The Christian churches, whether Protestant, Catholic or Orthodox, had all in some measure entered into the inheritance of what might be called Christian civilisation. Many of the greatest buildings in the world, whether Classical, Byzantine, Gothic or Baroque, were Christian churches. Much of the greatest painting in the world had been created to decorate churches or teach lessons to the unlettered faithful. Much of the greatest music in the world had been written for performance in the liturgy. Many of the greatest scientific advances were made by clergymen, and the intellectual life of Christendom was permeated with nearly two thousand years of Christian thinking. There also remained a widespread moral consensus rooted in the teachings of the Old Testament and the New. The English grew up to believe in decency and the obligation to serve others. Germans grew up to believe in duty and honour. Both admired the ancient world of Greece and Rome, and Christianity was intermingled with their national traditions. After centuries of conflict a synthesis of Barbarism with Graeco-Roman civilisation and Christianity had apparently been achieved.

Reversion to barbarism

Then in 1914, when the European peoples were within reach of conquering the world and missionaries looked forward to converting all the peoples of the world, the Christian civilisation of Europe split apart. A war began between the dominant tribes of Europe, which by now thought of themselves as nation states. It began as a European civil war, came to involve countries beyond Europe, and lasted from 1914 until 1945. Some aspects of it dragged on even longer.

It began as a struggle for power. Religion was irrelevant. On one side were ranged the predominantly Protestant German Empire, Catholic Austria-Hungary and the Muslim empire of the Ottoman Turks. On the other side was France, an anti-clerical republic with a substantial Catholic element in its population, the Orthodox empire of the Russian tsar and Great Britain, a union of Anglican England, Presbyterian Scotland, Methodist Wales and Catholic Ireland. The war was brutal. It was a denial of all that Christianity purported to represent, and yet from the start the leaders of the Christian churches in all nations entered into it with enthusiasm. The fighting on Germany's Eastern front resulted in the defeat of Russia, and a civil war within Russia ended in 1921 in victory for the overtly anti-Christian Bolsheviks, who were usually known in the West as Communists. The following year saw the seizure of power in Italy by an extreme nationalist group, the Fascists, and just over ten years later an even more extreme nationalist group, the National Socialists, or Nazis, came to power in Germany. Fighting began again in 1939 after what was in effect a twenty-year armistice, and the European tribes took to slaughtering each other again. The killing was on an even vaster scale than in the first round from 1914-18. It spread through the world and eventually ended with the saturation bombing, or systematic destruction, of German cities and the destruction of two Japanese cities by atomic bombs. Europe had demonstrated to the world how relatively shallow and vulnerable its Christian civilisation was.

Bolshevism and Orthodoxy

Early in 1917 Russia's failures in its war against Germany had led to the overthrow of the tsar and the establishment of a provisional democratic government. On 4th November the patriarchate of Moscow, suspended two centuries earlier by Peter the Great, was restored and very briefly the Russian Orthodox church glimpsed a bright future. But three days later the Bolsheviks seized power and the church suffered persecution on a scale which makes the persecution of Christians by Roman emperors pale into insignificance. The Bolsheviks took from the church its property and its freedom, and under the rule of Stalin, from the 1920s until 1953, restrictions, imprisonments and executions were used to ensure that the young were dissuaded from membership and that the church would gradually fade and die as the elderly died off. The Orthodox church, no stranger to tyranny, took refuge in the liturgy and in quiet spirituality. When the Bolshevik Empire collapsed towards the end of the century, the Orthodox church emerged remarkably strong after seventy years of persecution and with a continuing appeal to many Russians.

Fascism, Nazism and the Papacy

Bolshevism, of course, was overtly anti-Christian, and Pius XI, who was elected pope in 1922, a few months before the Fascists seized power in Italy, feared both Bolshevism and Socialism. His aim was to ensure the survival of a civil society which would provide support for the institution of the papacy and the Roman Catholic Church. He judged that Mussolini and the Fascists would do that and events proved him right. In 1929 he was able to agree the Lateran Treaty with Mussolini, who described him as 'a good Italian.' Mussolini agreed to establish the small territory of the Vatican City in Rome as an independent state, recognised Roman Catholicism as the official religion of Italy, and agreed that the state would enforce church laws on matters such as marriage. Pius XI recognised the united Italian kingdom and declared that Fascism, unlike Liberalism and Socialism, was compatible with Christianity.

He was anxious to reach a similar accommodation with Hitler as soon as the Nazis came to power in Germany in 1933, and he agreed a concordat with Hitler in the same year. Hitler had already begun an attack on the Catholic church, confiscating its property, destroying Catholic political parties and trade unions and dismissing Catholic civil servants. The pope accepted all that. He feared the complete destruction of the Catholic church in Germany and was prepared to agree to almost anything if the church was allowed to survive in principle. In 1937 he issued the encyclical *Mit brennender Sorge* ('With burning pity'), which criticised Nazi ideology as well as breaches of the concordat. But it had little effect. His successor, Pius XII, who was elected in 1939, was also anxious to establish good relations with Hitler, saw him as a bulwark against Bolshevism, and only condemned Nazism unequivocally in June 1945, once the war in Europe was over, Germany was defeated and Hitler was dead.

Nazism and the German churches

The Protestant churches in Germany had overall a similarly poor record in their response to Nazism. The Lutherans were used to being a state church, and their establishment in the sixteenth century was rooted in the idea that in each small German state a Godly Prince had an obligation to ensure reform. They had no tradition of opposition to lay authority and expected church and state to stand together. Large numbers of them, as well as large numbers of German Calvinists of the *Evangelische Kirche*, sought to accommodate their Christianity to Nazism. Hitler was widely seen as the incarnation of Germany, a modern saviour who would purge both Germany and Christianity of Judaism, and for many people the swastika replaced the cross as their preferred symbol of faith. Church synods passed anti-Jewish legislation and German Protestants for the most part supported Hitler with fervent nationalism, while he increasingly treated them as a contemptible irrelevance.

Many Catholics, anxious not to be outdone by the Protestants in patriotic fervour, competed in their zeal to support the Nazi party, and the hierarchy of the church required faithful Catholics to obey the lawful authority of the Nazi government. The churches, Protestant and Catholic alike, celebrated Hitler's birthday as if it were a church festival, and they encouraged the faithful to fight for the Fatherland. The churches were also, as it happens, the largest landowners in Germany after the state, so they benefited materially by being recognised by the Nazi government as state churches and getting from the state subsidies which were provided out of public taxation. Hitler took the view that they would accept anything 'in order to keep their material advantages.' That may or may not have been true, but what is clearly true is that most Germans genuinely and enthusiastically supported the Nazi government. German nationalism simply mattered more to them than did their Christian faith.

The war exposed the weakness of German Christianity. Most German Christians, whether Catholic or Protestant, professed a belief in the traditional teachings of the church. They knew that Jesus 'was conceived by the Holy Ghost, born of the Virgin Mary, suffered under Pontius Pilate', and so on. Believing that, they still went enthusiastically to war. They exterminated Jews in what is called the Holocaust. They killed people who were sick and no use to society, and others, such as gypsies and homosexuals. They enslaved their neighbours in the service of the German war machine. The exterminations, the enslavements and the killing in war all ran into millions. The nation of Martin Luther, of Bach and Brahms, Goethe and Schiller, Kant and Schopenhauer had reverted to barbarism on a scale the world had never seen before.

The most significant exception to this sad story of apostasy was the so-called Confessing Church, one of whose leaders,

Martin Niemöller, had been a successful German U-boat commander in 1914-18. It was a hesitant and uncertain opposition. But at least there were many Protestant pastors and Catholic priests who refused to co-operate with the Nazi regime and for varying periods were imprisoned or held in concentration camps as a consequence. After the war Niemöller made a statement in which he declined to claim innocence for himself or his colleagues: 'First they came for the Communists, but I was not a Communist, so I said nothing. Then they came for the Social Democrats, but I was not a Social Democrat, so I did nothing. Then they came for the trade unionists, but I was not a trade unionist. And then they came for the Jews, but I was not a Jew, so I did little. Then, when they came for me, there was no-one left to stand up for me.'

The weakness of the Christian churches

If Christianity was only skin-deep in Germany, it is questionable if it was any more deep-rooted in the other nations of Europe. The Catholic Croats took the opportunity to slaughter 350,000 Orthodox Serbs. The French, defeated in war in 1940, had to choose between making the best of things and collaborating with their former enemies, or continuing to fight, whether from abroad or in the so-called Underground. Many collaborated, and at the end of the war France was left with a national sense of shame which would take many years to overcome. The British had gone to war in 1914 with enthusiasm and an unjustified sense of self-righteousness. They went to war in 1939 without enthusiasm and a continuing sense of self-righteousness. The Christian churches generally went along with the national mood. Christian ministers served as chaplains with the armed forces, giving comfort to the fearful, the bereaved and the dying. But there was little questioning by the church either of the purpose of fighting in 1914-18 or the means used to pursue victory in the fighting of 1939-45.

Again there were exceptions. In the war of 1939-45 the Anglican Bishop of Chichester, George Bell, argued against both saturation bombing of German towns and the demand for unconditional surrender. He had thought carefully and clearly about the proper Christian approach to war. He was not denying the necessity to fight a just war. He was asserting the need for Christian conduct even in such circumstances. The bombing of civilian populations, whether to inflict reprisals or to break their morale, was wrong. It was wrong to cultivate an atmosphere of hatred. It was necessary to prepare for forgiveness and reconciliation. But his was a voice crying in the wilderness of a world in which the Christian churches had very largely failed. In Germany they needed to stand up to evil. Few did. In Great Britain they needed to face evil without hatred for its perpetrators and without pride. Few managed that.

Asia and Africa

The great European Civil War of 1914-45 destroyed any illusions the peoples of the rest of the world may have had of Europe being the centre of civilisation and the heart of Christendom. Civilisation and brotherly love were overwhelmed by trench warfare, revolution, saturation bombing, gas chambers and the use of atomic bombs. The peoples of Asia and Africa felt justified in breaking free from European rule, and they also saw the opportunity to do so. The Asian countries very largely had their own cultures and well-established religions: Hinduism, Islam and Buddhism, and although Christianity survived in parts of Asia, there was no longer an expectation that it would take over.

In Africa, on the other hand, Christianity had taken root. There was a particular problem in South Africa, which had been colonised by Dutch farmers, or *Boers*, whose descendants were mostly members of the Dutch Reformed Church. By the middle of the twentieth century three and a half million whites were outnumbered by fifteen million blacks, two million people of mixed race and half a million Asians. Only the whites were allowed to vote in elections, and in the election of 1948 the Nationalist Party came to power, imposed a policy of racial separation which was known as *apartheid,* and enshrined it in law. *Apartheid* was supported by the Dutch Reformed Church on the grounds that God had created the various races and intended them to be 'separate but equal.' It lasted until 1994, giving offence not only to the subject peoples of South Africa but throughout the world. It was widely expected to lead to large-scale bloodshed, but when the transition to black majority rule eventually came, it was managed by the black Methodist political leader, Nelson Mandela, and by the black Anglican Archbishop of Cape Town, Desmond Tutu, in a fashion which had something to teach the West about forgiveness and reconciliation.

In most of the continent, as the European colonies gained their independence, the Christian churches grew at an extraordinary rate and sometimes in extraordinary ways. In 1900 there may have been as many as nine million Christians in Africa. By 2000, despite a move to 'drive the white man's God out of Africa', there were about 380,000,000 – more than in either Latin America or Europe, and they were spread over as many as eleven thousand sects. If Africans were to follow Jesus, they would follow him in their own way and with new insights. Meanwhile the traumas of the twentieth century may have taught the European churches to exercise a measure of humility in dealing with their fellow-Christians in other parts of the world, and by the end of the century, as European material prosperity soared and European culture slid into self-satisfied, self-indulgent, post-Christian, hedonistic materialism, Europe began to look ripe for conversion not only by Christians from the U.S.A. but also by the churches of Africa and Asia. It was arguable that black African bishops of the Anglican communion could teach the English something, just as Latin American priests of the Roman communion could teach Rome something.

New forces in Christianity

At the same time two powerful Christian movements reached out to the poor of the world and flourished. One was the Evangelicals, who, as their name implies, concentrated on evangelism. The other was the Pentecostalists, whose emphasis, again as their name implies, was on the power of the Holy Spirit. Neither was a denomination in the sense in which that term is used of Baptists, Methodists and members of the United Reformed Church. Both movements cut across denominations. Evangelicalism was now something far wider than a somewhat fundamentalist movement within the Church of England. All through the world Evangelicals encouraged a yearning for simple, correct solutions to all problems. They held up the Bible and its interpretation, often by fundamentalist preachers, as the source of all answers. Meanwhile the Pentecostalists relied on the guidance of the Holy Spirit, usually expressed through emotion generated at revivalist meetings. Pentecostalism, which can also be thought of as the charismatic movement, was different from Evangelicalism, but the two things were related, and both were usually but not always fundamentalist.

Neither of these powerful and related movements should be thought of as Protestant in the conventional sense. The European quarrels of the sixteenth century about doctrine and the organisation of the church were irrelevant to them. The one sense in which they were Protestant was that they were clearly neither Roman Catholic nor Orthodox. Moved by the power of the Word of God or by the power of the Holy Spirit, or both, they sought to bring Jesus into the lives of the poor and the oppressed, and they were increasingly influential in the late twentieth century. Their strength lay partly in their interdenominational or non-denominational nature, and partly in their absolute assurance that they were right about everything – led as they were to the truth, either by the infallible words of Scripture, or by the infallible guidance of the Holy Spirit, or both. Their weakness was the lack of any central authority such as the papacy to speak authoritatively about the right solution to all problems of faith and morals.

The traditional churches

Meanwhile the papacy continued as an autocratic monarchy under Pope Pius XII (1939-58). He saw the Orthodox churches as schismatic, and he regarded Protestants as heretics. The Catholic Church, he asserted, was the universal church: it had always been, was still, and would always be the sole repository of truth on matters of faith and morals. It remained a sad consequence of the evil in the hearts of men, whether Orthodox or Protestant, Marxist or Agnostic, Hindu, Muslim or Buddhist, that they had not yet submitted to the divine authority of the Holy Father.

Then in 1958 Angelo Roncalli, patriarch of Venice, was elected pope at the age of seventy-six, and took the name John XXIII. He was supported by most of the more conservative cardinals and seen as a stopgap who would not do anything radical. But it could yet turn out to be one of the great turning points in the history of the church. He called the Second Vatican Council and suggested that Divine Providence was leading the church 'to a new order of human relations.' He rejected 'doctrinaire condemnation of error', preferring 'the medicine of mercy.' His successor, Paul VI (1963-78), took this new approach further. He spoke in terms of 'collegiality' rather than insisting on his own authority and he looked for reconciliation with other Christians, whether Orthodox or Protestant. Their two pontificates saw a revival within the Roman Catholic Church, and increasing respect and sympathy for the Roman church from other denominations. But demands among the faithful for progressive changes provoked conservative opposition and in many ways Paul VI was influenced more by the warnings of the conservatives than by the advice of the reformers. In 1967 he reasserted the requirement for clerical celibacy and in 1968 issued the encyclical *Humanae vitae* condemning artificial means of birth control.

Despite, or perhaps because of, the election of a Polish pope, John Paul II, in 1978, the leadership of the Roman Catholic Church remained conservative throughout the last two decades of the twentieth century. By the end of the century it had nearly a thousand million members and was the largest denomination of any religion in the world – though how many of them believed in the infallibility of the pope, understood the doctrine of transubstantiation or obeyed the papal teaching on contraception was another matter.

The Orthodox churches had a membership of more than a hundred and fifty million, nearly all of them in territories where Orthodoxy has survived for centuries. They had always, or almost always, been prepared to accept the primacy of Rome, but not its supremacy or the Doctrine of Papal Infallibility. They remained strongly opposed to the inclusion of the *filioque* clause in the Nicene Creed. The memory of how badly they were treated by the

Latin West survived, but despite that they remained committed to the Ecumenical Movement, which was seeking to bring the various churches together, and their relations with the traditional Protestant churches had become warmer.

It is more difficult to put a figure on Protestant numbers, not just in Africa and Asia, but also in Europe, where it was often no longer clear who was or was not a member of the church. The number of people attending services regularly on Sundays declined steadily and the Protestant churches were increasingly conscious that they were surviving in a largely non-Christian society. But many children were still baptised and many people thought of themselves as in some sense Christian, without having any connection with a particular Christian church. Meanwhile the churches were more tolerant of each other than in the past and more tolerant of other faiths. They prayed for unity but accepted diversity. Many of their members saw the danger of churchgoers being seen as a religious elite, a group of modern Pharisees, but they tried to avoid that and they still shared the conviction that faith in their crucified and risen Lord could lead them to transform their own lives and alter society for the better.

Chapter 20

The Dawn of a New Millennium

The divisions of Christendom

At the dawn of the third millennium the Christian Church can for convenience be divided into four main groups: Orthodox, Catholic, Protestant and Fundamentalist. The Orthodox churches had survived, guarding what they saw as 'correct belief' and attached to the liturgy and tradition of spirituality they had inherited from the past. The Catholic church had continued to spread through the world; but the liberalising movement, promised by the Second Vatican Council of 1962-5 and welcomed by Catholic laity, came to a halt in the Vatican, where the position on matters of faith, morals and church discipline was both conservative and authoritarian. The Protestant churches were divided into many different denominations, they were less self-confident than a hundred years earlier, and their membership had failed to keep up with population growth. Meanwhile the two fundamentalist movements which can loosely be described as evangelical and charismatic were flourishing and growing, both in the developed world, particularly in the U.S.A., and in Latin America and Africa. By the end of the twentieth century the Christian Church was growing in the wider world. In Europe it was divided and bruised. It had survived both paganism in its fascist form and atheism in its communist form. Materialism and cynical scepticism about what were seen as the comfortable certainties of the past were different, less dramatic, but more insidious problems.

The Ecumenical Movement

The very fact of Christian divisions was an incentive to seeking ways of coming together – if not in union, at least with understanding and friendship. Competition in missionary activity had gradually changed into co-operation and the World Missionary Conference at Edinburgh in 1910 was an important step towards Protestant and, in the long run, Christian unity. Warfare and the other upheavals of the twentieth century had divided the churches further, but the ecumenical movement, with its aim of Christian unity, continued, and in 1948 the World Council of Churches was formed. Twenty years earlier Pope Pius XI had condemned ecumenism and asserted that only a pope could summon an ecumenical council, and in 1948 the Orthodox churches also kept apart. But in 1961 the Orthodox churches joined the World Council of Churches and Pope John XXIII sent observers to its meeting at New Delhi in India. Relations began to improve in a range of ways. In 1965 Pope Paul VI and the Patriarch Athenagoras of Constantinople met and jointly deplored the schism of 1054. In 1982, roughly fourteen hundred years after Pope Gregory the Great conceived the idea of converting the Angles, Pope John Paul II became the first pope ever to visit England, and he even shared in worship in Canterbury Cathedral, where he embraced Michael Ramsey, the retired 100th Archbishop of Canterbury.

All over the world Christian churches tried to find ways of uniting. Sometimes, as when Anglicans, Methodists, Presbyterians and Congregationalists came together in the Church of South India in 1947, or when the English Congregationalists and Presbyterians came together as the United Reformed Church in 1972, or when the Anglican churches entered into communion with most of the Lutheran churches of Scandinavia and the Baltic in 1992, they were successful. But there were many failures, and the rate at which new sects came into existence always outstripped the movement towards unity.

Christianity on the defensive

Active Christians were a minority in many of the countries of Europe, and their churches were divided from each other largely for historical reasons, which were no longer of interest to most of their members. In England an individual might attend the local Anglican parish church, or the Roman Catholic, United Reformed, Baptist, Methodist or Unitarian church, or any of a range of new Christian groups or churches, either as a result of family upbringing or schooling, or the influence of friends or neighbours, the personality of a priest or minister, the architecture of a church or its distance from home, the style of its service or the quality of its singing. Any one of these things might be more significant in determining membership than the theological issues which had seemed so important a few centuries earlier. Those who attended these churches were conscious of being Christian while much of society around them was not. Most were attached to the Bible, and their religion usually centred on the personality, teaching and example of Jesus. As in the past they saw good reason to spread the good news to others. But now they often felt the need in a hostile world to defend what they thought of as 'the Faith' against its critics.

That defence sometimes took the form of asserting the historical truth of events described in the Bible for which the evidence was inadequate, and asserting the literal truth of metaphorical statements, so that angels and evil spirits, heaven and hell were seen as having a physical reality. Some would, for example, assert a belief in the perpetual virginity of Mary the mother of Jesus, because it was asserted by the church to which they belonged, even though apparently contradicted by scripture. They might find it difficult to draw a line between myth, which can be illuminating, even if not literally true, and history, which seeks to understand the past by getting as close to the truth as evidence allows.

The problem of mythology

The stories in the Old Testament of the creation of the world in six days, of Adam and Eve, of Noah's Ark, of Abraham, Moses and so on were an integral part of European culture. The stories told about Jesus in the gospels, about his birth, his miracles and the extraordinary events following his crucifixion, were also part of that culture, and they had contributed over the centuries to emphasising and confirming his very special nature, and in particular his divinity. The virgin birth, the miracles, the physical resurrection were all widely believed to be true, as were the Old Testament stories, and whether or not they were literally true was simply not an issue before the rationalism and scepticism of the Enlightenment of the eighteenth century. The fact that other people, including the leaders of society, believed them made it all the easier for an individual to accept them. The miraculous nature of the stories, whether in the Old Testament or in the gospels, had helped to support Christianity.

What was seldom recognised was that one could lose sight of the significance of Jesus's teaching, his life and death and subsequent influence, behind the screen of these remarkable stories about him. In the twentieth century, as scientific knowledge advanced, as education spread and as teachers encouraged critical thought and scepticism among the young, it inevitably followed that more and more people would doubt the literal truth of at least some of the bible stories. In the first half of the twentieth century fewer and fewer people in the traditional Christian heartland of Europe believed in the literal truth of the stories about the Creation and about Adam and Eve. Since a belief in those stories was widely thought to be an essential part of Christianity, this may have led to an erosion of the membership of the Christian churches. In the second half of the century fewer and fewer people believed in the literal truth of the New Testament stories of the virgin birth and the physical resurrection of Jesus. Since those beliefs appeared to be required, that may have helped to produce a further erosion of church membership. The stories which had once been such powerful supports for

Christianity were now very often barriers cutting people off from the church.

Authoritarian reactions

The various different Christian churches reacted in a range of different ways. The Roman Catholic Church accepted a metaphorical interpretation of many of the early stories in the Old Testament. Pious Catholics might believe that the world was created in six days, but they were not required to do so. On the other hand, on matters related to Jesus and his mother the church was clear about its teaching and required its members to accept papal authority. It held to the doctrine of transubstantiation. It held that Mary was not only a virgin when Jesus was conceived but also that she always remained a virgin; in 1854 Pius IX had proclaimed that she was conceived without the taint of original sin; as late as 1950 Pius XII proclaimed the doctrine of her bodily assumption into heaven.

Fundamentalists, whether they were in the evangelical tradition, attached to the authority of the Bible, or in the charismatic tradition, relying on the guidance of the Holy Spirit, had similarly clear and assured views. They usually interpreted the New Testament literally, and many of them were more inclined than the Roman church to cling to a literal interpretation of the Old Testament. They also placed their own distinctive interpretation on the scriptures, asserting, for example, that true salvation required a personal conversion such as Saul had experienced on the road to Damascus (*Acts 9.3-6*).

Both Roman Catholicism and fundamentalism appealed to the yearning in humankind for certainty and clarity in an insecure world in which traditional teachings and moral standards were being challenged. Roman Catholics saw themselves as speaking with the authentic voice of the one true church, whose leader had divine authority to provide the right answers on all matters of faith and morals. Evangelical fundamentalists spoke with the authority of their own interpretation of the Bible. Charismatics spoke with the authority of the Holy Spirit. All three seemed sure that they were always right, and it sometimes appeared that they were asserting that eternal salvation depended on getting one's beliefs right.

The Protestant conscience

In the mainstream Protestant churches, where they were not affected by fundamentalism, views were less clear-cut. Many clergy taught, or at least were sympathetic to the view, that it was less important to believe any particular doctrine than to visit 'orphans and widows in their distress' (*James 1. 27*), and remember that Jesus had told his followers to follow him and preach repentance, forgiveness and the need for reconciliation. Jesus had said that he came not to destroy the law but to fulfil it (*Matthew 5.17*), but he also made it clear that the law was made for the convenience of humankind rather than the other way round (*Mark 2.27*). He told stories to illustrate his vision of the kingdom of heaven, and he summarised 'all the law and the prophets' as a requirement to love God and one's neighbour (*Matthew 22.37-40*).

By the end of the twentieth century it was not unusual for conscientious Protestants, whether in Europe or America, to assume that they ought to obey the laws of the society they were living in and beyond that look to the teachings and example of Jesus for an ideal of how to live. It was not for the church to dictate what they should believe or how they should live. It could offer guidance, but all men and women needed to take moral responsibility for their own beliefs and decisions and act in accordance with conscience. But while Christians often looked to their leaders for guidance rather than for assertions of authority, non-Christians sometimes indicated that, while not believing in Christianity themselves, they expected Christians to accept what they saw as the traditional beliefs of the church, and they expected church leaders to condemn vice unequivocally and applaud virtue. The church, in fact, was expected to be a useful support for conventional morality, which was one of the very things Jesus had objected to in the attitude of the religious people of his own time.

When Bishop John Robinson of Woolwich in 1963 suggested in his influential book *Honest to God* that one should not think of angels or evil spirits as physical beings, or of heaven and hell as physical places, he was widely seen as undermining the faith of ordinary people. The shock and horror was even greater when David Jenkins, Bishop of Durham from 1984 until 1994, said of the resurrection that it was 'more than a conjuring trick with bones.' Many members of the church might well feel a sense of freedom in finding that even some bishops would express their trust in Christ as their Lord and Saviour in a different way from that in which it had commonly been expressed in the past. But many people found it difficult to accept Christianity without the associated mythology.

Christianity in a post-Christian society

A large part of the problem facing the Christian church was the way it was perceived by those outside it. At first sight it might seem that the Roman Catholics and the fundamentalists were jointly winning the battle for hearts and minds. In their different ways they were apparently entirely self-confident and clear both about what one should believe and about how one should behave. The Orthodox churches were quieter. The Protestant churches were divided and uncertain. But that view of things is misleading. In the political life of the twentieth century there were strong temptations to seek either a left-wing ideological solution to all problems or, alternatively, a right-wing authoritarian solution. Both the right and the left used force and both were prepared to use virtually any means to achieve their ends. But an open society is healthier, and the triumph of what is loosely called 'democracy', for all its failings and its internal divisions, offers some hope for the future in a sadder, if not much wiser, world. Similarly there are temptations in the religious life to turn to fundamentalism for ideological solutions or to Roman Catholicism for authoritative solutions to all problems. But in religion, as in politics, an open society is healthier, and already in the nineteenth century many theologians had been pointing the way to greater openness of thought. While Pope Pius X was still fighting a rearguard action against 'modernism', Archbishop Randall Davidson of Canterbury declared in 1914: 'Follow the truth, do your utmost to find it, and let it be your guide, whithersoever it may lead you.' The Roman position was that scholarship should always be guided by the authority of the church, but many Protestant scholars appealed to reason and to the individual Protestant conscience, and they expected and even welcomed disagreements. Not surprisingly it was largely theologians and biblical scholars from the mainstream Protestant churches who pointed to new ways of looking at traditional beliefs and at new ways of expressing them. In the United States prosperity had resulted in the founding of universities throughout the country, and in the twentieth century American learning extended into every area of academic study, including theology. It was particularly American Protestant theologians who found ways of translating the traditional faith of the church into the modern world and of looking differently at ideas of God, heaven, prayer and the experience of conversion.

The new theology

There was a need to look at God differently. The traditional Western picture of an omnipotent, omniscient Superbeing is helpful to some people but unhelpful to others. The Eastern and mystical view of God as invisible, intangible and inapprehensible satisfies some and leaves others bewildered. The rationalism of the eighteenth century led more and more people to question the existence of God, and that in turn led to many unsatisfactory arguments, because so much hung on what was meant by 'God.' At the end of the first millennium St Anselm had suggested that God is 'that than which nothing greater can be thought', and few, if any, have ever improved on that. One of its great merits is that it is not so tied to any one description, picture or myth as to get in the way of greater understanding.

But twentieth century theologians have tried to rethink the idea of God, and one outstanding example is Paul Tillich, one of the first American theologians of distinction since Jonathan Edwards at the time of the Great Awakening. He was by origin a German and had been Professor of Theology at Frankfurt University before finding refuge from the Nazis in the U.S.A. in 1933, and he was interested in the interaction between theology and human experience, which, he appreciated, necessarily varies from one culture to another, both in time and place. He faced the problem that, in the light of modern understanding of cosmology, there are difficulties in thinking of God as a 'person', since, if the word 'person' means something recognizable, then God would need to be located in a particular place. Rather, thought Tillich, God should be thought of as 'the infinite and inexhaustible depth and ground of our being', and while the Father was 'Being itself', Jesus should be recognized as the 'New Being', in union with the Father and revealing how that saving union is open to all other human beings; he is the symbol of our perception of the transcendent God. Salvation, moreover, was not to be seen as victory over those external, or objective, forces of evil, such as the devil and evil spirits, with which early Christians had contended, but rather as victory over those internal, or subjective, forces which corrupt and distort human lives. Tillich was a 'liberal' in the sense that he respected and sought to understand the views of others, but evangelicals who disliked his thinking tended to use the word 'liberal' as a term of abuse.

Theologians also revised the way they wrote and spoke about the kingdom of heaven. As Jesus so clearly said, it is not a place with a specific physical location (*Luke 17.21*). It is a spiritual kingdom, and when he told his followers to pray 'Thy kingdom come....on earth as it is in heaven' (*Matthew 6.10*), he was telling them to seek the transformation of ordinary life by the power of God.

Similarly they looked at prayer differently. It was at least questionable whether it made sense to ask God to intervene in our lives to give us what we want. God did not necessarily work that way, and there has been good reason to avoid thinking in those terms for at least three hundred years. But that, they saw, could enhance rather than erode the value of prayer. Prayer should not be an occasional activity cut off from normal life and seeking the intervention of an external agent. It should be a matter of holding up every aspect of one's life before God, seeing problems in the context of the ideal of love, listening to his 'still, small voice of calm' (*1 Kings 19.12* and *The English Hymnal*

383), seeking to align oneself with God, and acting and reacting accordingly.

Finally it was necessary to look at the idea of conversion differently. Too often the idea of the Pauline transformation had led those who were 'converted' to assume that they now knew the answer to all spiritual questions. But being 'new born' should mean becoming as a new born baby in the spiritual life and needing to spend the rest of life seeking to convert one's nature towards the likeness of Christ. The conversion of an individual's life, like the transformation of society, is a slow process with many slips and wrong turnings on the way.

Faith and Works

These ideas filtered down only slowly and by the late twentieth century there was a clear need for them to be proclaimed explicitly. That was especially so over the issue of faith. In the Reformation Luther, quoting St Paul, had asserted that salvation was by faith (*Romans 3.28* and *Galatians 3.11*) rather than a reward for buying indulgences or going on pilgrimages and doing penance. Protestantism, it seemed, was a religion of faith, Roman Catholicism of good works. But by the late twentieth century Catholics and Protestants very largely agreed over the relationship between faith and good works and would explain it in much the same way. Of course faith was important. It was a divine gift which would free men from the bondage of sin, and just as a good tree would bring forth good fruit, so Christians saved by faith would do good works. By their fruits you would know them (*Matthew 12.33*). The good works were evidence of salvation rather than a price paid for entry to heaven.

But there remained a difference over what was meant by faith. The Roman Catholic and Orthodox churches both emphasised the importance of correct belief, or 'orthodoxy', and required their members to accept the faith of the church. Protestants often believed that faith was far more a matter of trust than belief. It was not principally a matter of giving assent to intellectual propositions. It was a matter of trusting in God and in the teaching and example of Jesus Christ. That is not a suggestion that theologians should abandon the search for truth or that all opinions are of equal value. But it does involve the idea that differences of opinion are inevitable, and that it is stultifying for anyone to believe that he or she has the final answer to theological problems.

Meanwhile there was also a problem with what used to be called 'good works.' The churches in the so-called 'developed' world had lost many of their traditional roles to the state. In past centuries the church had provided education and had looked after those who were ill or in need. Members of religious orders taught in schools and universities and cared for the sick and dying in hospitals and hospices. Parish priests cared for those in distress and the social activities of a community centred on the parish church. By the time the state had taken over the provision of education, health and social services, the church had lost a large part of its traditional role. Clergy were likely to find much of their time taken up with regular religious services, weddings and funerals, and also with meetings and visiting the sick. However much else they did, they could easily be seen as engaged primarily in the performance of rituals which had only occasional or peripheral relevance to most people's lives. Many clergy took the problem seriously and tried to solve it. But it remained a real and intractable problem, all the more because it was largely a matter of perception.

Morality

At the same time there remained a widespread assumption that the function of the church was to maintain public and private morality, and that if only the clergy, together with the police, the schools and social workers, would do their jobs properly, there would be less juvenile delinquency, fewer unwanted pregnancies and abortions, less drug addiction, less crime and less divorce. If only the churches would speak out clearly against sin, it was suggested, ordinary people would be able to live their lives in greater security. But that is to lose sight of the fact that the morality which was central to the teaching of Jesus was to do with a way of looking at things, a new perspective on life, rather than a matter of adherence to rules, however admirable those rules might be. Repentence is not so much a matter of being sorry for the wrong one has done as a matter of looking at things in a different way.

The danger was that the church was coming to be seen as an institution for telling people what they should not do. The Roman Catholics appeared to be best at it. They were quite clear that pre-marital sex, homosexuality, abortion and divorce were all and always wrong. They were widely seen as the original and true church, particularly prohibitive and condemnatory. Protestantism was sometimes seen as watered-down Catholicism. Protestants would accept the use of contraception. They would accept divorce under some circumstances, but would not want to celebrate the second marriage of a divorced person. They would agree reluctantly to abortion in specified circumstances and were probably against pre-marital sex, but they recognised that it happened very widely and did not want to put people off the church by condemning it too loudly. They were divided over the issue of homosexuality, with some believing it to be both unnatural and distasteful, others rather unhappily accepting it, while not wanting to see it flaunted, and a minority seeing it as a matter of a person's God-given nature and an expression of the glorious diversity of divine creation.

A new moral vision

What was widely lacking in the way Christians expressed themselves publicly was an emphasis on positive ideals and aspirations rather than on restrictive rules. When Christian leaders were asked in public about the Christian view on any moral issue, they often felt obliged to condemn the action in question but not the perpetrator. What they seldom, if ever, did was refer the questioner to the law, but then go on to give examples or tell stories to illustrate an ideal which went beyond the law. They were unlikely to say that the important thing was to love and then do whatever flowed naturally from that. But that is just what St Augustine had said sixteen hundred years earlier: *dilige et fac quod vis* ('Love and do as you wish'). The consequence was that those who spoke for Christianity too often sounded suspiciously like the religious people of Jesus's day whom he attacked for their self-satisfaction and for adhering meticulously to rules rather than caring about 'the justice and the love of God' (*Luke 11.42*).

A new insight into the issue of the relationship between Christianity and morality was given by another American theologian, Reinhold Niebuhr, who is sometimes described as being 'neo-orthodox', and who tackled the problem that moral issues are usually far from simple. He argued that the choice for Christians often lies somewhere between the ideal and the practical. On the one hand Christians saw peace and mercy, and even poverty, as noble ideals. On the other most believed it was right to fight Nazi Germany, imprison criminals, and work hard to accumulate wealth. So did Niebuhr. But he was aware of the contradictions and sought to resolve them. For example, he was clear that, while society needs mercy, mercy only makes sense in the context of justice, which has to come first. It was therefore all the more important for Christians to cultivate humility, in order to avoid a sense of moral superiority. Then they should take whatever practical action appeared to be appropriate in a particular context; they should recognize their own fallibility; and finally they should forgive the sins of others as they themselves would wish to be forgiven.

The dawn of the third millennium

The Christian church at the dawn of the third millennium was faced, as it always had been, with enormous challenges. Because it is made up of ordinary human beings it is *semper reformanda*, always in need of reform, and it needs to change. A less authoritarian Roman Catholic church would be better able to provide the leadership, organisation and examples of pastoral care which are its strengths. The Orthodox churches could both teach their fellow Christians and learn from them. Protestant churches which cared more about understanding and mutual love than about clinging to the principles which divide them might find ways of bringing the Christians of the world together. If evangelicals and charismatics were prepared to recognise that there are various different ways of finding and following Christ, they might find it possible to share their insights more gently with others and avoid alienating even more than they convert.

Something which had improved was the relationship between the Christian churches and Judaism. Old Testament scholarship, an increasing awareness of the Jewishness of Jesus and St Paul, and above all the shock of the Holocaust combined to cause Christians to be ashamed of anti-Semitism.

There was further to go in relations with Islam. At the beginning of the twentieth century the Muslim world and Islam appeared to be in decline. By the end of it they were resurgent. Christian theologians and Islamic scholars could meet and reach amiable and mutual understanding of their differences and of what they had in common. But Christian fundamentalists looked at Islamic fundamentalism as if in a mirror and failed to see their own reflection.

In the seventeenth century the Copernican revolution had moved the earth from its position at the centre of the universe to that of a planet orbiting a star somewhere in infinite space. In the nineteenth century the Darwinian revolution set humankind in the context of eternity. The history of the Christian Church covers less than a thousandth part of the time humans have existed, and far less than a millionth part of the time that there has been some form of life on earth. The church has scarcely begun the task set in the prophetic vision of Jesus's mother Mary: to put down the mighty, lift up the humble, feed the hungry, and send the rich empty away (*Luke 1.52 and 53*). A glance at the world today, its divisions, cruelties and inequality, shows how much needs doing. The Christian Church needs to find how to put aside most of its internal disagreements, learn to agree to differ, and co-operate with others in uniting the world under the rule of justice, moderated by mercy and humility, and in the context of love.

Suggestions for further reading

Several good general histories of the Christian Church were published in the last half-century. They are all more detailed than this book.

The Penguin History of the Church, published between 1960 and 1970:

1 The Early Church	Henry Chadwick	1967
2 Western Society and the Church in the Middle Ages	R. W. Southern	1970
3 The Reformation	Owen Chadwick	1964
4 The Church and the Age of Reason 1648 – 1789	Gerald R. Cragg	1960
5 The Church in an Age of Revolution 1789 to the Present Day	Alec R.Vidler	1961
6 A History of Christian Missions	Stephen Neill	1964

A History of Christianity by Paul Johnson (Penguin 1976). A good read.

The Oxford Illustrated History of Christianity, ed. John McManners. Essays by nineteen scholars on their own specialist areas (OUP 1990).

A History of Christianity by Owen Chadwick. A beautifully illustrated, reflective account of the development of Christianity (Phoenix 1997).

Christianity. The First Two Thousand Years, by David L. Edwards (Cassell 1997). A thoughtful and wide-ranging work, giving attention to the Orthodox Church and to Christendom beyond Europe.

Christianity: Two Thousand Years (OUP 2001), ed Richard Harries and Henry Mayr-Harting. A short, elegant and readable collection of essays based on a series of lectures by distinguished scholars.

A History of Christianity – The First Three Thousand Years by Diarmaid MacCullough (Allen Lane 2009). A detailed and remarkably well-balanced account in more than a thousand pages of text.

Almost all of these books neglect the Middle Ages and the churches of the East, by comparison with the attention given to the western church from the Reformation onwards. One only has to look at the titles of the six volumes of the Penguin History of the Church to see the problem. MacCullough's massive book avoids these problems, but the price paid for a detailed examination of both the Middle Ages and the churches of the East is that it is very big – more than five times as long as this book.

Index of Persons

Abdul Malek, Caliph (685-705) 118

Abelard, Peter (1079-1142) 161, 162, 170

Abraham 5, 17, 41, 270

Adam 2, 3, 270

Adrian IV, Pope (1154-59) 170

Agatho, Pope (678-681) 101

Alaric, Visigothic king (395-410) 80, 89

Albert of Brandenburg (1490-1545) 200

Alexander the Great (356-323 BC) 12

Alexander III, Pope (1159-81) 170-72, 176, 178

Alexander VI, Pope (1492-1503) 196, 225

Alexius I Comnenus, Byzantine Emperor (1081-1118) 148, 152

Alfred, King of the West Saxons (871-99) 132

Amadeus, Duke of Savoy – see Felix V, Anti-pope 191

Ambrose, St, Bishop of Milan (374-397) 64, 77, 88

Amos, the Prophet 7

Anacletus II, Anti-pope (1130-38) 171

Anastasia, Constantine's half-sister 52

Anna Comnena (1083-1153) Byzantine princess and historian 153

Anne of Bohemia, wife of Richard II, Queen of England (1382-94) 188

Anne of Cleves, 4th wife of Henry VIII, Queen of England in 1540, 214

Anthony, St (c.251-356) 67

Anselm, St, Archbishop of Canterbury (1093-1109) 153, 160-62, 274

Antiochus IV, King of Syria (175-164 BC) 13

Antoninus Pius, Emperor (138-161) 85

Aquinas, Thomas, St (c.1225-74) 165, 166, 194

Aristotle (384BC-322BC) 12, 41, 51, 166

Arius (c.256-336) presbyter in Alexandria 53, 58, 71

Arthur (1486-1502) elder brother of Henry VIII 212

Athanasius, St (296-373) 59, 60, 74, 109

Athenagoras, Patriarch of Constantinople (1948-72) 104, 268

Augustine of Canterbury, St (died c.605) 96, 131, 132

Augustine of Hippo, St (354-430) vii, 77-80, 109, 135, 157, 167, 200, 204, 218, 278

Augustus Caesar, Emperor (c.30BC-AD14) ix, 14, 17, 85, 113

Bach, Johann Sebastian (1685 1750) 260

General Index

Lightning Source UK Ltd.
Milton Keynes UK
UKOW04f1404271215

265371UK00002B/281/P